636
.68
Tro
1992

Trollope, Jeffrey.
Seed-eating birds : their care and breeding : finches and allied species-- doves, quail, and hemipodes / Jeffrey Trollope. -- London : Blandford, 1992.
336 p. : col. ill. ; 22 cm.

Rev. ed. of: The care and breeding of seedeating birds. 1983.
Includes bibliographical references (p. 329-333) and indexes.
06882803 LC:92224940 ISBN:0713722703 (pbk.)

(SEE NEXT CARD)

2259 93JUN26 10/ 1-00606321

# Seed-eating Birds

# Seed-eating Birds

## Their Care and Breeding

FINCHES AND ALLIED SPECIES — DOVES, QUAIL AND HEMIPODES

JEFFREY TROLLOPE

BLANDFORD

A BLANDFORD BOOK

First published in the UK 1992
by Blandford
(a Cassell imprint)
Villiers House
41/47 Strand
London WC2N 5JE



Distributed in the United States
by Sterling Publishing Co., Inc.
387 Park Avenue South, New York, NY 10016–8810

Distributed in Australia
by Capricorn Link (Australia) Pty Ltd
P.O. Box 665, Lane Cove, NSW 2066

**British Library Cataloguing in Publication Data**
Trollope, Jeffrey
Seed-eating birds.
1. Pets: Seed-eating birds
I. Title
636.68

ISBN 0–7137–2270–3

Typeset by Fakenham Photosetting Ltd,
Fakenham, Norfolk
Printed and bound in Great Britain
by Biddles Ltd, Guildford and King's Lynn

# Contents

# Acknowledgements

My thanks are due to Martin Trollope and Ron Grace for photography:

Martin Trollope 2, 5, 6, 7, 8, 9, 10, 11, 12, 15, 16, 17, 18, 19, 20, 21, 22, 23, 24, 26, 27, 28, 29, 30, 31, 32, 33, 34, 35, 38, 40, 41, 44, 47, 48, 49, 50.

Ron Grace 1, 3, 4, 13, 14, 25, 36, 37, 39, 42, 43, 45, 46.

I would also like to thank Stuart Booth and Miranda Walker for their help with editorial matters.

The publishers would like to thank Anita Lawrence for the line illustrations.

# Introduction

In this introduction I have included, where they are valid, extracts from a previous version of this book, *The Care and Breeding of Seed-eating Birds*. The main objective of this edition, as with the first, is to provide information which will help aviculturists to achieve greater success in breeding seed-eating birds.

The majority of species covered are exported from the Indian subcontinent, Hong Kong, South-east Asia, Africa and Central and South America. They are therefore regarded as foreign birds by aviculturists in the primary areas of importation — the USA, Europe and the UK. British breeding species have been omitted.

Since the first version appeared, the need to establish captive-bred stocks of imported birds has changed from urgent to imperative. Since the 1970s, worldwide legislation has reduced and controlled the trade in wild birds, which had reached unacceptably high proportions. No responsible aviculturist will regret the demise of unrestricted bird importations which has led to an increased commitment to breeding birds.

In this book the number of species described has been increased to include those that have become available in recent years. Species that are now seldom imported have been retained, where it appears that there are sufficient stocks for their establishment in aviculture. The chapters on management and breeding have been revised. The section on sickness and health contains only the very basic information required for precautions against disease. There are currently many books, usually written by veterinary surgeons, which cover diseases, injuries and their treatment in detail.

In response to many species becoming endangered as the result of habitat destruction, especially rainforests, many zoos, bird gardens, conservation trusts and related organisations have initiated and maintained captive breeding programmes. These have mainly involved waterfowl, pheasants, parrots, birds of prey, a few dove species and passerines, such as the Rothschild's Grackle. With this commitment to the larger and endangered species, it is unlikely that these institutions will ever use their limited resources to establish the more common and smaller seed-eating birds. This therefore, will inevitably become the role of private aviculturists, who have already established in captivity almost all of the Australian parakeets and grass finches since the ban on commercial exports from Australia in 1960.

Private aviculturists have also played a significant role in the breeding of endangered species, especially psittacines. The breeding biology and behaviour of many taxonomic groups has been studied in aviaries (for example, hemipodes, tinamous, parasitic whydahs, birds of paradise) and the information gained would have been difficult and, in some cases, impossible to obtain from field studies.

During the last few years the total number of wild-caught birds imported into the UK has been drastically reduced. This has resulted in a much needed improvement in shipping and reception standards.

Bird importations have always been erratic and unpredictable. Currently some of the factors affecting 'foreign bird' availability include: restrictions imposed by the exporting and importing countries; political, economic and agricultural conditions in the countries of origin; the economics of civil aviation; airline routing; and public and press perceptions of aviculture in the importing countries.

The opportunity to establish captive-bred stocks of wild birds from the countries of origin will inevitably be further reduced or, in many cases, cease. It is therefore essential that aviculturists in the countries of importation establish in captivity species such as doves, serins, waxbills and munias. It has been done with Australian finches and other taxonomic groups, and there is no reason why these successes cannot be repeated. Australian aviculturists have established many species of birds in captivity since the ban on commercial imports into their country.

As far as I can ascertain at the time of writing, none of the species listed in this book are considered endangered by the authorities. Therefore they are not listed in Appendix 1 of CITES (Convention on International Trade in Endangered Species of Wild Fauna and Flora). However, although many of these species are under no threat currently, they are at risk from the agricultural protection needs in their countries of origin.

In the battle to maintain and develop their agricultural economies, these countries are forced to increase the use of pesticides to protect crops. These will inevitably become an increasing hazard to bird life in the countries of origin, as they did in the 1950s in the UK, Continental Europe and the USA. Despite the advances in the control of pesticides, they are likely to remain a serious hazard to birds in the forseeable future, especially in developing countries.

In addition to the destructive impact of pesticides on bird life, many bird species are regarded as serious agricultural pests, both in their countries of origin and where they have been introduced. The species covered in this book include some of these agricultural pests, which come under the following taxonomic groups: mannikins and munias (*Lonchura*), sparrows (*Passer*), finches (Fringillidae), weavers (*Ploceus*, *Euplectes*, and *Quelea*), the pin-tailed parrot finch (*Erythrura*) and *Streptopelia* doves.

The African Red-billed Quelea or Weaver (*Quelea quelea*) is probably the world's most numerous species of bird; it is also the most serious of agricultural pests. The estimated average annual adult breeding populations in African regions range from 19 million for Kenya to 94 million for the Lake Chad basin. The Red-billed Quelea has a vast distribution in sub-Saharan Africa and has a negative impact on the agriculture of more than 25 countries, damaging and destroying small-grain cereal crops. National governments and international agencies in the affected countries carry out a total war against the Quelea. The main methods of destruction used are fire bombs and explosives, aerial chemical spraying and spraying from the ground. These methods are very effective; an estimated 120 million Red-billed Queleas were killed in Zimbabwe in 1985. This number was assumed to be half of the total population at that time.

The risk to bird populations other than the target species is high at the lethal control-levels operated against the Red-billed Quelea and other pest species. It is inevitable that other species are killed; in one operation 43 non-target species were found dead after one spraying of a quelea colony, the species ranging from waxbills to goshawks. There have been many reports of a wide taxonomic spectrum of non-target species being destroyed during operations. As the result of crop protection against both invertebrate and vertebrate pests, many seed-eating bird species, currently numerous, but with a limited distribution, could become vulnerable or endangered in a short time span. Therefore aviculturists breeding these species could find that they are playing an unexpected role in conservation. Many seed-eating birds, although imported in large numbers in the past, have seldom been bred in captivity, or their breeding has been a comparatively rare event. So, apart from the pleasure of breeding these birds, the aviculturist has the opportunity to add to our total knowledge of these species.

One of the problems associated with the establishment of captive-bred stock of wild birds is the desire of some owners for stock 'improvement' once the species has become domesticated, or established in captivity. This improvement initially takes the form of developing the colour mutations that inevitably occur when birds are bred in large numbers. I think it is a mistake to try and 'improve' species which are prolific in captivity; the wild imported Java Sparrow (*Lonchura* [= *Padda*] *oryzivora*) is, in my opinion, a far more beautiful bird than the domestic white variety, although colour can be bred back. It is very likely that, in the constant striving for ever more colour varieties, the original 'wild' coloured birds will become the rarities in captive stocks.

An example of a more fundamental deviation than colour variety is the modern show Budgerigar, in which 'improvement' has involved a change in shape and an increase in size, resulting in stock far removed from the elegant, fast and far-flying wild birds. With regard to hybrids, they can be useful to assist in proving or disproving a taxonomic relationship, besides having a curiosity or rarity value. However, I feel that both stock 'improvement' and hybrid breeding have little significance for current and future aviculture, if it is to retain credibility as an important factor in conservation.

In this book I have defined captive breeding as successful if one or both parents complete the full breeding cycle, from egg-laying to rearing the young to independence. Although artificial incubation and rearing methods may be necessary to prevent wastage of bird life and to retain the viability of captive stocks of rare birds, I think that these methods (especially artificial incubation) can be both good servants and bad masters. The domesticated Japanese Quail (*Coturnix japonica*) has lost the ability to incubate its own eggs, and instances of hens successfully incubating their own eggs are extremely rare. The Chinese Painted Quail (*Excalfactoria chinensis*) is going the same way and, in this case, I think the problem is largely due to their egg-rolling behaviour, which causes aviculturists to resort to artificial incubation and rearing methods to prevent wastage. Even with stock that has good natural incubation and rearing records, I cannot argue that the success rate is anywhere near the percentage achieved by well-managed artificial incubation and rearing methods. However efficient these methods may be, they are closer to commercial poultry-farming than aviculture and could leave us with stocks of gallinaceous birds which are totally dependent for their maintenance on these techniques.

During the last few years, an increasing number of aviculturists have realised the crucial importance of establishing captive bird species. In the UK, the avicultural societies have initiated an exchange-and-mart scheme for birds. This enables aviculturists to obtain single birds, in order to make up a breeding pair, or pairs in order to establish a breeding group. The avicultural organisations also publish a yearly breeding census, which provides a valuable record of the species and numbers of birds bred by contributors to the census — a very small percentage of the total number of non-domesticated species bred in the UK.

These and other initiatives by these societies and similar organisations worldwide are both welcome and timely. If aviculture is to survive, it is essential to maintain breeding records of species which have been, and are currently, imported.

# Notes on the Text

The first part of this book consists of general information on housing, feeding, selection and establishment of stock, care and breeding, and is applicable to all the birds discussed in the book. More specific details are given in an introduction to each taxonomic group, followed by individual descriptions giving the scientific and common English names, description, distribution and habitat. The breeding and breeding period in captivity (which refers to outside aviaries without artificial heat and light, unless otherwise stated), description of nests, eggs, chicks or immature birds and behaviour are given for a representative species in each genus. For some homogeneous groups these details would be repetitive and superfluous and have therefore been omitted. Whenever possible, the listing of Howard and Moore (1980) has been followed, although present changes and debates on the systematic position of many species have been indicated where they are of concern to the aviculturist. I have used the term 'established', to indicate that a species can be maintained in captivity from current stocks, without continuous importation. The term is also used to describe a period of successful adjustment to a new environment for recently acquired birds. I think 'established' is preferable to 'acclimatised', especially for those birds that have been imported. The text is based on 40 years of personal experience, recording my successes and failures, coupled with reference to the material of aviculturists, museum workers, ornithologists and others, whose work is known to me, or is relevant.

# *PART ONE*
# *General Care*

# 1
# Accommodation

The two main factors to be considered when housing birds are their security and the local climatic conditions. Security, apart from the obvious need of containing the birds inside the aviary, includes keeping out rodents and predators — weasels, for example, or snakes in countries such as the USA and Australia. It also means preventing cats, as far as possible, from harassing the birds. In cold and temperate countries, the second factor, climate, can be tackled in one of two main ways. One is to provide shelters for each aviary or range of aviaries in which the birds can be shut during periods of hard winter weather. The second is to house the birds in aviaries in the spring, summer and autumn and in a bird room during the winter. This latter method has a number of advantages; power for heating and lighting need only be supplied for one site and having the total stock housed in one building makes feeding, watering, and stock checks easier. As the aviaries are empty for the winter, rodents can be eliminated without risk to the birds, and repair and maintenance work can be carried out more efficiently and does not involve the movement of stock.

Nevertheless, having enclosed shelters attached to the aviaries also has its advantages; the stock has a stabilised environment throughout the year with the benefit of good weather at any time. I work with a compromise; the more hardy species are sometimes kept throughout the year in an outside aviary with an enclosed shelter while the less hardy birds are transferred to a bird room for the winter. In both cases my remarks refer only to birds fully established or bred in my aviaries and not to those recently acquired, regardless of whether they are imported or have been aviary bred elsewhere.

In countries with temperate climates the question of providing heat and light for many species is a controversial one. I personally favour heating to provide a temperature of approximately 10°C (50°F) for most species once established. I no longer believe in providing heat for a fixed 'winter' period as I once did; instead I make use of a thermostat and keep a flexible approach to the current weather conditions, which in a variable climate can keep you on your toes. This same approach applies to birds housed outside in aviaries with an unheated shelter; in very prolonged periods of hard weather I move them into a bird room. Although the birds might well survive, and even thrive, outside without heat it is risky to expose birds to very severe conditions. Artificial lighting should also be provided during the longer winter nights, as in many areas of the USA and Europe it is too long a period for many birds, such as the more delicate Ethiopian-region waxbills, to go without food and resist the additional stress of low temperatures. It is that deadly combination of cold and lack of food that kills so many native wild birds in hard weather. It is true that you will hear aviculturists say 'My cordon-bleus wintered outside without heat and light, and never lost a feather', but there are so many variables to be taken into account. Was it a hard winter? What sort of aviary were they in? Did it have a shelter or a protected roof and sides? Were covered roosting sites provided? Was the aviary in a protected situation? Were the birds' food and water checked and replenished once a day, twice or more often? These variables must be considered with the regional climatic conditions in mind. And finally, two very important questions to ask ourselves of birds that have survived hard weather in outside aviaries in apparent good health are; how long did they live afterwards and what was their breeding record?

## AVIARIES

In considering aviaries in detail, we shall be discussing the security factor in all its aspects. I have yet to come across the perfect aviary cage or enclosure. All one can do is ensure that the essential features are present for the type of stock you intend to keep and for any purposes you may have in mind, in our case the production of healthy breeding birds. The types of commercially built aviaries and do-it-yourself designs are almost as varied as the species one can keep. As well as buying an aviary which simply has to be bolted together, ready-made frames or panels can be bought, so that you can start with a small unit and add more panels later, ending up with a block of aviaries as large and complex as you wish to make it. My aviaries are designed to accommodate and breed the species covered in this book, which includes birds varying in size from that of the Golden-breasted Waxbill (*Amandava subflava*) at 90 mm (3½ in) to that of the Emerald Dove (*Chalcophaps indica*) at 250 mm (10 in). I use the available space for mixed collections, and consider the size of the birds, although important in relation to space, secondary to species compatability and their reproductive biology and behaviour. (These aspects will be discussed in detail later.) The main cause of many problems such as poor breeding results and the spread of disease is overcrowding, a temptation which must be avoided. Of the three types of aviary described here, the first two have the rear and approxiinately one-third of the roof and sides covered.

**Type 1**

4.3 × 2.4 × 2.4 m high (14 × 8 × 8 ft), used to house four pairs of waxbill/finch-sized birds 90–152 mm (3½–6 in), or two pairs of cardinal-sized species 190–228 mm (8–9 in) and one pair of larger doves or quail 254–279 mm (10–12 in).

**Type 2**

3.1 × 1.1 × 2.4 m high (10 × 3½ × 8 ft), used to house two pairs of waxbill/finch-sized birds, or one pair of cardinal-sized birds, one pair of small doves and one pair of quail up to 190.5 mm (8 in).

**Type 3**

2.4 × 1.8 × 2.1 m high (8 × 6 × 7 ft). This type has a completely enclosed shelter and is used to house the more hardy species during the winter. The size and number of birds housed is the same as Type 2.

Alternative methods of housing include keeping one pair of birds to each unit, which can be much smaller, depending on the size and species of bird. This method is generally considered to be optimal for breeding results; however this does not allow for the species which are colony breeders and need the stimulus of being housed with conspecifics for successful reproduction.

## PLANNING AN AVIARY

Before either buying or making an aviary, the site should be selected with care and a plan of the aviary and garden made, as well as one of the selected site and alternatives. The aviary should not be sited near trees or fences, as these will make it easy for cats to get on the roof. Wild birds might perch on branches above the aviary and their droppings can cause disease; and in the autumn, leaves falling on the aviary roof can create problems. The site chosen should also avoid any obvious source of disturbance such as a garage. Other factors to consider are easy access by path and enough space to extend the aviary should you wish to do so. Protection from prevailing winds and use of any features already present in the area, such as brick walls, should be taken into account. I prefer to leave a clear space of at least 90 cm (3 ft) around the perimeter of the aviary or range of aviaries to make checking of the structure and maintenance easier.

## BUILDING AN AVIARY

Probably the most widely used method of constructing an aviary is to make wooden panels which can be bolted together. This method has the great advantages of making it easy to add an extension and if the aviary has to be moved, it can be dismantled and taken to another site. A convenient size of panel to make is 1.8 m (6 ft) high × 91 cm (3 ft) wide; this size gives adequate strength and standard 91 cm (3 ft) or 1.8 m (6 ft) wire mesh or welded square netting can be fitted with a minimum of cutting and waste. The panels can be made of

25 × 25 mm (1 × 1 in) battens, but these, in my opinion, are incapable of withstanding an accidental hard blow. Larger panels can be constructed if there is no possibility of adding an extension to the aviary. Stapled to each panel should be some 12 × 12 mm (½ × ½ in) 19 gauge wire mesh or welded square mesh. (If you can buy even smaller mesh size then do so, because the 12 mm size will not exclude all mice. Although more expensive, I always fit small mesh wire to my aviaries.) A larger mesh size of 25 × 25 mm (1 × 1 in) will effectively contain many kinds of birds, but the aviary will have limited use should you decide to keep smaller birds, such as waxbills or many finch species.

The panels for the shelter can be covered with tongued and grooved wooden boards for the roof and floor, and with shiplap boards for the sides. Alternative materials are heavy-duty exterior grade plywood, treated hardboard and PVC interlocking plastic panels. The roof of the aviary can be sloping or the ridged apex type. I have built aviaries with flat-roofed flights and created a sheltered dry area with a false apex roof of translucent plastic panels or other material fixed to a raised centre batten. The ends of this roof must be covered with wire or other material to prevent the entry of rodents and wild birds. An important point to remember when making an enclosed shelter is to provide adequate light by means of glazed windows. This is because birds are reluctant to fly into a darker area.

When making the panels, the wood can be creosoted and the wire and metal fittings painted with black bitumen paint before assembly. Alternatives to creosote include clear or coloured wood preservative, and paint; you can also use plastic-coated wire mesh which needs no painting. To support the aviary and prevent the wood rotting, one course of bricks or breeze blocks should be laid on a concrete foundation; a concrete fillet laid on top of the brick course makes it easier to get a perfectly level result. The wire mesh should be extended under the ground and bent outwards to prevent rodents burrowing under the aviary (Fig. 2). The floor of the shelter section of the aviary should first be concreted, then a wooden floor supported on battens laid on top. The flight section floor can also be concreted, provided it has adequate drainage; alternatively, gravel can be laid, or an earth floor can be used.

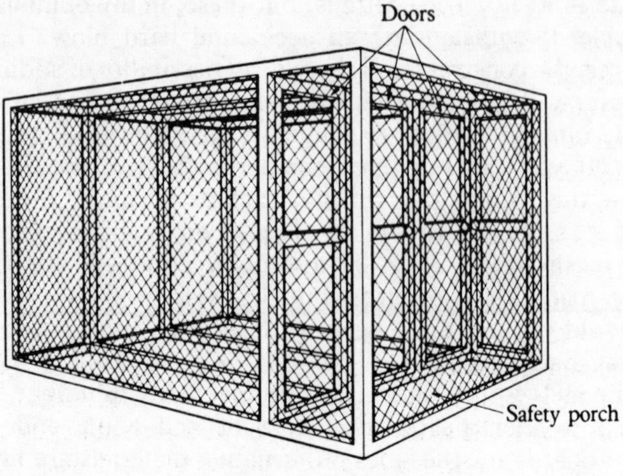


Fig 1 Plan of three aviaries with safety porch

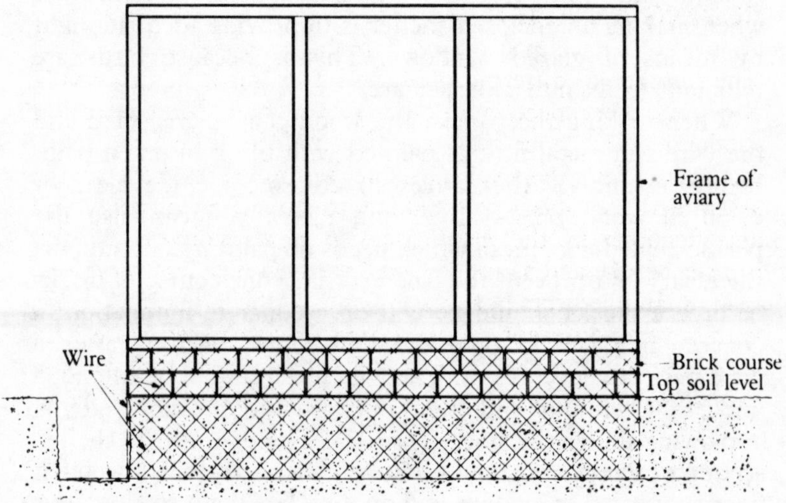


Fig 2 Method of extending wire underground to prevent rodents burrowing under brick courses.

If quail are to be kept in the aviary, an entrance must be made at ground level in the shelter section.

I consider that a safety porch to prevent birds escaping is essential for all aviaries (Fig. 1). It should never face the aviary door or doors. Although a small entrance door is often considered adequate, a lot depends on the size of the aviary and the species of bird.

The flight area roof can be covered completely or in part with translucent or opaque plastic panels to provide a dry sheltered area for nesting sites. The cat problem can be overcome by adding a false roof of larger mesh; if constructed to overhang the sides of the true roof by some 45 cm (18 in), cats will be unable to climb up the sides of the aviary to reach the roof. Down the sides of the flights you should have double mesh; simply fit removable wired panels secured with button fasteners over the aviary panels so that they can be easily maintained and painted as required.

As an alternative to wooden panels for aviary building, rustic poles can look very attractive. Metal tubing is another possibility, but it is more difficult to obtain the same flexibility allowed by wooden panels.

## BUYING AN AVIARY

The number of different types and sizes made commercially will suit every need and money available. Comprehensive catalogues and price lists can be obtained from the manufacturers, but whenever possible I think it is best to see assembled the aviary you intend to buy. The pictures and specifications in the catalogue can never convey the full impact of size and space. As well as their business premises, many manufacturers have trade stands at the larger bird shows with several different types of aviaries assembled. It is also very helpful if you can talk to a representative so that you can explain your needs and the type of site available.

## BIRD ROOMS

Whether you are lucky enough to have an existing building such as a conservatory you can convert, or a spare room in the house you can use, or whether you have to buy or build a bird room, the most important factors are adequate light, ventilation, and temperature control, the last of which is difficult to achieve without electric power. Most aviculturists end up buying a commercially made bird room or standard portable wooden building — the workshop type with plenty of window space is preferable to the garden shed which usually has fewer windows. As with aviaries I think it is best to see the building type you are intending to buy assembled before purchase. It is important that as many windows as possible can be opened but at the same time all the windows must be protected by removable wire panels. A protective double door of wire or a safety porch will enable you to leave the building door open in warm weather to prevent heat reaching an unacceptable level. Ventilation grills with sliding covers are essential and an extractor fan is a very desirable asset, even vital in some climates.

The minimum size for a bird room is, in my opinion, 2.4 × 1.8 m (8 × 6 ft). A concrete base should be made for the building to prevent wood rot, keep out rodents and to provide a level surface to build upon. Portable buildings of this type are often used as a shelter for an aviary, the flight frames being attached to the building. The bird room can be lined — I have always used hardboard — which will reduce heat loss in the winter. Insulating material such as glass-fibre can then be placed between the outer wall and the lining.

## HEATING AND LIGHTING

The safest and most effective method of heating a bird room or aviary shelter is an electric enclosed tubular heater, or electric fan heater, controlled by a thermostat. There are many alternatives, such as paraffin and Calor-gas heaters, but, in my opinion, both for temperature control and safety, they are inferior to electric heaters.

Electric lighting is best provided by fluorescent tubes, which produce a shadowless light. In the winter months, a minimum of 14 hours light from 06.00 to 20.00 hours is available in my bird room and shelters, controlled by means of a time switch. A dimmer is incorporated into the lighting circuit, which slowly reduces the light intensity before switching off, so the birds are not suddenly left in the dark.

### Power Cuts

Electrical power cuts and circuit failures can occur without warning, so alternative battery-powered lighting and heating must be available for an emergency.

## CAGES

There are many circumstances in which cages are used for breeding. Some Australian finch specialists prefer their use to that of aviaries, and for other semi-domesticated and domesticated species, and for imported birds which adjust readily to captivity, breeding cages are a viable alternative to aviaries. Cages are also used for the isolation of newly purchased stock, sick birds, and the housing of young birds removed from the aviaries. As with aviaries the number of commercially produced designs are too numerous to list, but for the breeder of

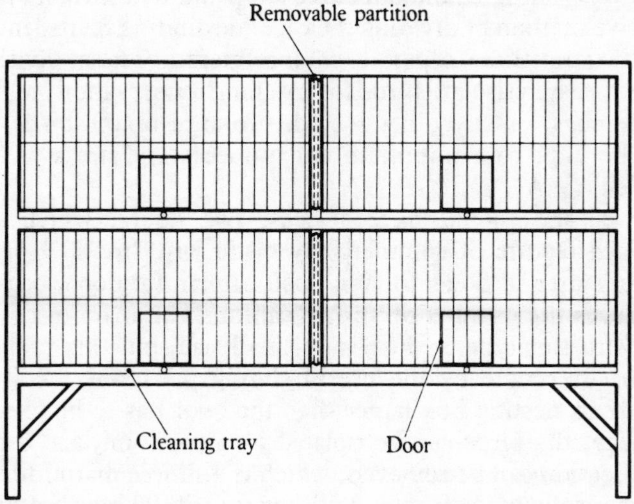


Fig 3 Block of box cages

birds, the only really useful type of cage is the box design. Single box cages, double-sized breeding cages and blocks of breeding and stock cages are commercially available. If you decide to make your own, welded metal cage fronts of various sizes can be purchased. I always use blocks of cages (Fig. 3) which will make the most effective use of bird room space. The space required, as with many aspects of aviculture, is the subject of much debate; for finch/waxbill-sized birds I use a minimum area of approximately 91 × 45 × 45 cm high (36 × 18 × 18 in), and for birds the size of small doves, cardinals and larger, a minimum area of approximately 120 × 61 × 61 cm high (4 × 2 × 2 ft).

Overcrowding or housing incompatible birds together can result in an insidious decline in health which in many cases cannot be readily detected until too late. As a rough guide, for stock cages I use the smaller type for housing three pairs of waxbill/finch-sized birds, and the larger type for one pair of cardinal-sized birds and one pair of doves or quail, or four pairs of the smaller birds. For breeding purposes, one pair of birds per cage is the only realistic number. An important feature for box cages whether used for housing surplus stock or breeding, is a sliding partition both wire and solid. These partitions sliding in and out along a top and bottom slot are an effective method of dividing the cage, depending on its length, into two or three separate compartments. These divisions make it easy to isolate birds for catching, observation, replacing perches, or any other job; disturbance of the birds will thus be kept to a minimum and unnecessary stress will be avoided.

Each cage should have at least two doors, which is a standard feature of commercially made wire fronts. I prefer the slide up and down foreign finch pattern for doors because it reduces the chances of birds escaping. The main disadvantage with this type of door is its small size, but this problem can be overcome by the use of sliding partitions. So if for example a nesting box larger than the door has to be fixed in the cage, the birds can be isolated by a partition, and a cage front section can be removed, which is a simple matter for the commercially made fronts. A sliding tray at the cage bottom is essential for cage cleaning, and a spare set of trays for each cage makes cleaning quicker and more efficient.

## CAGE AND AVIARY FURNITURE

With the exception of the non-perching quail such as *Coturnix*, and hemipodes, perches are essential for all the birds described in this book. Oval or round wooden perches can be bought at any pet shop, and for commercially made cages they are fitted or supplied with the cage. However, these perches are usually designed for budgerigars or canaries and come in only a small range of sizes. Natural perches of fruit tree branches are a better idea, as they give a wide range of perch sizes to suit the individual bird of any species. The perches should be positioned so they are not above feeding sites, thus ensuring that food and water are not contaminated by defecation; an uninterrupted flight space should also be guaranteed. The perching surfaces should also be clear of the aviary wire or cage sides, so that the birds' tails will not be damaged by friction (Fig. 4).

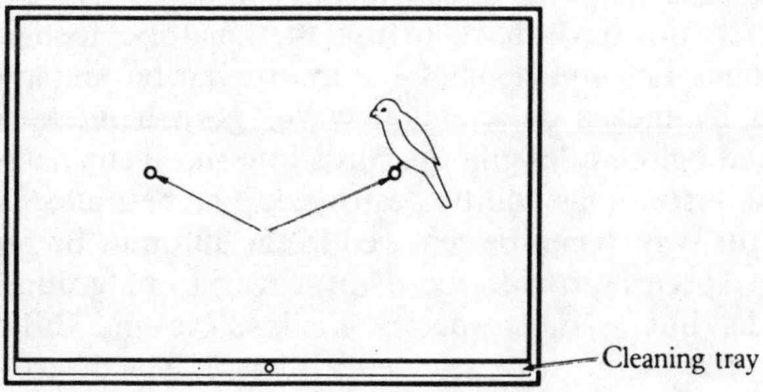


Fig 4 Perches arranged to prevent birds damaging their tails

## PLANTED AVIARIES

The question of the planted aviary is a matter of choice, I personally think that an aviary needs to measure at least 3 × 1.8 × 1.8 m high (10 × 6 × 6 ft) to look effective — in smaller aviaries plants rapidly become soiled. Some species of birds will damage the plants and so prevent growth. It is also important to remember that the effective working space can be reduced so that if birds have to be caught, or any emergency task carried out, what should be a simple job can become very difficult. The alternative to a planted aviary with soil is wooden tubs or other containers for the plants which can be placed on a concrete or other type of solid floor. For aviaries with or without plants, branches of gorse (*Ulex*), broom (*Saothamnus*) and conifers can be cut and hung up to provide cover and nesting sites. I do this in my aviaries by nailing lengths of 25 × 25 mm (1 × 1 in) wooden battens inside the aviary and wiring the branches very tightly to the battens.

## PLANTS

The advantages of a planted aviary, apart from the obvious one of making the aviary attractive, include visually breaking up the lines of the aviary to make it blend more naturally with the garden. Plants attract insects and other invertebrates, provide cover, nesting sites and in some cases a food source for which the birds have to use their natural food-seeking behaviour. The soil floor of the aviary can be prepared and grassed by means of seeds; however growth must be well advanced before releasing the birds into the aviary, otherwise the young seedlings will be destroyed. The best alternative is to use turf which can be renewed in the autumn. Bamboos of various species provide excellent cover from ground level upwards, but as most species are invasive and difficult to uproot, the site must be selected with care. The dwarf species of bamboo are easier to control and so are preferable.

Other shrubs for planting inside the aviary include privet (*Ligustrum*) which is fast growing, hardy and seldom loses its leaves even in very hard winters. Although privet can be accused of too rapid a growth, I have found it invaluable for providing nesting sites and cover, and it can easily be controlled by hand clipping or pruning twice a year. The hawthorn (*Crataegus*) is another useful shrub which will stand hard pruning and the blossoms are attractive. Its height must be watched when established, but a judicious annual pruning will prevent this becoming a problem. The cotoneasters — *C. horizontalis* which has prostrate growth and the upright-growing *C. rotundifolia* — are both excellent aviary shrubs which have attractive flowers and are hardy. Broom and gorse are both suitable shrubs for nesting sites, the densely growing gorse being best. As with the hawthorn, gorse 'thorns' or 'spikes' must be treated with care and thick gloves worn, but in over 30 years I have had only one accident involving a bird, and that was when a waxbill caught its leg ring on a thorn (but fortunately it was released without harm). If growing gorse is difficult, branches of gorse pushed into the soil retain their cover value for a long time. A shrub often used in aviaries is berberis (barberry), the majority of which species thrive in either sunny or shady situations. Mahonia is another useful aviary shrub, the different species varying from the very hardy to the delicate. The evergreen box shrub (*Brescas*), although not the most attractive of shrubs, can easily be controlled and is not difficult to establish. Along with the bushy shrub, Baggessen's Gold (*Lonicera nitida*), it provides excellent nesting sites and cover. In mild climates like that of southern California, plants such as the deciduous magnolia, tulip trees, mimosas, banana plants and thornless palms have all proved suitable for the aviary.

For the outside of the flights the attractive clematis is a favourite. Most species prefer their heads in the sun and their roots in the shade — a flat stone placed over the roots will help to provide this condition. The fast growing Russian vine provides excellent cover and is a great attractant for insects. I allow and even encourage the growth of convolvulus (bindweed) although this confession will arouse horror in the minds of any gardener. However, the rampant growth can easily be controlled by snipping the climbing stems at the bottom near the roots; these stems soon wilt and die, and provide excellent nesting material for the larger birds such as cardinals, grosbeaks and hawfinches. Bindweed flowers are very attractive although short lived.

What you would like to grow in the aviary and what will grow can sometimes be two different things. The type of soil, space available and the situation of the aviary all have a bearing. It would be helpful to consult an experienced gardener or nurseryman who could advise you on the species of plants most suitable for your soil, situation, and regional climate.

I have yet to hear of any case where the toxicity of plants has been implicated in the death of a bird; however plants which are very suspect, such as yew and laburnum, should never be used. The use of insect sprays, weed killers and other toxic chemical agents should obviously be banned either in or anywhere near the aviary. And remember, what could be a safe distance away for their use can be negated by wind, liquid chemicals draining under the soil, and similar factors.

## BATHING AND DRINKING FACILITIES

The common type of bird bath or pool is usually made of concrete or similar material. Whatever the type or material, the pool or bath must have a gradual slope to a maximum depth of 12 mm (½ in) for waxbill/finch-sized birds, and 25 mm (1 in) for the larger birds. The sides of the pool should be roughened, as slippery surfaces are dangerous. The pool should be sited in a clear space away from overhanging branches, and cleaning will be assisted if a concrete or flat stone surround is made. The pool should not be too large. Concrete caps used for chimney pots I have found ideal; they can be obtained from a second-hand material builder's yard. When inverted and placed in the soil on a gravel bed, these caps are not too large, they have a gradual slope to a depth of approximately 25 mm (1 in) and they have a rough surface. An alternative to concrete pools are flat earthenware dishes which can be obtained in sizes suitable for cage, bird room or aviary. In many ways they are superior; they are more hygienic, for instance, because instead of scrubbing and cleaning, you simply replace a dirty dish with a clean one. In hard weather the same routine is much more efficient than de-icing a concrete pool with hot water. Flat stones or pieces of flat concrete can be placed in the dishes to adjust the depth and prevent even the smallest bird from drowning. I do not advise the use of pools made of plastic materials that can be obtained from aquarium suppliers, garden centres and pet shops, as the surfaces are too smooth and they are usually much too deep to be used as bird baths.

# 2
# Nutrition and Food

The greatest danger to providing and maintaining adequate nutrition for the birds described in this book is if the term seed-eating is taken too literally. It is not a matter of chance that the species which have been successfully domesticated or semi-domesticated and which represent a wide taxonomic spectrum, are those that can more easily be maintained and bred on a diet consisting largely of seed. The Budgerigar, Bengalese Finch, Zebra Finch, Canary, Japanese Quail and Diamond Dove are well known examples. Many other seed-eating birds belonging to families such as the buntings (Emberizidae) and the waxbills (Estrildidae) need live food in the form of insects and other invertebrates (or adequate substitutes) if they are to retain health and fitness in the long term and breed successfully.

For feeding requirements, birds can be divided arbitrarily into four basic groups: seed-eaters (hardbills), softbills (which are further subdivided), nectar feeders and carnivorous birds. With the exception of a few highly specialised feeders, all these groups overlap to some extent in their choice of foods and needs.

Large-scale research into the nutritional aspects of avian husbandry was originally initiated to meet the demands of the commercial poultry industry and resulted in the production of complete diets, such as chick and turkey starter crumbs. These diets have benefited the rearing of quail and other avicultural gallinaceous birds. Other nutritional research was in response to the requirements of the pet bird market, pigeon fanciers and to a lesser but increasing extent, aviculturists keeping a wide variety of birds from softbills to nectar feeders. This has resulted in many commercially produced diets covering a wide range of needs from canary rearing foods to products for hummingbirds. These diets have given the aviculturist keeping seed-eating birds useful food supplements and substitutes which in some cases can partially fulfil the requirements of seed-eating species for which live food is essential for successful breeding.

There is little doubt that many cases of ill health in birds are caused by a nutritional deficiency. Classic examples could often be seen among dealers', pet shops' and private collections in the days of unrestricted bird importations. Waxbills and many species of small finches were often fed on a diet of pannicum millet and little or nothing else; happily, this is now a rarity. The response to critical comment was usually 'the birds lived a long time' and mortality was low. I was always reminded by this reply of a response to a similar statement attributed to the late Duke of Bedford, a skilled and dedicated aviculturist. When a lady was boasting to him of the longevity of her far from healthy parrot, the Duke's reply was, 'Madam, your parrot has not lived a long time; it's merely taking a long time to die'.

## BASIC NUTRITION

A complete diet should consist of proteins, carbohydrates, fats and oils, vitamins, minerals and water. These various constituents have a complex metabolic interrelationship within the bird's body. The largest percentage of a bird's diet provides energy; protein and carbohydrates give an energy equivalent of four calories per gram, fat yields nine calories per gram. These food sources have to be broken down into more simple substances by digestive enzymes before they can be utilised in the body.

### Proteins

Proteins are needed in the diet for building up and replacing the body's tissues, with a greater amount being required during growth and reproduction. Excess protein is used by the body for energy, and if the main energy sources — carbohydrates and fats — are insufficient, an increasing percentage of dietary protein will be used for energy, resulting in a breakdown in the body's proteins, with associated muscle wastage and loss of body weight. Proteins are composed of amino-acids, the essential and non-essential; the essential amino-acids must be provided in the diet. Animal proteins are much better sources of the essential amino-acid lysine than plant proteins.

### Carbohydrates

Carbohydrates, which are the most readily available source of energy, are broken down within the body into simple sugars, then metabolised into carbon dioxide and water, with the resultant release of energy. Sugar and starches are carbohydrates, as is cellulose (fibre or roughage). Some animals such as ruminants, have the ability to use cellulose which is broken down by micro-organisms in the gut. Although this ability is probably limited in birds, due to food passing quickly through their short digestive tracts, some roughage is needed to provide a suitable environment for micro-organisms which have a role in the production of certain vitamins. It is also required to exercise and maintain the gut muscles, although an excess of roughage can result in a diet of poor nutritional quality.

### Fats and Oils

The term 'fat' in a nutritional sense also includes oils of animal and plant origin. Apart from providing the bird with its second source of energy, fats and oils (unstable fats) have other important functions. They are needed in the diet to promote the absorption of fat-soluble vitamins and they also provide a source of fatty acids, some of which are essential. The oils obtained from plants are better sources of the essential fatty acids than animal fats. Besides these nutritional considerations, stored body fat has a protective function and also provides insulation.

### Minerals

Minerals are important for both the structure and functioning of the body. The minerals calcium, phosphorus and to a lesser extent, magnesium, are the chief constituents of bone and egg shells. Calcium also plays a role in the blood clotting mechanism, but neither calcium nor phosphorus can be utilised unless vitamin D is present. Other minerals present in the body tissues include potassium, iron, sulphur, zinc and copper. Others, sometimes known as trace elements, are required only in minute amounts, although they are essential if the body is to function correctly. Sodium and chloride are found mainly in the body fluids; they are concerned with the acid-base equilibrium and play an important part in water metabolism.

## Vitamins

Vitamins are required as accessory food factors to the protein, carbohydrate, fats and minerals which constitute the main food substances. By acting as catalysts, they play an essential part in many metabolic reactions, remaining unchanged at the completion of these processes. Certain vitamins also function as co-enzymes in the breaking down of complex food substances. Some vitamins are excreted from the body more quickly than others which are retained for periods of time that vary with metabolic demands and other factors. Providing a variety of good quality fresh foods are available, vitamin deficiencies, like many other nutritional disorders, are rare.

### FAT-SOLUBLE VITAMINS

Vitamin A (retinol) is sometimes known as the anti-infection vitamin, as a deficiency leads to a degenerative change in the epithelial body tissues, so reducing their effectiveness as a barrier to infection.

The normal growth and development of young birds is also affected by a deficiency of this vitamin; they become stunted and weak, and sometimes show symptoms of the nervous system being affected. Carotene and related pigments which are found in plant foods are converted into retinol within the alimentary tract, but foods of animal origin are the only direct source of retinol.

Vitamin D can be produced by the action of the sun's ultra-violet rays on precusors which are present in the skin, but this process cannot be relied on for providing adequate sources of vitamin D, even with birds in outside flights. This vitamin is required in order that calcium and phosphorus can be utilised in the formation and maintenance of bones and in the production of egg shells. Vitamin D deficiency causes rickets in young, growing birds and osteomalacia (adult rickets) in mature birds. Breeding in the early stages is also affected, as when hens lay thin and soft-shelled eggs.

Vitamin K plays an essential role in the blood-clotting mechanism of the body, and thus a deficiency results in haemorrhages in the skin and muscles. In certain animals, deficiencies under normal circumstances are rare, due to the synthesis of this vitamin by the action of micro-organisms in the gut. This action is limited in some bird species, depending on their natural diet and variations of their alimentary tract (notably the development of the caecum). Green-leafed plant foods are rich sources of vitamin K.

Vitamin E has a wide distribution in natural foodstuffs such as cereals and green plant materials, so a deficiency is comparatively rare. The metabolic functions of vitamin E are far from clear but a lack of it is known to have varying effects on a wide taxonomic spectrum of species. It has been called the fertility vitamin as a deficiency causes a variety of reproductive problems in rats, mice and hamsters. Muscular weakness and paralysis are demonstrated in species from sheep and pigs to rabbits and guinea pigs which have been deprived of vitamin E. In birds the best known and documented effects of vitamin E deficiency occur in poultry — the so-called 'Crazy Chick Disease' (encephalomacia). A deficiency in birds in general has been associated with reproductive problems — mainly embryos dying during incubation (dead-in-the-shell). Muscular and tissue disorders, which are probably analogous to those found in animals, have also been reported.

### WATER-SOLUBLE VITAMINS

Vitamin C (ascorbic acid) is a vitamin which birds are able to produce within the alimentary tract, and apart from the Red-vented Bulbul (*Picnonotus cafer*) and possibly some other fruit- and nectar-feeding species, a deficiency is unlikely in the majority of bird species. The vitamin is essential for the formation of intercellular material in soft tissues and bones, and in animal species which require vitamin C in their diet, notably simians and guinea-pigs, a deficiency can cause a breakdown of this material. This can result in the weakening and possible fracture of bones, or the rupture of blood vessel walls with associated haemorrhaging in the surrounding tissues.

The B complex vitamins are concerned with the metabolism of digested and absorbed components of food, without which the utilisation of energy sources and proteins cannot take place. Apart from laboratory experiments where the effects of a single vitamin deficiency can be observed by administering 'purified' diets, the clinical picture outside of the laboratory is usually that of a multiple B vitamin deficiency. Neuromuscular disorders such as tilting back of the head, convulsions, uncoordinated movements, clenched toes, weakness in the legs, poor feathering and many other symptoms, can all be indicative of a single or multiple B vitamin deficiency. It is important to remember, however, that these same clinical signs can have many other causes, such as injury or infectious disease.

## Water

Clean water for drinking and bathing must be available at all times. It is known that a bird's intake of water is dependent on many variables, such as diet, ambient temperature, humidity, species of bird and breeding activity, but there appears to be very little data on the subject, other than on pet birds and those of economic or research importance, such as poultry, pigeons and quails. Bice investigated the daily water intakes of adult non-breeding canaries and budgerigars and found the average intake of canaries was 5.4 ml and budgerigars 3 ml. As there is evidence that budgerigars are more resistant to the adverse effects of dehydration, the canary intake would appear, to some extent, to be similar to that of the majority of bird species described in this book.

The withdrawal of water can produce symptoms of distress, quickly followed by collapse and death in many species, especially when the surrounding temperatures are high and when the birds are under stress — for example, during transportation. I never rely on one water container even if a cage or aviary houses only one bird, and the container is a clip-on, enclosed type to prevent the bird from bathing (and thus wasting water). I think the minimum of two water containers is necessary whether of the enclosed or open dish type (Figs 5 and 6); ideally one of each type is a safeguard.

## Filtration of Drinking Water

In the UK, in recent years, there have been various reports from aviculturists who have alleged that water from the mains supply has had deleterious effects on their birds. The presence of substances in minute amounts, although no hazard to human beings, could well be a health threat to small birds. If there is cause for concern, consider using a suitable filter, and contact your local water authority.

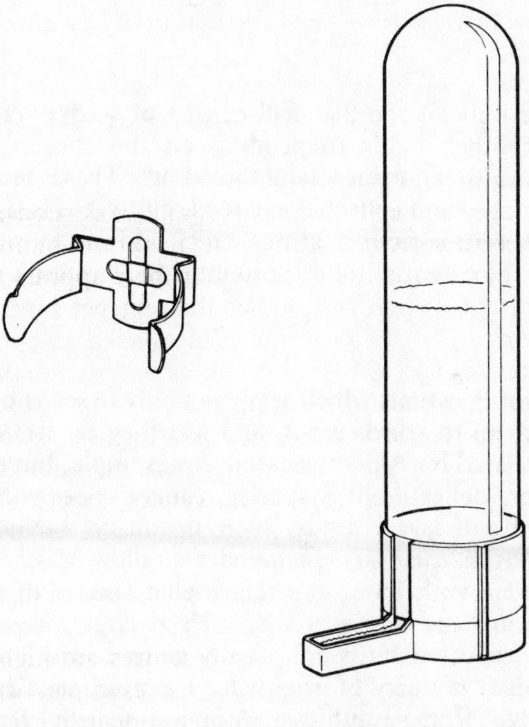

Fig 5 Fountain-type water container showing metal clip for container

Fig 6  Open water dish

## FOODS

Although the bulk of the diet will consist of seeds, varying quantities of other foods (depending on the species) are needed for health and successful breeding. These include commercially bred and collected live food, cultivated and wild plants, commercial softbill mixtures, chick and turkey starter crumbs, and the essential soluble minerals and insoluble grit.

### Seed

Two important questions which apply not only to seeds but to all foods are: can the birds eat it, and will they eat it? Many finches and related birds de-husk seed, for example, but some of the smaller, delicate-billed species, cannot cope with the medium-sized and larger seeds, such as canary, hemp and sunflower. Doves, quail and hemipodes swallow small seeds whole, complete with husk, but the smaller species of these birds cannot manage certain items, such as large maize and maple peas. Imported birds are usually given foods that are available in their country of origin; for example, seed-eating birds imported from South-east Asia are usually fed on pannicum millet or paddy rice — the smaller birds such as avadavats on millet, and the larger birds such as Pin-tailed Parrot Finches and buntings on paddy rice.

Before statutory quarantine was imposed by the USA, UK and some European governments, the aviculturist had to accustom newly imported birds to a balanced diet, but this is now largely the responsibility of the commercial importer. However, some importers and retail businesses still feed seed-eating birds on a spartan diet and although it is generally much easier to accustom these birds to a new diet than softbills, new foods of any kind should be introduced gradually, making sure that the amounts of the previous diet given continue to be adequate. It is always worth while finding out what the previous owner has fed the birds; this includes items other than food, such as grit and minerals, which are essential if the birds are to utilise their food efficiently.

Table 1 shows the results, in percentages, of three food value analyses of seeds commonly fed to many bird species; the lowest and highest figures of the three results are given in

*TABLE 1*
*SEED FOOD VALUES**

| | Proteins % | Carbohydrates % | Fats % | Minerals % |
|---|---|---|---|---|
| Canary | 14–16 | 52–61 | 5–6 | 2–7 |
| White millet | 11–15 | 60–70 | 4–5 | 2–4 |
| Yellow millet | 11 | 63 | 4–5 | 2–3 |
| Hemp | 16–19 | 16–18 | 32 | 2–4 |
| Maw | 17 | 12 | 40 | 6 |
| Niger | 17 | 15 | 32–33 | 7 |
| Rape | 19–24 | 10–12 | 40–42 | 4–6 |
| Linseed | 21–24 | 24–30 | 34–36 | 3–6 |
| Sunflower | 16–24 | 20–21 | 22–29 | 3 |
| Wheat | 10–12 | 70–81 | 2 | 2 |
| Maize | 10 | 65 | 7 | 2 |
| Oats | 11–12 | 53–56 | 5 | 2–3 |

* Showing highest and lowest percentage results of three analyses. A single result indicates uniform percentage

each case; a single figure indicates a uniform percentage. Analyses of the same seeds can vary for many reasons, from the type of soil in which the seed was grown to the amount of time the seed has been stored before analysis. The table shows that three of the main seeds fed to many species of finches and related birds — canary-seed, and white and yellow millet —

have a lower crude protein and fat content than the oily seeds, such as hemp, maw and niger. Furthermore, many investigations into the protein content of canary and millet seeds in general have shown them to be seriously deficient in the amino-acids lysine and arginine, as well as the B complex vitamins, especially riboflavin and biotin.

The possibility of obesity is frequently given as a reason for not increasing the nutritional value of basic millet and canary-seed by the addition of oily seeds. In many cases obesity is due not only to overfeeding with these seeds, but also to insufficient space for exercise. For example, active birds such as cardinals (which in my opinion are never at their best in a cage) are often kept in cages that are far too small. And yet it is not always wise to keep a bird on its own, as it tends to become sluggish and so more prone to obesity. Although the injudicious mixing of birds is to be avoided, an established population of compatible birds in the same cage has the advantage of stimulating more movement — perhaps through competition for a favourite perching point, for example.

Apart from increasing the seed variety given, another way of enhancing the nutritional value and interest of seeds is to soak them until germination has commenced. The seed should be soaked in cold water for three to five days, depending on the ambient temperature, and the water changed daily. Before feeding to the bird the seed should be thoroughly rinsed in clean running water and allowed to dry. The seeds I have found most suitable for germination are panicum millet, white millet and canary. Millet sprays (the seed heads of panicum millet) complete with stalk, so they are easy to hang in cage or aviary, can be offered either dry or soaked until germinated. In many cases I have found some birds will ignore or eat very little of the unsoaked sprays, but seldom fail to consume germinating sprays avidly.

Different types of seeds are best offered in separate open dishes that should be replenished continually. I never use hoppers for seed as they easily become clogged through moisture. Although it is tempting to provide a mixture in one dish, this means that you have little idea of which seeds are being eaten and how much. It is essential to make sure that husks are blown off before refilling a dish, otherwise what may appear to be an adequate seed supply might actually be empty husks, and this can lead to disastrous results for the birds. At least once a week each seed dish should be replaced with a clean one, otherwise dust will build up and the slightest moisture will cause mould growth. Only clean, good quality seeds should be purchased, whilst the amounts to be bought and stored will depend largely on the space available and number of birds. It is cheaper to buy in bulk, but the seeds must always be used in the order in which they were received. Vermin-proof containers, such as metal bins with tight-fitting lids, will keep the seed dry and free of dust.

## Plant Foods

Plant foods, both cultivated and collected, are an excellent source of vitamins and make a diet more interesting for the birds. Wild plants such as shepherd's purse (*Capsella*), dandelion (*Taraxacum* spp), chickweed (*Stellaria* spp), plantain (*Plantago* spp), sow thistles (*Sonchus*) and many others will be readily accepted. Seeding grasses of many species provide an excellent food and constitute a major dietary source for many wild seed-eating birds. The ubiquitous annual meadow grass (*Poa annua*) is taken by nearly all seed-eating birds, from waxbills to quail. Cultivated plants which can be given include spinach, lettuce, brussel sprout leaves, watercress and cabbage leaves which I shred for the smaller birds. All green food fed to the birds must be fresh; it should be washed before being offered and any uneaten food removed before it becomes stale.

The major problem with the use of either collected or cultivated plant foods is the danger of contamination from the ever increasing number of chemical agents used against insects, weeds and other 'pests'. I never use sprays or any pest controls, and primarily because of my bird keeping, I am tolerant of weeds, allowing them to grow and cropping the leaves and seed heads, or controlling their spread by digging them up to feed to the birds. If you are a keen gardener, an alternative is to keep a 'wild' kitchen garden, isolated from the areas where weed killers are used. Another source of wild plant foods is to find an area near your premises where sprays or other chemicals are not used. I have found that if you explain your reasons for the enquiries, official bodies and local residents are very helpful.

## Live Food

There are very few birds which will not take live food in the form of insects and other invertebrates, and for many species, live food provides the animal protein needed for the successful rearing of their young. For some years mealworms and maggots were practically the only commercially produced live food available for bird feeding. Now many other invertebrates can be obtained, such as house crickets and locusts. The results of analyses carried out on mealworms and blowfly maggots and published by Clive Roots show that although the protein content is 16.2% for maggots and 20.8% for mealworms, the calcium and phosphorus percentage is only 0.02–0.2 for maggots and 0.03–0.27 for mealworms. There is little doubt that this lack of minerals is responsible for leg and other skeletal deformities in young birds when the parents are provided with mealworms and maggots as the only rearing food. I have tried in the past to overcome this problem by dusting the mealworms or maggots with mineral preparations and powdered cuttle fish, after first making them sticky with multi-vitamin preparations and other additives, but I met with limited success. When a variety of commercial or collected live food is supplied in addition to mealworms and maggots, the young birds have been reared without any problems. Gibson was able to rear healthy chicks fed almost solely on mealworms, provided that at least a third of the mealworms were smeared daily with soft margarine. However, the whole question of live food for rearing young is dependent on the species of bird and the size of live food required by the nestlings during the first few days of life. These requirements will be detailed under the taxonomic groupings.

### MEALWORMS

Mealworms are the larval stage of the beetles *Tenebrio molitor* and *T. obscura*. *T. molitor* is the species usually bred in vast numbers commercially to supply the retail pet trade; they are used for feeding birds, reptiles and insectivorous mammals.

Because of their size and protective skin, mealworms are difficult for the smaller birds such as waxbills to cope with — usually, they manage to eat them only after much prodding and mangling of the larvae. I feed only the smaller larvae and those that are white and grub-like after casting, to waxbills, and leave the full-sized larvae to the larger birds, such as buntings. The mealworms can be cut up before feeding, or as an alternative (though I have not tried it) they can be dipped in boiling water, but as this would kill them, I would have thought they no longer attracted the birds because all movement would have ceased.

Mealworms are expensive, but you can breed your own. Success depends on temperature and humidity, and it is these factors that control the length of the life cycle, which is about six months at 21°C (70°F) and four months at 26.7°C (80°F). I breed mealworms at normal room temperature (about 20–22°C [68–72°F]), but if the surrounding temperature remains at over 30°C (86°F) for any length of time, it is doubtful if the life cycle will be completed. The usual breeding method is to use boxes of well-seasoned wood at least 30.5 cm (1 ft) deep, the overall size depending on the quantity of mealworms required. On the floor of the culture box place a piece of soft cloth or hessian covered with bran to a depth of approximately 25 mm (1 in), and then introduce some adult beetles or larvae. As the bran is used up, add some more, then lay newspaper or soft cloth over the culture. The beetles will chew through this layer and lay their eggs. Pieces of bread and root vegetables should be placed on top of the cloth or newspaper. When small larvae are spotted, a shallow tray filled with grated root vegetables and bran should be placed on top (lettuce may also be given). The vegetables and lettuce must be replaced every few days to stop mould growing. As the larvae grow, the amount of root vegetables must be increased. A piece of damp sacking should be placed under the lid of the box, as this, together with the root vegetables, will maintain the humidity which is essential for successful breeding. Maintaining the humidity level, along with the removal of the beetles, also helps to prevent cannibalism. However, the culture should never be allowed to become too damp, otherwise mite infestation and mould growth will occur. When the larvae are fully grown, they will collect in the newspaper and can then be removed for feeding to the birds, or to start another culture box.

Some breeders advocate having three or four layers of bran in each box, separated by hessian or sacking. Personally I have found it best to have two or three single-layer culture boxes going at the same time, as I find it easier to collect the adult larvae; also, the multi-layer boxes seem more likely to suffer from mould growth and mite infestation, but this is a matter of opinion. Besides wooden boxes, I have also used well-ventilated plastic containers, and in laboratories large glass containers have been used, obviously to facilitate cleaning when ending a culture and thus preventing mite infestation.

### BUFFALO WORMS

I first became aware of this live-food source in 1982, when I found some buffalo worms (lesser mealworms, *Alphitobius diaperinus*) in a shipment of house crickets. They are now part of a wide range of invertebrate species bred commercially and readily available. For most if not all of these species, a home culture is only useful as a standby; a commercial supply can be obtained by phone and return of post, or from a retail shop. These larvae can be bred in screw-top jars with a fine gauze-and-muslin panel for ventilation in the lid. The culture food can be bran with poultry chick crumbs, or bran and fishmeal.

### MAGGOTS

In the UK and Europe maggots are produced commercially for the angler on a vast scale, but are rarely available in the USA and Australia.

The three main types of maggots of interest to the bird keeper are the 'standard' maggot (the larval form of the blue-bottle fly), the 'pinkie' (greenbottle) and the 'squatt' (house-fly).

The main disadvantage with standard maggots is their size — they are too large for many birds to feed to their young, and some smaller adult birds also find them difficult to cope with. However, they are accepted by larger birds such as buntings and cardinals, quail and some dove species. Some of the larger birds will feed them to their young a few days after they have hatched.

'Pinkies' are much smaller than standards, and I have found them very useful as a basic live food for the smaller birds, such as serins, pytilias and waxbills, to feed to their young. Pinkies are also softer skinned than standards, so the smaller birds find them much easier to manage. They are very active and will easily escape from any small container without a tight-fitting lid (the ventilation holes must be the size of a pin-head).

It is important to place any bought maggots in clean bran for at least four days before feeding to the birds, to allow them to excrete any contaminated food matter they may contain. *Bird deaths from botulism have occurred when fed maggots reared on contaminated food material*, but when well-cleaned maggots have been used, I have not experienced any trouble. *Do not use maggots if you have any doubts about your supply.*

HOUSE CRICKETS

These can be bred without much trouble, but unless you have premises isolated from your house, then it is better to buy them as escapees can prove troublesome house pests. Many retail pet shops stock house crickets and they are also available through mail order. With their wide range of sizes, house crickets provide a very useful source of live food for many bird species.

FRUIT-FLIES

Fruit-flies (*Drosophila*) are easily bred, and providing an approximate temperature range of 21–25°C (70–77°F) is maintained, they will breed throughout the year. Extremes of heat are more damaging to the culture than extremes of cold, although the optimal temperature for breeding and a short life cycle of about six to seven days is 24°C (75°F). Although in laboratories the rearing medium consists of sugar, yeast, sucrose, or similar, for avicultural purposes a tin containing rotting fruit placed on a bed of wood-wool works very well. It is important to make sure that the birds cannot come into contact with the rotting fruit, as any mould growing on it might cause problems.

WHITE WORMS

These small worms (genus *Enchytraeus*) can be bred in peat in boxes or tins. The peat should be made moist, then enough placed in the container to make it about two-thirds full. A white worm culture should then be obtained from an aquarist shop and placed on top of the peat, followed by a sloppy mixture of bread and milk, or porridge, to feed the worms. A fine mesh wire fixed to the top of the container will allow ventilation and keep out any unwelcome visitors such as mice, and finally, a board or other solid covering will do the job of keeping the culture dark.

It is important to keep the peat moist, but *not* wet, and to protect it from extremes of heat and cold. In the warmer weather I keep the culture outside in a location which is protected from sunlight and rain. I have found it best to keep three or four cultures going and use them in rotation. To feed the birds I simply take a trowel full of peat and worms and scatter it on the floor of the aviary — spiders or insects which have invaded the container make a welcome bonus for the birds.

### WAX-MOTHS

Wax-moth larvae are an excellent bird food and, as with other live foods, are available from commercial breeders, by phone or return of post. One of the pioneers in breeding live food for aviculture is Frank Meaden, who developed techniques for breeding wax-moths, and many other species, long before they were well known or available commercially. The most often used and bred is the Greater Wax-moth (*Galleria mellonella*).

They can be cultured in screw-top jars, with the usual gauze-and-muslin ventilation panel; a temperature of approximately 30°C (86°F) is optimum for breeding success. Meaden (1979) recommends a food consisting of 6 parts rolled oats, 1 part glycerine and 1 part honey. When mixed to a crumbly consistency, add a sprinkling of yeast and mix well into the food.

### STICK INSECTS

The Indian Stick Insect (*Carausius morosus*) is widely kept in schools and laboratories, or as a 'pet'. A nocturnal insect, it feeds on privet and is easily kept and bred at room temperature. It reproduces parthenogenetically. The Corsican Stick Insect (*Bacillus rossius*) is also readily available from many pet shops, but not so commonly kept as the Indian. The Corsican comes from southern Europe and feeds on bramble; it is also parthenogenetic, and easily kept and bred, but it is less nocturnal than the Indian.

Practically any sort of escape-proof and ventilated container can be used to house stick insects — an old aquarium with the top covered with fine gauze, or rigid, clear plastic tubes with the top and bottom covered with fine gauze and sealed around the edges with tape. Place the tubes on absorbent paper on a tray, along with a jam jar of water containing the food plants (the cut leafy stems of privet or bramble). The lid of the jam jar should be pierced and the plant stems pushed through so that the young insects cannot drown in the water. The food plants will keep fresh in water for about a week, but must then be replaced. Spray the leaves lightly every day, taking care not to wet the sides of the container. The height of the container is important, as the insects moult while clinging to the stems, so they need at least twice their own length clear of the base of the container for a moult to be successful — and remember, stick insects can measure as much as 75 mm (3 in).

The tiny eggs that are laid fall to the floor, and although the recommended practice is to collect them and keep them on clean, moist sand in a plastic box, I put plastic trays on the container floor with a layer of sand and let the inoffensive droppings and eggs fall directly onto it (but I always remove dead leaves and suchlike to prevent mould growth). The incubation period for stick insects is a long one; depending on the species, it would appear to vary from three or four months to nine months. The hatched nymphs must have food plants available soon after hatching, and my method of leaving the eggs in the container means the nymphs do not have to be moved to obtain food.

In my opinion, the main advantages of stick insects as live food are the vast numbers which hatch and the comparatively slow growth rate, which means that you have a wide variety of sizes to use as food. The insects and their droppings are totally inoffensive and without smell, and if they escape there is no danger of them becoming pests (unless they escape in a greenhouse). For some reason I cannot explain my sticks breed from May until September, with very few hatchings outside this period. (I assume that as I lack the benefit of central heating the slightly lowered temperature inhibits egg laying and hatching.) As with all live food breeding I never rely on one culture, but keep at least three containers in operation. The disadvantage of stick insects as live food is their protective behaviour of playing 'dead' when disturbed, but this appears to be more pronounced with the larger insects. The birds are often deceived by this at first, but I noticed when a pair of cardinals with young in the nest were fed on stick insects, it took the parent birds about 20 minutes to realise this, and as with any live food, the parent birds were soon waiting for me to put the next lot of insects into the aviary.

COLLECTED LIVE FOOD

The variety of species and size of collected live food means that collection is superior to any commercial or home-bred supply. As with plant food collection, the area you search for food should be near your home if possible and free of spraying with insecticides and weed killers. Collection is worthwhile during late spring and all through the summer. During this period I go collecting armed with a walking stick, pair of leather gloves, galvanised tub, plastic bags and trowel. I use the handle end of the stick to pull nettles, hedges and bramble stems down into the tub, then I shake and beat them vigorously to dislodge the live food. The tub is then emptied into a plastic bag and sealed with a rubber band. In this way I can gather a good crop of spiders, earwigs, moths, greenfly, caterpillars and other invertebrates, depending on the month and the weather.

On the ground I turn over any rotting logs, stones, old lino and other dumped household items looking for woodlice, beetle larvae. I spend about 30 minutes on collection every morning or evening, but if I cannot go collecting, I at least have a supply of home-bred and purchased live food available. When collecting, local residents (once they realise you are a harmless eccentric!) are often very helpful and will let you collect any plagues of caterpillars, for example, which have invaded their garden but you must always ask that essential question, 'Do you use sprays and other chemical agents?'. I am often surprised at the number of people who, although keen gardeners, have rejected the use of chemicals out of concern for wild birds, butterflies and other vulnerable creatures.

If you have no suitable collection area nearby, an expedition at the weekends to collect as much as possible is the best alternative. On warm sunny days ant pupae, which are an excellent rearing food for young birds, can be collected from the nests of many species of ant such as the meadow and wood ants. In Australia, termites are used by many aviculturists to feed the more insectivorous species of birds.

## Supplementary Foods and Additives

Commercial insectivorous mixtures, fine grade for the smaller birds and a coarser mixture for the larger species, are useful both for enhancing the nutritional value of a diet and as a rearing food. It is sometimes difficult to get the birds used to this supplement; if you are using it as a rearing food, for example, it is no good suddenly offering it when the chicks are hatched, so always mix a small amount with seed and increase the amount during the breeding season.

There are numerous commercial soft foods with a wide spectrum of ingredients now available. If you can get species which rear young on live food to take these substitutes, instead of live invertebrates, it is a great advantage. There is always scope for experiment; recently an aviculturist was successful in breeding several species of waxbills using frozen freshwater shrimps. The method used was to place the thawed shrimps in a shallow dish, with just enough water to cover them.

There are many vitamin preparations in a powdered form, which can be dusted on live food, and multi-vitamin solutions which can be added to drinking water. In the winter only, I use this method once a week, being careful to follow the manufacturer's instructions. It must be remembered that overdosing with vitamins, especially the fat-soluble vitamins, like A and D, which are not readily excreted from the body, can lead to toxicity problems.

## Minerals and Grit

Minerals are supplied by broken pieces of cuttle-fish and oyster shell. I also find that Kilpatrick's pigeon minerals (not the large variety, but the dark powdered form which Goodwin has described as looking like iron filings) are readily taken not only by my doves, but by all the seed-eating birds I keep, including the quail; they should be offered in separate dishes.

Grit is supplied by commercial bird sand, and 'sharp' sand can be obtained from builders' yards. Mineralised grit can also be purchased from pet shops and seed merchants.

# 3 Obtaining Stock and Management

There are four ways that the majority of species described in this book can be obtained, apart from breeding them. You can buy from a commercial importer, pet shop or private breeder, or import them yourself. This last method is not to be recommended because of the legal and commercial documentation involved, let alone the quarantine and other legal requirements of countries such as the USA and the UK. So all things considered, the importation of birds by the private aviculturist is a difficult process and best left to the commercial importer. The keeping of native species in captivity is subject to legal controls in many countries and in some, such as the USA, it is prohibited. It is easy to see, therefore, that the newcomer to aviculture must acquaint himself with the legislation regarding the keeping in captivity of all avian species, both native and imported. In the UK the Ministry of Agriculture, Fisheries and Food and the Department of the Environment provide current informaton, and similar government departments in other countries can do the same. One of the best ways for the beginner in aviculture to receive guidance is to join a local avicultural club or society.

## BUYING BIRDS

Wherever you buy your birds, always observe them carefully before making a purchase. Stand back away from the cage or aviary so that the birds relax and you can spot the active bird as opposed to a sick bird which is frightened into activity.

A healthy bird should be tight feathered, active and clear eyed, the area around the eyes, nostrils and beak clean and free of lesions or discharge. Around the vent there should be no matted feathers or soiling, and the feet and legs should show no sign of injury, inflammation or puffiness. It is often stated that if a bird is healthy, poor plumage is not important; however, if large areas of feathers are missing, the bird is very vulnerable to low temperatures and draughts, and special care must be taken. If birds are obtained from a commercial source, in many cases they are kept in high temperatures, and therefore in any new environment, they must initially be kept at similar temperatures. In warmer weather these temperatures can slowly be reduced as a first step towards the birds becoming acclimatised to their new surroundings. In some countries, such as the UK, it is possible when buying from many commercial sources to have the birds sent to you by rail or road carriers. This has two main disadvantages: firstly, you have not selected the birds yourself and secondly, there is the additional risk of a transport method over which you have no control. From whatever source the birds are obtained, they should be kept isolated from other stock until you are satisfied that they are healthy and well established. Although birds imported into the USA, UK and some other countries have been quarantined, it must be remembered that quarantine has one primary objective, and that is to protect the commercial poultry industry from the devastating effects of contagious diseases such as velogenic Newcastle disease. Therefore quarantine is no guarantee that the birds you buy are not suffering from a nutritional deficiency or other disorders. Also, these birds are a long way from being either acclimatised or established, especially as they have had the additional stress of being moved from quarantine to the importer's retail section or to a pet shop, and then on to another change of environment when you buy them.

It is always best to buy birds in the late spring or summer, especially if they have been imported. Although all your stock should be carefully observed, fresh arrivals must be checked as often as possible in their isolation quarters. Even if the birds are obtained from a breeder, they should never be released into an aviary straightaway. In the less complex environment of an isolation cage, it is easier to check the birds for signs of ill health and for them to find their food and water and generally become familiar with their new surroundings. If the birds are received late in the day, especially in the winter, light should be provided for some hours so they can feed and drink, and this should be continued until they are established. A dimmer control incorporated in the lighting circuit is essential, so that the birds are not suddenly plunged into darkness, with resulting shock. The dimmer ensures that the light intensity is slowly reduced over a period of 30 minutes or so, then automatically switched off.

Whether you are a beginner buying birds for the first time, or an experienced aviculturist, it is essential to select the species and number of birds in relation to the accommodation and the time you have available for their care. If your work means that you are away from your birds even for a day, you must have someone reliable to care for them. Holidays are another factor which is sometimes overlooked. The ideal solution is a reciprocal arrangement with another bird keeper who lives near you; otherwise, a member of your family or a friend to whom you can show your routine of care in detail, leaving them clear and concise written instructions.

## MANAGEMENT

It is always best to stick to a routine for cleaning, feeding and watering to which the birds can adjust, and as far as possible this routine should not be changed. Any work in the bird room or aviary must be carried out without any sudden movements or undue haste.

### Cleaning

Cages can be kept clean by lining the dirt trays with newspaper and laying bird sand on the paper, or the sand alone can be used. The trays can then be emptied into a large plastic bag, relined and replaced. If any cage shows signs of soiling, the birds can be transferred to a clean cage and the dirty cage washed with a solution of disinfectant specially recommended for use with livestock and mixed according to the manufacturer's instructions; the cage should then be washed with hot water and dried.

A vacuum cleaner, especially the heavy-duty industrial type, is very useful to clean the bird room floor and remove dust from awkward corners, and it is much quicker and more efficient than sweeping. Perches of the commercial type can be cleaned by scraping with a hacksaw blade, but remember that all perches, whether commercial or made of natural twigs and branches, must be frequently replaced with new clean ones. As the birds often clean their bills by rubbing on the perches, soiling can quickly lead to eye infections.

The way an aviary is cleaned depends on its type of flooring. Flight areas with a soil floor can be dug up and replaced with fresh top soil or turfs. Solid floors such as concrete can be swept and washed down. When birds are breeding, cleaning must be curtailed and providing the aviary is not overcrowded and the feeding areas are cleaned, no problems should arise. It is important, not only for hygiene but also to maintain an aviary in good condition, to clear it once a year for creosoting, painting (lead-based paint must not be used), and repairing brickwork.

Cut branches used for cover and nesting sites should be burnt, and nesting boxes, baskets and similar items should be cleaned or replaced. Wire netting should be checked, painted and replaced as necessary to ensure that rodents are kept out as far as possible, and that the birds cannot escape.

## Rodent Control

Effective rodent control is essential, as mice and rats not only eat and contaminate food, but disturb breeding birds; rats can also kill both young and adult birds. Although the best defence against rodents is to prevent them gaining access to birdrooms and aviaries in the first place, sooner or later mice will get in. Control is best carried out with traps of various types and poisons. The break-back type of sprung mouse or rat traps have two basic designs; one relies on bait fixed to metal prongs which release the trap when the animal takes the bait; the other uses the same principle, but the animal must first step on a platform to trigger the trap. I have found that setting one trap, with or without bait, is useless, especially as mice seem to prefer seed to other food. Even if they should be attracted to the bait, their fantastic agility and reflex actions often allow them to jump clear of the sprung trap. Therefore, in areas where the birds have no access, I set traps of the platform type in groups of four, placing them against the side of a wall or other perimeters that the mice run along. An alternative trap consists of an enclosed box with small holes through which the mice can enter. The box should be placed on the ground with the holes about 50 mm (2 in) away from a wall (Fig. 7). Enough traps are set inside the box so that as a mouse enters, it cannot avoid triggering one, and if it jumps, it is bound to land on the other traps.

Inside the aviary the best method of control is the type of trap which catches rodents alive. It consists of a ventilated box with two holes from which funnel-shaped, wire tunnels project to allow mice to enter but not to get out. For a couple of nights the lid of the box should be left off so that the mice can enter and feed on the bait, then when the lid is replaced the mice will be trapped the next time they enter. A similar type of trap has a paddle operated by clockwork; no bait is required because on entering the hole the mice are knocked into a ventilated compartment by the paddle. Rats can be caught in a wire cage in which the trap is operated by a spring-loaded platform.

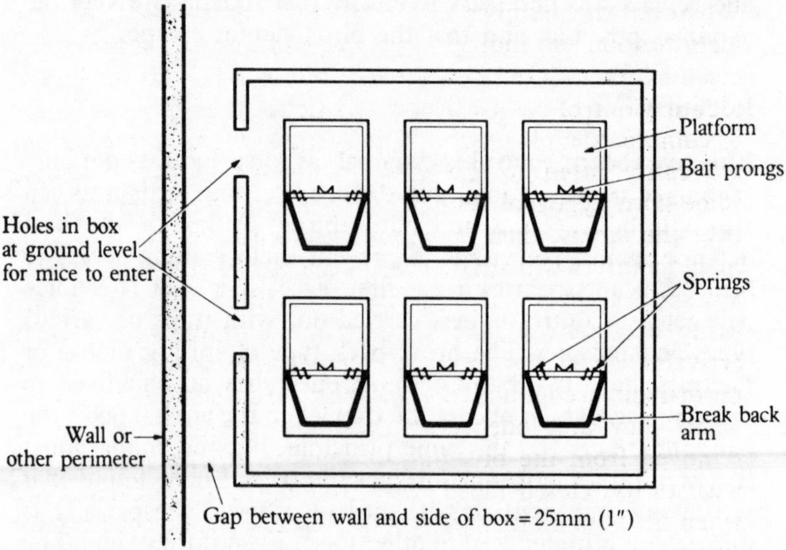


Fig 7 Plan view of six platform type spring traps set in cardboard box

## Poisons

Poisons must be used with caution and common sense and only in areas where the birds have no access. It is essential that the manufacturer's instructions are read and followed. A simple and efficient method of dispensing poison is to use a wooden box with holes so that the mice can enter, and of course, it should be fitted with a waterproof lid to protect the poison from rain and wind. Rodents can become immune to one type of poison, so changes must be made when results indicate this is happening.

## Cat and Rodent Repellers

These apparently repel cats and rodents by ultra-sound and are, I believe, comparatively new in the UK. I have no experience of them myself, but any device which may repel cats and rodents, without causing them harm, is well worth investigating.

## Record Keeping and Ringing

Whatever the number and species of birds you have, the identification of individual birds and record keeping are essential for long-term effective breeding. The best method of identification is the use of split plastic rings of various colours or combination of colours. Whatever age the bird, these rings are easily fitted to the tarsus with the aid of a simple 'shoe-horn' type tool. The ring is opened with the tool, slipped over the tarsus, then pinched closed with your fingers. The manufacturers will advise you on the size of ring required for any species; the tool is supplied along with the rings which are easily obtained by mail order. The best time to ring new arrivals is when they are moved from their isolation quarters to permanent accommodation. Young birds should be ringed when they are independent of their parents and can be removed from the breeding quarters to stock cages. If you wish to use closed metal rings, ringing must be carried out when the young birds are still in the nest (the optimal age for ringing is dependent on species).

Records can be kept in stock books or on cards. I prefer a book, as cards can be easily mislaid. Use the book to record long-term breeding data, purchases, deaths and hatching. Cards are useful, however, pinned to cages and aviaries with the details of the birds housed in each.

## Computer Records

Computers are widely used for the recording of breeding and other data. They have the great advantage of instant retrieval of information and documentation. Records from books or cards can be transferred and act as a safeguard against loss.

## Catching and Handling

The best method of catching birds is to use a net — the short-handled, circular type is easy to use. If the bag of the net is made of soft, finely woven cloth, or similar material, the birds' claws will not get caught, and provided the wire rim of the net is well-padded, no injuries will occur. Birds must be caught with decisive and co-ordinated movements — something which is achieved with experience. The isolation of the bird you wish to catch in the shelter or safety porch of an aviary, and the use of cage partitions, make the job much easier and cause the other birds less disturbance. Even in a fairly large area, if you stand still and keep the birds on the move without causing panic, their movements will become predictable and the catch can be made quickly and efficiently.

Once caught, a bird must be held firmly but never tightly: enclose it in your cupped hand, restraining the body and preventing wing movement, whilst holding the bird's head between your first and second fingers. Clumsy handling not only causes the birds stress, but feathers can be lost, especially with soft-feathered species such as doves.

## Escaped Birds

Even with safety porches and the careful checking and maintenance of aviaries, escapes can sometimes occur. For recapture an important factor can be whether you have other birds of the same species as the escapee. For example, if one bird of a pair escapes, you stand a good chance of recapture, but if both birds of a pair escape and it is the only pair you have, the chances are not so good because the draw of contact calls and the visual attraction of conspecifics is lacking. Exceptions can occur when a pair bond has been formed, even between different species. An amusing example of this happened when I had a cock St Helena Waxbill (*Estrilda astrild*) whose mate had died, and until I could obtain another hen, I caged him with an unmated Zebra Finch hen for companionship. They immediately formed a pair bond and built an enormous nest where she laid and incubated eggs, with her noisy and energetic mate fussing around. Due to a fault in the cage front which had gone unnoticed, he escaped and spent the rest of the day flying around the garden. That night he roosted in a hedge, and although I kept watch at dusk, I missed the exact location, so I could not use the method of shining a torch and catching him at the roost. The next day I left the bird room door open, and he flew in immediately and was soon trying to rejoin his mate in the cage, so all I had to do was close the door. Needless to say, the tireless reproductive efforts of this odd but cheerful couple were fruitless.

Escaped birds can also be caught by placing a caged mate or opposite sex conspecific in a safety porch and propping the door open with a stick attached to a long cord. Baiting the porch with seed or live food and baited trap cages are other alternatives.

## Overgrown Bills and Claws

Claws, and more rarely bills, sometimes grow to an excessive length; it occurs more frequently with birds housed in cages than aviaries. Some species such as *Lonchura* mannikins (also known as nuns) are prone to rapidly growing claws which, if not trimmed, can easily be caught in aviary wire and nesting material. If overgrown bills are neglected, feeding can become difficult for the bird, with serious results. For the simple but important procedures of claw and bill trimming, all that is required is a *sharp* pair of nail scissors or clippers and an extra light source such as a portable lamp. Handling a bird for whatever reason causes it a certain amount of stress, so having everything you need to hand will reduce the time involved and therefore the stress. For claw cutting, the toe and claw are held between the thumb and forefinger so that the claw can be examined in a good light for the vein. The cut should be made clear of the vein, otherwise bleeding will occur. When bill cutting, the bird's head and the base of the bill should be secured with your fingers then the bill trimmed back to its normal length; overcutting can also result in bleeding.

## SICKNESS AND HEALTH

It was once true to say that the majority of veterinary surgeons had little interest in birds. This is no longer the case, since aviculture has been elevated from the status of a hobby to that of a science, due to veterinary and technological developments. An ever-increasing number of veterinary surgeons are both interested and have great expertise in avian species. The aviculturist, whenever possible, should establish a working relationship with a local veterinary practice, even if he has only a small number of birds.

With intelligent management, a varied diet of good quality and the owner's empathy, the health and longevity of birds are remarkable. Laymen are surprised when I tell them that small birds such as serins and mannikins can have an active and healthy life of 15 years, and 20 years plus is not exceptional — in some cases certainly, a bird's lifespan exceeds those of cats and dogs. Longevity records can be misleading, but my own data show that successfully established imported birds and captive bred stock have an average active life of eight years, counting from the time of purchase for imported birds, as their age is unknown. However, birds like any other living creatures act as hosts or can be invaded by a wide spectrum of organisms, ranging from viruses and bacteria to ecto and endoparasites, some of which are or can be pathogenic. With the exception of some overt pathogens, healthy birds can act as host to a population of organisms, without ill effects, providing they are not further challenged by bad management, accident or injury. If the stock is well managed, the other essential precaution against disease is careful observation. A bird which may appear fit to the novice can show subtle signs of something wrong which alerts the experienced aviculturist. If any of the many signs of ill health such as respiratory distress, diarrhoea, listlessness or fluffed out plumage is noticed the bird must be isolated and heat provided within the temperature range of 29–32°C (85–90°F). Always finish attending to the other birds before you remove and handle a suspect bird, otherwise you may be spreading contagious disease throughout your stock. Heat and isolation implemented at the first signs of ill health result in complete recovery in many cases, without further treatment. The heat is best provided by a hospital cage (Fig. 8) which has a thermostatic control and an observation panel or glass front — the problem of birds knocking themselves against the glass can be overcome by drawing bars on the glass with a felt tip pen.

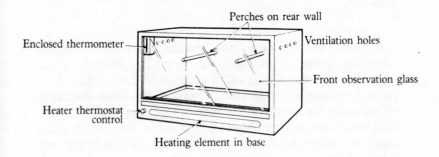

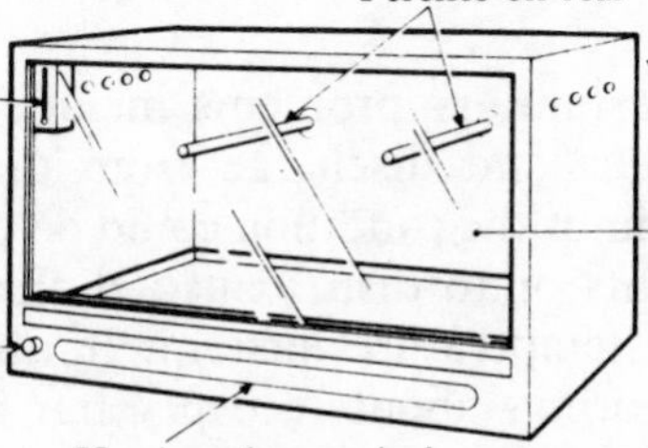


Fig 8 Hospital cage

An alternative is an infra-red heat lamp, but I prefer the hospital cage, as it gives a more consistent high ambient temperature. Lamps are useful for larger birds, for whom most commercially made hospital cages are too small. Once a sick bird has recovered the temperature must be slowly reduced until it is approximately that of the bird's normal environment and only then should it be returned to its cage or aviary.

It must be remembered that many conditions such as rapid breathing or wheezing are only symptoms of what may be infectious disease. If a bird does not respond to heat treatment within 24 hours a veterinary surgeon should be consulted and in many cases treatment with wide spectrum antibiotics, such as the tetracylines, is the next step. In the event of a death for which there is no obvious cause a *post mortem* examination should be carried out, either by a veterinary surgeon or a specialised laboratory which undertakes bird post mortems on a commercial basis.

Sick birds are more likely to drink than eat, so antibiotics are usually given in the drinking water. The most effective method of administering antibiotics is by injection, usually by the subcutaneous or intra-muscular route. This is not a problem with the larger birds, but unfortunately when the patient is a waxbill weighing perhaps eight to ten grams and liable to die suddenly from the additional stress imposed by handling even a veterinary surgeon accustomed to treating birds may consider it unwise to inject intra-muscularly.

## Ailments

### RESPIRATORY

Symptoms of respiratory problems include rapid breathing, wheezing, gasping and discharge from the nostrils. If the symptoms are minor the condition could be due to chilling as a result of draughts or to disturbance at the roost leading to exposure to low temperatures or rain. In these circumstances heat treatment brings about recovery but if recovery is not rapid, treatment with wide spectrum antibiotics obtained from a veterinary surgeon is essential.

The fungal infection known as candidiasis and usually indicated by whitish lesions in the mouth, can cause respiratory distress when it invades the air sacs. The condition often appears after prolonged treatment with antibiotics. Birds infected with gape worms *Syngamus trachea*, demonstrate symptoms such as gaping, coughing and wheezing. Of the seed-eating birds the ground-dwelling species such as quail are the most susceptible. Eggs of the parasites are coughed up from the trachea and then swallowed, and passed out in the droppings thus contaminating the floor of the aviary. The condition can be successfully treated, and good management (including the transfer of quail to a different aviary every season, and the removal of old fouled soil) offers sound preventive measures. Respiratory distress can also come about in simpler ways: nasal passages may become blocked by seeds, or dust particles may cling to sticky layers inside the nostrils.

### ALIMENTARY

Probably the commonest symptom of an alimentary problem is diarrhoea, often accompanied by discolouration of the droppings. Diarrhoea may be due to overfeeding with green food or stale food, in which case isolation and heat treatment combined with a plain diet and no green foods will ensure a rapid recovery. Commercial preparations are available to treat those cases of diarrhoea which are not due to infectious disease. If the bird does not rapidly recover or shows signs of listlessness, loss of weight and deteriorating condition, infectious disease is likely. Pathogenic organisms of the genus *Salmonella* are sometimes implicated and treatment with antibiotics obtained from a veterinary surgeon will often bring about recovery. Coccidiosis is another possibility; it is a protozoal disease often caused by species of the genus *Eimeria*. It is most likely to occur in gallinaceous birds such as quail, especially if there is any chance of infection from poultry. Symptoms can vary from a loss of condition and listlessness to severe emaciation and blood stained diarrhoea. The infected birds excrete oocysts in their droppings, and in damp, warm conditions, if the litter of sand, soil and grit is not regularly cleaned the oocysts will produce spores which are ingested by the birds, thus causing further infection. A number of drugs like the nitrofurans are used to treat this disease and some commercial poultry foods containing coccidiostats can be purchased. The best defence (as with many infectious diseases) is good management. If coccidiosis or salmonella is suspected a veterinary surgeon should be contacted without delay.

Constipation, another common alimentary symptom, is usually caused by faulty nutrition, primarily insufficient roughage in the diet. The bird will sit on a perch straining with jerky movements and appear distressed. A few drops of cod-liver oil can be put into the beak, taking care to avoid any pressure on the abdomen when handling the bird. At the same time, the vent can be gently massaged with olive oil.

### EXTERNAL PARASITES

Mites are the most serious ectoparasites that can attack birds, as both adults and nymphs suck blood from the host. Heavy infestations can result in severe and sometimes fatal loss of blood and the formation of scabs which can lead to secondary bacterial infections. The Red Mite (*Dermanyssus gallinae*) feeds on the birds at night, leaving its host during daylight hours to hide in cracks and crevices in perches and other woodwork. A second species, the Northern Mite (*Ornithonyssus sylviarum*) lives out its entire life cycle on the host. Eradication of mites can be achieved by means of commercial sprays for both birds and cages, the infected birds being sprayed and transferred to a clean cage. Regular cleaning and painting of cages and renewal of perches are sound preventive measures. I always use creosote on the wood of aviaries and bird rooms as it is more effective than paint because it soaks into the wood. (Paint when chipped or cracked provides hiding places for mites and exposes wood.) Furthermore, creosote will kill practically anything, including your birds if you are unwise enough to release them into an aviary before the creosote is really dry. I allow a minimum of ten days for drying, irrespective of the weather conditions, and longer for exposed woodwork. Many species of biting lice (*Mallophaga*) can infest birds. They eat the debris on the skin surface and cause so much irritation that the bird pulls out feathers. Lice can be easily eradicated by using the proprietary bird sprays available.

### INTERNAL PARASITES

Apart from gapeworms, which have been covered separately as a parasite which affects respiration, birds can have both round and tapeworms. Tapeworm (cestode) infestations are less likely in seed-eating birds than insectivorous species, which consume a larger number of intermediate hosts. Birds with severe infestations will become weak, anaemic and lose weight. Eradication of tapeworms is difficult, as treatment with certain drugs can leave the head (or scolex) still attached to the intestinal epithelium. Should a *post mortem* examination reveal the presence of tapeworms, which is more probable with recently imported birds, a veterinary surgeon should be consulted.

The life cycles of roundworms (nematodes) can sometimes involve an intermediate host. Some species in the genera *Ascaridia* and *Capillaria* are common parasites of pigeons, and gallinaceous birds such as quail. Infections can occur as a result of wild birds perching on aviaries and contaminating the floors with infected droppings. The signs of heavy infestations are similar to those of tapeworms, the bird becoming weak, listless, anaemic and emaciated. Treatment with drugs can be effective against certain species but as with all anti-parasitic drugs, the level of dosage can be critical. The best defence is the prevention, as far as possible, of the conditions leading to severe infestations, such as keeping birds in the same aviary throughout the year, without having it empty for a thorough cleaning, disinfection and renewal of floor materials. Failing to do this is asking for trouble, especially with a soil floor, as it provides the ideal conditions for the parasites' life cycles.

### EYE INFECTIONS

Conjunctivitis is an infectious ailment often caused by bacteria picked up when the bird wipes its face on a perch contaminated by droppings. The feathers become fouled and the eyes are easily infected. Sometimes a foreign body such as a particle of dirt or grit can cause the condition. In the early stages the only indications might be that the bird frequently opens and closes the eye; later the eye will water, become swollen and then close up. The bird must be isolated and the infected eye bathed with warm water or, better still, physiological saline (0.9% saline solution). When bathed, the eye can be treated with veterinary ophthalmic ointment. It must not be forgotten that eye infections can be symptomatic of other disorders, such as ornithosis, so if the condition does not respond rapidly to treatment or is accompanied by other symptoms, such as respiratory problems, a veterinary surgeon should be consulted.

### EGG BINDING

The egg-bound bird will become listless and weak, its plumage fluffed out; sometimes it loses the ability to fly, or at least becomes too weak to fly efficiently. Although various treatments have been suggested, the only method I have found effective is heat treatment in a hospital cage at 29–32°C (85–90°F); when the egg is passed, the heat is slowly reduced until it is approximately that of the ambient temperature. The bird must be kept in isolation until it is completely fit, and only then returned to breeding accommodation. If this fails, a veterinary surgeon may be able to help; a number of drugs are useful and in some cases surgery may be indicated. However, the most important factor in saving an egg-bound bird is to spot the trouble before the bird becomes too chilled and weak. Catching and handling an egg-bound bird must be done with great care, otherwise if the egg is broken inside the bird's body, death is inevitable. Egg binding can be caused by factors such as a sudden drop in temperature, disturbance at the nest, a mineral imbalance such as dietary calcium difficiency, or the bird attempting to lay a large or misshapen egg.

POISONS

Prevention is better than attempted cure with poisoning of any sort, and with sensible precautions incidents can be avoided.

When painting or using wood preservatives make sure that lead based paint is not used. The freshly painted or treated accommodation must be thoroughly dry, and enclosed areas well ventilated before being used to house birds. It is important to remember that the birds in adjoining accommodation may be affected by fumes or spray droplets. Disinfectants must also be used with caution and the manufacturers' instructions read and followed. Suitable disinfectants, aerosols and similar products can be obtained from pet shops and other retail businesses trading in livestock products and they will also give advice on the product best suited to your needs.

As outlined in the section on rodent control, rodenticides must never be used in areas to which birds have access. The dangers of using toxic chemical agents such as insect sprays and weed killers have been referred to in Chapter One. However, I will re-emphasise that they should not be used near bird accommodation. Plants like yew (*Taxus baccata*) and nightshade (*Atropa belladona*) can be poisonous when eaten and should not be used in aviaries or allowed to grow near them. There is some evidence that plants without an apparent reputation for being poisonous can affect birds in some avian families and not others. It has been reported that convolvulus or bindweed has been implicated in the death of some budgerigars who had eaten its leaves, while waxbills with access to the plant were not affected. I have kept birds from doves and quail to finches and waxbills in aviaries with rampant convolvulus growth for nearly three decades without evidence of ill effects. It may be that the budgerigars were affected because they ate the leaves and possibly the waxbills did not. However, many of my birds are avid eaters of any green plants including convolvulus especially serins, weavers and quail.

Apart from accidental poisoning due to the thoughtless use of paints, sprays, disinfectants etc., the most likely form of poisoning is botulism which is a blood poisoning from the bacterium *Clostridium botulinum*. The poisoning is caused by the metabolic by-products of the bacterium, which can occur in any decomposing organic material. The occurrence of botulism in wild birds is related to their feeding behaviour. The incidence in gulls is particularly high due to their feeding on waste food from rubbish tips. *The risks to captive birds arise from the spoiled food itself and also from maggots fed on fish or meat. To my knowledge on two occasions in the last four years there have been well-documented cases of maggot-fed birds being poisoned*. However, I have used maggots regularly for bird feeding for well over twenty years without any problems. When the maggots are purchased, I use a fine sieve to separate them from the stale material they have been kept in and from any remaining food materials, dead maggots, etc. They are then kept in clean bran for a minimum of four days and sieved again before being fed to the birds.

My personal experience of confirmed botulism cases is confined to gulls. Affected birds show muscular weakness, paralysis, and eventual collapse, due to involvement of the central nervous system, and these clinical signs are apparently observed in all species. Occasionally diarrhoea and trembling can also be seen. If botulism in captive birds is suspected the first step is to remove the source of poisoning, e.g. spoiled food or maggots. Then a veterinary surgeon must be contacted without delay. This is essential if any type of poisoning is suspected.

INJURIES

One of the commonest causes of injury is birds flying into wire when frightened by mice, or by predators such as owls and cats. This can be prevented to some extent by the methods outlined in Chapter One. Plenty of cover provided by plants, cut branches and nesting baskets, as well as boxes in which some species will nest, all help reduce these incidents. An enclosed shelter attached to the aviary in which the birds can roost is a useful asset, but unless they are 'trained' to be shut in at night, they are often perverse and roost outside in a hazardous site. The only way of *almost* completely preventing these incidents is inside accommodation, or a large outside aviary, in which the roosting and nesting sites are well away from the aviary perimeter and roof.

Other common accidents are caused by overgrown claws catching in wire netting. Nesting material such as fibres and fine stems can become wrapped around legs and toes. Leg rings which are too small can cause injury and those too large can catch on twigs etc. in an aviary, so the bird is trapped and injury caused in attempts to escape.

In my experience injuries from fighting are rare in the avian species covered in this book. Guidelines on compatible species are given in Chapter Four and in introductions to the taxonomic groups.

Anything other than superficial wounds are best treated by a veterinary surgeon. Cuts and scratches which are minor, involving a small area of skin or the underlying tissues can be bathed with physiological saline (0.9% saline solution) obtainable from any pharmacist. The area can then be treated with an anti-bacterial spray. Split plastic leg rings which are too small or due to an accident have damaged the tissues, can be removed with a small sharp pair of nail cutters, of the surgical type. Closed metal rings are more difficult especially if the ring has become embedded in the tissues. If you are not experienced in these 'first aid' techniques it is best to enlist the help of an experienced aviculturist or consult a veterinary surgeon.

With any injury, immediate isolation of the patient in a box or hospital cage is imperative. Food and water should be placed in a situation where the bird can reach them without effort. The bird should be kept in a quiet and secluded situation. This is especially necessary if the injury is a dislocation or fracture. Treatment of these injuries by the inexperienced can do more harm than good and for the application of splints and other immobilizing dressings a veterinary surgeon should be consulted.

# 4
# Breeding

For the aviculturist intending to breed the birds covered in this book, there is a large number of advantages. Accommodation is not so expensive as that required for most psittacines for which aviaries have to be made of heavy gauge wire, metal or protected wood to resist the birds' destructive powers. And generally speaking, seed-eaters are less aggressive and territorial than softbills, which means you can breed more than one pair in the same aviary. With the exception of some quail species which occasionally call at night, seed-eaters cause no auditory annoyance to neighbours. This is a factor which cannot be ignored, unless you live in an isolated rural area, as aviculturists keeping birds such as *Aratinga* conures can testify. Other advantages are the reproductive potential of species such as quail which lay large clutches and have early sexual maturation. Doves lay two egg clutches, but will often rear five or six broods in a season; finches and related birds lay medium-sized clutches and some species will rear three or four broods.

There are many species which can be established in captivity, especially if your efforts are not handicapped by wanting to breed to show standards or establish a colour mutation. These objectives must involve deliberate inbreeding to some extent, depending on the numbers of your initial stock and the degree of inbreeding required to achieve and maintain the desired characteristics. Without these demands, deliberate outbreeding can be adopted, or perhaps the term minimal inbreeding is preferable, as the number making up the nucleus stock and the availability of fresh blood are variables which control any captive breeding programme.

Unless a species is well established and sufficient numbers are bred in captivity, dependence on importations for new blood is inevitable. Bird importations are notoriously erratic and current trends for seed-eating birds, like finches, waxbills, munias and doves indicate an increasing decline in the numbers and species available from the countries of origin. For the UK, secondary imports from Continental Europe have, to a limited extent, replaced these shipments. A few Oriental/Asiatic munia species, some of which were probably not imported before 1980, have been available in small numbers. From Central and South America, a few bunting species in the Emberizinae have been available recently on occasion. These have included Sierra, Dicua, Warbling, Catamenia and Sporophila Finches.

Most species in the cardinal-grosbeck subfamily, Cardinalinae, are currently rarely available in the UK, in common with cardinals of the genus *Paroaria* (Pope and Red-crested Cardinals), although formerly they were frequently imported.

## BREEDING METHODS AND COMPATIBILITY

There are two basic methods of breeding seed-eating birds; you can keep one pair of birds to each cage or small aviary, or use a larger aviary to house either birds of the same species that breed in colonies, or pairs of birds which are taxonomically unrelated. Although species that are established in captivity and which have nutritional needs that are met largely by a seed diet will breed readily in cages (and these two factors are related), aviary accommodation is required to breed many of the imported feral species, as they need the seclusion and space it provides, as well as the benefit of 'natural' live food. As with all generalisations there are exceptions; some 'wild' species adapt readily to captivity once acclimatised, and will breed in cages or aviaries if the diet and management provided is of a high standard. Whenever possible I use aviaries for breeding. (A rough guide to the number of birds that should be housed in relation to aviary space is given in Chapter One.) When using an aviary to breed more than one pair of birds, an important consideration is compatibility. There are a number of guidelines (given below) which the aviculturist can follow; they can help to reduce not only overt aggression but also the more subtle interference and harassment which can prevent birds even starting to breed.

1 Apart from colony breeders (which present other prob-

lems), birds of different species and colour are more likely to be compatible than closely related species or two cocks both of which have red plumage, for example.

2 Ground-dwelling birds such as *Coturnix* quail can live in perfect harmony with other birds which are not terrestrial. The only problem which may arise is with quail which need a perch to roost — for example, the California Quail (*Lophortyx californica*) — as these can cause disturbance to passerines and doves.
3 Most species of doves can be kept with other birds, but more than one pair of doves in the same aviary will usually lead to conflict. Depending on the size of the aviary, two pairs of taxonomically unrelated doves will sometimes breed successfully in the same aviary, but a careful watch must be maintained for signs of aggression. Doves which are terrestrial in behaviour should not be kept in the same aviary as quails.
4 Competition for nesting sites can be a major source of conflict. Therefore, housing species which invariably use a nest box together with birds which make an open nest will reduce the chances of trouble.

## PAIR FORMATION

The nature and establishment of a pair bond vary throughout the taxonomic spectrum and may be brief or lasting, sometimes involving more than one partner of the opposite sex. As examples, some weaver and whydah species are polygamous, whilst finches are monogamous and hemipodes polyandrous. Pair bonds are initiated and maintained by displays, courtship feeding, mutual preening and vocalisations. Usually, the bonds formed among birds that breed in colonies are vague; monogamous species, on the other hand, often form lasting pair bonds and are more territorial than social breeders. There are exceptions to these generalisations within taxonomic groups both large and small. The monogamous Greenfinch (*Carduelis chloris*) and other species of cardueline finches will sometimes nest in loose colonies.

Whatever the nature of their pair bonds, social behaviour, or breeding biology, a group of birds should be released into the breeding enclosure at the same time. Introducing additional birds, especially after the group has become established in their new environment, will often cause disruption and conflict.

It is a common occurrence for a pair of healthy, sexually dimorphic birds to fail to breed and later prove their reproductive competence with different partners. The usual comment on the failure of the first pairing is 'They didn't like each other'. I have no doubt that this can be true, but in many cases I suspect that when other conspecifics are present a bond has already been formed which can be made with just auditory or visual contact. As an example, I once housed two pairs of Green Singing Finches (*Serinus mozambicus*) — pairs A and B — in separate cages in a bird room for the winter, with only auditory contact. In the spring both cocks began to sing and I noticed that the hen of pair B constantly called to cock A, which responded with song and contact calls. In April both pairs were released into separate aviaries approximately two metres (six feet) apart, but they had visual contact. Cock A and hen B spent most of the time flying up and down the aviaries contact calling and trying to keep each other in sight. Neither pair made any attempt to nest, so later in the year, I changed the pairing by moving the cocks, then both pairs bred successfully. Although the 'evidence' in this case is circumstantial, this apparent pre-bonding with only visual and auditory contact has happened on various occasions and has involved birds belonging to other genera and families.

## SELECTION OF SPECIES

A number of factors with regard to this question must be taken into account, especially if you intend to concentrate on breeding a few species or group of birds. These include sexual dimorphism, nuptial plumage, whether the species breeds in colonies or is territorial, and increasingly important, availability.

Some bird groups contain many species in which the sexes are alike — for example, the munias and mannikins (subfamily Amadinae) which are still available, comparatively cheap to buy, and which breed in small colonies, thus ensuring that the difficulty of sexing is not a major problem. A number of methods have been developed in recent years to determine a bird's sex and they have been used successfully on the larger, rarer and more expensive species, among them psittacines and softbills. The methods include a surgical technique that enables an endoscope to be used, the analysis of steroids in droppings and a similar technique using the pulp of feathers. All the methods are expensive and the surgical method impractical for the smaller seed-eaters; however, steroid analysis might be useful for some of the rarer and expensive species.

Aviculturists are often confused by the usage of the names 'finch' and 'bunting' for birds which, although related taxonomically, have only a superficial resemblance to the well-known species of true finches and buntings, such as the Goldfinch (*Carduelis carduelis*) and the Yellow Bunting (*Emberiza citrinella*). Further confusion arises as 'finch' is also applied to several species in the family Estrildidae (waxbills, munias, and others), and some species of North American buntings are known as 'sparrows'. Detailed breeding information for each taxonomic group and species will be given in the following chapters, so the general notes given here will act as a brief, preliminary introduction to the families.

## Emberizidae (Buntings)

This family includes the true buntings of the genus *Emberiza* and a wide variety of New World species. Many Asiatic and neotropical species commonly imported until the late seventies are now rarely seen, and a few have apparently not been imported since. I do not know of any species established in captivity but the captive breeding potential of species such as the Saffron Finch (*Sicalis flaveola*) and some true buntings has been demonstrated on many occasions.

## Fringillidae (Finches)

The finches are distributed in Eurasia, Africa and the Americas, and include well-known groups of birds such as the hawfinches, grosbeaks, siskins, linnets and rosefinches. Some species of finches, for example the Greenfinch (*Carduelis chloris*), are established in captivity. One of the finch groups best known to foreign bird enthusiasts are the African serins; their potential for becoming established in captivity is good and several species are still occasionally imported into Europe and the USA.

**Estrildidae (Waxbills, Munias, Mannikins, Grass and Parrot Finches)**

Many species in this family are established in captivity, the popular Australian grassfinches being a well-known example. A number of waxbill and mannikin species are imported occasionally from Africa and are comparatively low in price compared to many other seed-eating birds and softbills. A few species have been established and Australian aviculturists have been very successful with some waxbills and munias, which shows what can be achieved even with a ban on commercial imports.

**Ploceidae (Weavers, Whydahs, Bishops, Sparrows)**

The cocks in many species belonging to this family have a nuptial plumage and nest in colonies. All the evidence indicates that, in general, the whydahs and bishops are polygamous. Whydahs of the subfamily Viduinae are parasitic, the hosts usually being waxbills of the genera *Estrilda*, *Uraeginthus* and the *Pytilia*. Although breeding successes are fairly frequent, to my knowledge establishment in captivity of any species has yet to be achieved. There are several species of sparrow which could be easily established — the attractive Yellow Sparrow (*Passer luteus*) has proved to be a prolific colony breeder when given the opportunity. Importations of many species in this family are decreasing.

**Phasianidae (Quail)**

The quail species which have been bred most often in captivity are New World species, the best-known examples being the California Quail (*Lophortyx californica*) and the Bobwhite (*Colinus virginianus*). Old World quail have also adapted readily to captivity and include the long domesticated

Japanese Quail (*Coturnix japonica*) and the recently established Chinese Painted Quail (*Excalfactoria chinensis*). Their small size and terrestrial behaviour make the *Coturnix* quails ideal subjects for a mixed collection. Commercial imports have ceased and opportunities to breed species such as bush quails (*Perdicula* spp.) from the Indian subcontinent have probably been lost.

### Turnicidae (Hemipodes)

The hemipodes or button quails are a most interesting group because of their polyandrous reproductive behaviour. Although over the years they have been bred with some success, to my knowledge captive breeding has never been consistent and even in the days of unrestricted bird imports, shipments were small in number and erratic — often a few hemipodes would be found in a large quail consignment. Like the *Coturnix* quails, the terrestrial hemipodes are excellent birds for a mixed aviary.

### Columbidae (Doves, Pigeons)

The smaller species of this family, the doves, has long been represented in aviculture by the domestic Barbary Dove (*Streptopelia roseogrisea*), and more recently by the Diamond Dove (*Geopelia cuneata*). Other species, particularly from the genus *Streptopelia*, breed freely in captivity and several large collections have been established in the USA and Europe. Doves, like quail, can fill an ecological niche in an aviary, adding to the interest and pleasure to be derived from it.

## BREEDING POTENTIAL AND AVAILABILITY

In the following table I have listed some passerine and dove species which, in most cases, have been frequently imported in the past. Many of those selected probably have sufficient stocks available in captivity for their potential establishment as a breeding species, allowing for the decreasing numbers of imported birds. This is very important for species in which the sexes are alike, so that pairings can be achieved by allowing 'natural' selection from a group. There are of course other species which could be considered, but a detailed account of those listed and others, is given in Part 2 of this book. I have not included quail, as a number of species are established and commercial imports are not available for others.

*TABLE 2*
*SEXUAL DIMORPHISM AND ORIGINS*

| Common Name | Scientific Name | Sexual Dimorphism | Origin |
|---|---|---|---|
| FINCHES AND ALLIED SPECIES | | | |
| Saffron Finch* | *Sicalis flaveola* | + | South America |
| Jacarini Finch | *Volatinia jacarini* | + | Central and South America |
| Green Singing Finch | *Serinus mozambicus* | + | Africa |
| Grey Singing Finch | *S. leucopygius* | – | Africa |
| St Helena Seed-eater | *S. flaviventris* | + | Africa |
| Red-winged Pytilia | *Pytilia phoenicoptera* | + | Africa |
| Red-billed Fire-finch | *Lagonostica senegala* | + | Africa |
| Red-cheeked Cordon-bleu | *Uraeginthus bengalus* | + | Africa |
| Blue-headed Waxbill | *U. cyanocephala* | + | Africa |
| Red-eared Waxbill | *Estrilda troglodytes* | – | Africa |
| St Helena Waxbill | *E. astrild* | – | Africa |
| Rosy-rumped Waxbill | *E. rhodopyga* | – | Africa |
| Orange-cheeked Waxbill | *E. melpoda* | – | Africa |
| Red Avadavat | *Amandava amandava* | + | India, South-east Asia, China |
| Golden-breasted Waxbill | *A. subflava* | + | Africa |
| African Silverbill | *Lonchura malabarica cantans* | – | Africa |
| Indian Silverbill | *L. m. malabarica* | – | India, Sri Lanka |
| Bronze-winged Mannikin | *L. cucullata* | – | Africa |
| Spice Finch | *L. punctulata* | – | India, South-east Asia, China |

| | | | |
|---|---|---|---|
| White-headed Munia* | *L. maja* | – | Malaysia, Indonesia |
| Chestnut Munia* | *L. malacca* | – | India, Sri Lanka, South-east Asia |
| Cut-throat Finch | *Amadina fasciata* | + | Africa |
| Red-headed Finch | *A. erythrocephala* | + | Africa |
| Sudan Golden Sparrow | *Passer luteus* | + | Africa |
| DOVES | | | |
| Laughing Dove | *Streptopelia senegalensis* | + | Africa, Arabia, India |
| Tambourine Dove | *Turtur tympanistria* | + | Africa |
| Masked Dove | *Oena capensis* | + | Africa |
| Zebra Dove* | *Geophila striata* | + | Malaysia, Indonesia |
| Gold-billed Ground Dove | *Columbina cruziana* | – | South America |

* = Birds not bred by author.

## NESTS

There are a number of standard nesting receptacles (Fig. 9), many of which are made commercially, but some bird species will always prefer to use a bush or shrub. Seclusion is another factor which must be given some thought, as a site will often not be used unless sufficiently screened. A knowledge of the nesting behaviour in the wild is often a help; for example, I could find no reference in bird literature to rock sparrows (*Petronia* spp.) nesting in any site other than a hole, and of the two species I have bred, a nest box with an entrance hole has always been their choice, even when a wide variety of receptacles and sites have been available. However, like all living creatures, the behaviour of birds can be unpredictable. With the obvious exception of quail and hemipodes, over 40 per cent of the nesting sites used by birds in my collection (which includes species from seven avian families) have been in clumps of cut gorse. Both in captivity and in the wild the choice of site can be bizarre. I have seen a pair of Cinnamon-breasted Rock Buntings (*Emberiza tahapisi*) build their nest in

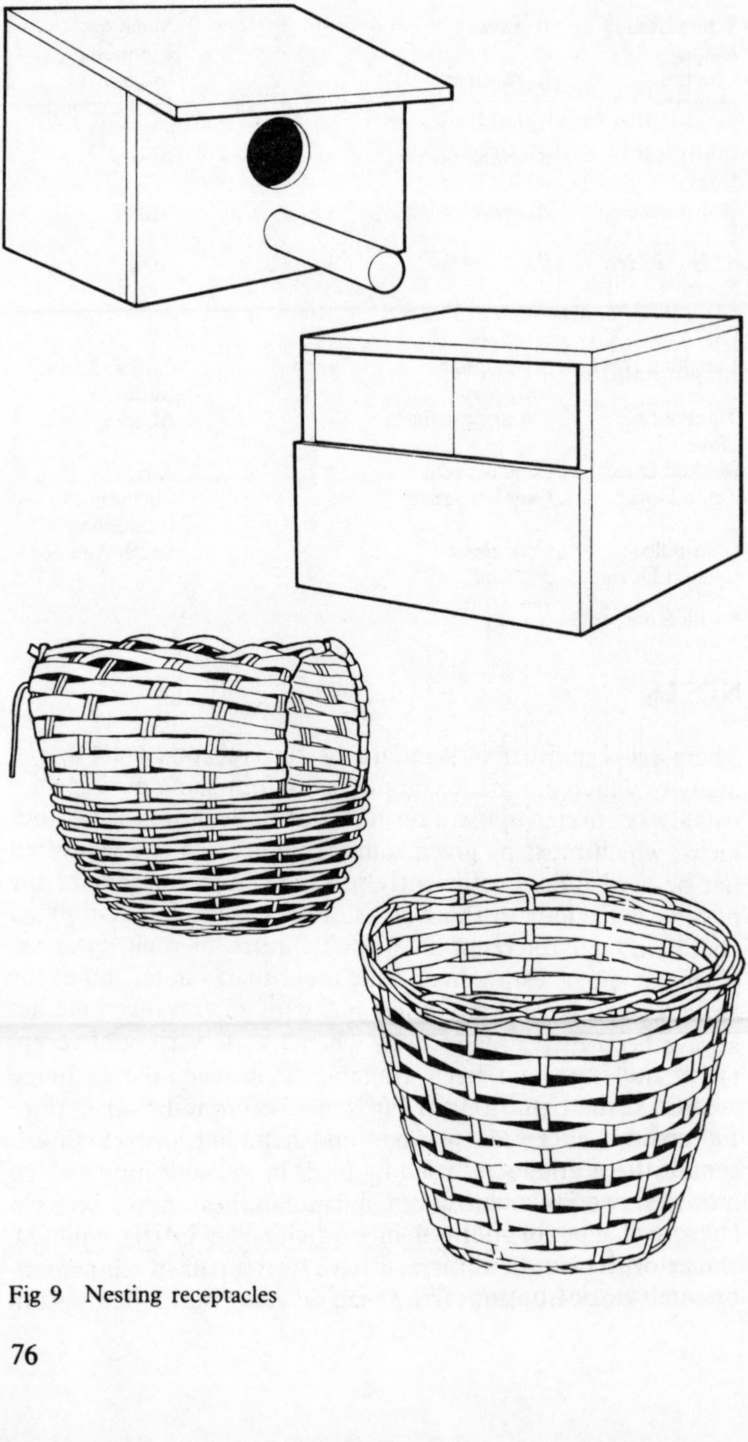

Fig 9 Nesting receptacles

a seed dish in an aviary with a wide variety of nest sites and receptacles.

An important consideration in providing nest sites is shelter — it is not much use fixing nest baskets in a situation which is completely exposed to rain and wind. Always supply more baskets and boxes of every type than the number of breeding pairs and fix a minimum of three or four at different levels. I have had some success in my 'type 2' units which are 3.1 × 1.1 × 2.4 m high (10 × 3½ × 8 ft), by using 25 × 25 mm (½ × ½ in) wire mesh platforms of approximately one metre square at the rear of the aviary. These platforms are fixed at varying heights and act as supports for nesting baskets and branches for cover (Fig. 10). The birds nesting on the platforms have no

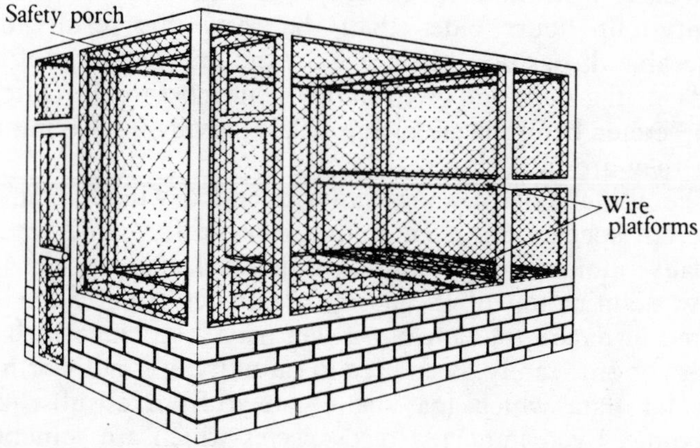


Fig 10 Wire platforms at rear of aviary acting as support for cut branches providing cover and nest sites

physical contact at their nest sites with those above or below, thus reducing the likelihood of conflict. As nesting materials I provide dried grasses, rootlets, moss, kapok (used for padding cushions), wood-wool (industrial packing material) and twigs. The longer types of animal hairs and similar fine material must be used with caution as they can become entangled around the legs and toes of both nestlings and adult birds. I find that a little material placed in a nest basket or box, and old wild birds' nests, always help to stimulate your birds to nest. Cover for ground-dwelling species should not be forgotten; conifer branches and tussocks of grass can be used and quail will sometimes nest in a box with one open side.

## INCUBATION AND REARING

There are variations within the taxonomic groups, but as a general rule true incubation among passerine species commences when the last egg of the clutch is laid. Among the exceptions are the serins, such as the Green Singing Finch (*Serinus mozambicus*) which will sometimes incubate when the last but one egg of the clutch is laid. Quail start incubation when the clutch is complete. Some dove species will start incubating with the first egg, and as one chick will be roughly twenty-four hours older than the rest, this results in a noticeable disparity in their size for the first few days of life. Birds of all groups will often sit on the nest before the clutch is complete or before even an egg is laid, giving a false impression they are incubating.

The amount of nest inspection tolerated will vary among different species and even among pairs of the same species. Usually, domesticated and semi-domesticated species will allow examination of the nest without deserting. Some imported birds are tolerant but if you have a species which has never, or only rarely, been bred in captivity, it is not worth the risk for data which may be obtained from a subsequent breeding. Even imported bird species which are sometimes intolerant will get used to regular inspections. I know a lady aviculturist who simply unhooks a nest basket, takes a look inside, then replaces the basket, and her birds' breeding results are excellent. I examine the nests of most of my birds but would hesitate to copy her method. The situation of the nest may make inspection impracticable; a nest built in a clump of gorse, for example, is best left alone. Nest inspections should be made early in the day to avoid any disturbance near nightfall. If all goes well and the parents rear the chicks, it is usual practice to remove the young from the cage or aviary when they commence to feed themselves. With many species, by this stage a second clutch is being incubated and sometimes the cock bird will become aggressive, especially towards the male chicks. However, the chicks are still often fed by the cock, so if there is no sign of trouble, you can risk leaving them with the parents for the benefit of this extra feeding.

Deserted eggs can be artificially incubated and chicks hand-reared. For passerine birds and doves the techniques are difficult. The artificial incubation and rearing of precocial birds such as quail are much easier, especially as data for temperature and humidity parameters are readily available. Foster parents are another method for passerines which rear their chicks largely on a seed diet, the Bengalese Finch (a domesticated form of *Lonchura striata*, also known as the Society Finch) being widely and successfully used. For seed-eating dove species, the Barbary Dove, a domesticated variety of the African Collared Dove (*Streptopelia roseogrisea*), makes an excellent foster parent. The smaller varieties of Bantam domestic fowl have been used as foster parents for quail.

## HAND-REARING

Successful hand-rearing is largely dependent on the time-lag between the last food and warmth from the parents and the first provided by you; the longer the delay, the less chance of success. The chicks can be kept in a lined cardboard box, although I prefer a hospital cage which will give temperature control. Another alternative is to use a horticultural heating pad in a box; the pad is completely enclosed and perfectly safe to use, and operates at a low power of about 25 watts. A wall thermometer fixed inside the box will give a temperature check. Whatever type of container you use for the chicks, a nest of soft tissue which can be frequently changed will ensure that the chicks are kept clean. Food should be given often and for young chicks at least every hour for the first few days. The last feed of the day and the first morning feed should be given as late and early as possible. Fine-grade, commercially available softbill mixture, to which is added powdered cuttle fish and enough milk to mix it to a paste, is a good rearing food; chopped mealworms and other live food can also be used. The food is given with a fine spatula, small syringe or a plastic cocktail stick with the points snipped off. When the chicks show signs of trying to take the food from the feeding implement, a shallow dish containing the rearing food with small seeds scattered on top should be provided. At this stage the temperature can be slowly reduced, and when the chicks start feeding themselves they can be transferred to a conventional box cage. However, I continue to hand-feed them twice a day for a few days to supply the nutritional 'boost' they would receive from their parents.

It is important to remember that many (but not all?) *Estrildid* species, e.g. waxbills and munias, solicit food from their parents with a different posture from most other passerines. Instead of the head with open gape being directed straight towards the parent, the nestling estrild begs in a prone posture, with the neck turned to such an angle that the gape is directed upwards towards the parent. When fledged, the young birds use a similar posture; when perched the head of the chick will often be slightly below the perch when begging. In many cases the head is swung from side to side during the begging. Goodwin (1982) remarks that most estrildids do not use the wing-fluttering movements generally seen with young passerines when soliciting food.

## BREEDING STIMULUS

Of the many external factors controlling reproduction in birds, light has long been considered of primary importance. Much of the experimental work and field studies on reproduction have concerned temperature zone birds. Many of these early investigations so dramatically emphasised the importance of photoperiod that people lost sight of other factors which are also extremely important (Marshall). These include temperature, food availability and rainfall — not rainfall as such, but the environmental changes that occur because of rain. It has long been known that in the temperate and colder regions some captive birds, especially the Gouldian and other Australian finches, attempt to breed in the winter months — that is at a time that would synchronise with their breeding period in the wild. This was particularly marked with the Gouldian Finch when these birds were still imported from

Australia. For the aviculturist in the UK, the USA, and many areas of Europe, it has been standard practice to keep foreign birds in heated or frost-proof quarters with or without artificial light during the winter. The breeding season in outside aviaries is usually from May/June until September. Some aviculturists, notably breeders of Australian finches, have used artificial heat and light to breed their birds during the winter. For many years I used the accepted breeding period for outside aviaries and considered that after July or August the season was finished. However, in 1964, after successful breeding attempts in outside aviaries in the late summer and autumn, I extended the season experimentally from April to November. Since then a number of breeding successes without artificial heat and light have occured in a period of declining photoperiod and temperature. The records that follow only include acclimatised or aviary-bred birds, but apart from the Chinese Painted Quail and perhaps two Estrildidae species, probably none is established in captivity anywhere in the world. The number of species is small, as I remove the birds to heated quarters if hard weather should occur in the October–November period.

## Passerine Species

From a total of 18 passerine species, 16 bred successfully from the end of June onwards and 9 of these reared young as late as October/November: Blue-headed Waxbill, Cordon-bleu (*Uraeginthus*); St Helena Waxbill, Orange-cheeked Waxbill (*Estrilda*); Red Avadavat, Golden-breasted Waxbill (*Amandava*); Crimson-winged Pytilia (*Pytilia*); Pearl-headed Silverbill (*Lonchura*); Cut-throat Finch (*Amadina*); Green Singing Finch, St Helena Seed-eater (*Serinus*); Bush Petronia (*Petronia*); Red-crested Finch (*Coryphospingus*); Red Cardinal (*Cardinalis*); Collared Warbling Finch (*Poospiza*); Jacarini Finch (*Volatina*). Four of the species which reared young in the October/November period — the Red Avadavat, Crimson-winged Pytilia, Orange-cheeked Waxbill — were the most consistent and reliable breeders.

## Quail

Two quail species bred successfully after June, one reared young in September/October: Chinese Painted Quail (*Excal-*

*factoria chinensis*); Harlequin Quail (*Coturnix delegorguei*). A single record for successful breeding as late as September/October would appear to be unusual for quail species.

## Doves

All five species of doves were consistent breeders after June and as late as October/November: Gold-billed Dove (*Columbina cruziana*); Talpacoti Dove (*Columbina talpacoti*); Plain-breasted Dove (*Columbina minuta*); Black-billed Wood Dove (*Turtur abyssinicus*); Cape Dove (*Oena capensis*). The production of crop-milk giving the doves independence from the need to supply live food for their young, is possibly the reason for the late successful breeding in Columbidae.

## Hemipodes

A single hemipode species, the Barred Hemipode or Bustard Quail (*Turnix suscitator*), reared young from June until September.

Apart from captive birds retaining a breeding period that coincides with that of the country of origin, probably for many generations of captive breeding, many tropical and subtropical species are opportunistic breeders with rainfall initiating the start of their reproductive cycle. However, it is apparent from my records that in average weather conditions in southern England at least, established foreign birds can successfully rear young in a period of declining photoperiod and temperature. The reason for this I would suggest is the (hopefully) optimal and constant food supply available. Aviculturists in some areas of the USA and Australia can take more advantage of this opportunistic reproductive drive than their colleagues in areas of Europe and the UK.

# PART TWO

# Descriptions of Species and Their Maintenance

# 5
# Emberizidae — Buntings and Allied Species

Included in this family are groups of birds ranging from the 'true' buntings, i.e. the Old World genus *Emberiza* and related species, to diverse New World forms. Sharing a position in the subfamily Emberizinae with the true buntings are New World genera, some of which are well known in aviculture. Among these are the saffron finches (*Sicalis* spp.), cardinals of the genus *Paroaria* and grassquits. The grassquits, at 90–100 mm (3½–4 in), are probably the smallest seed-eating birds in the family. The subfamily Cardinalinae contains the largest birds in the family, such as the well-known Red or Virginian Cardinal (*Cardinalis cardinalis*) and the little known saltators. 'Typical' buntings and related species are a fairly homogeneous group and are, for seed-eating passerines, of medium to large size, 127–203 mm (5–8 in). The bills are usually conical and somewhat attenuated, the tails are fairly long and most species are sexually dimorphic, the males often attractively but not brightly coloured. The most brightly coloured cock birds are found in the New World subfamily Cardinalinae. The grosbeak–cardinal species possess heavy and in some cases decurved bills.

With a family containing such diverse groups of species, which include the Thraupinae (tanagers, honey creepers and related species), it is hardly surprising that a good deal of taxonomic revision has occurred. In the past the buntings were placed in the Fringillidae, the tanagers and honey creepers each having the status of their own family. The majority of North American buntings are known as 'sparrows' or 'finches'.

Although there are exceptions, a number of generalisations can be made about the family. The most important for the aviculturist is the buntings' need for live food when rearing young (or substitute foods the parents will accept). Furthermore, the adults of some species cannot be maintained in good health and condition, in the long term, without live food.

## Subfamily Emberizinae

### Accommodation and Breeding

The species in this subfamily are predominantly terrestrial, finding their food, and in some cases nesting, on the ground. Their nests are open and cup shaped, although some tropical species construct a domed nest, and the sites can vary, from holes in rocks to high in a tree. The eggs are blotched and spotted, sometimes with irregular lines, or unmarked. Incubation, which is, in most cases, 12–13 days, is carried out by the hen alone or shared with the cock. The majority of buntings are active and restless birds, best housed in an aviary. Cages should be of the box type, and for the larger species should be at least 1.2 m × 45 cm × 61 cm high (4 × 1½ × 2 ft). I have kept pairs of buntings with other carefully selected, unrelated birds in the same aviary without any trouble. However, in most cases buntings should not be housed with birds which cannot 'hold their own', such as waxbills. Suitable nesting receptacles for Old World species are canary nest pans or wire cups fixed in bushes or cut branches, half-open nest boxes and piles of rocks or bricks, leaving cavities for nest building. Nest baskets will be used by some Central and South American species.

### Food and Care

A very basic diet consists of a mixture of millet and canary seed, although this can be improved with the addition of seeds such as rape, hemp and commercial softbill mixture. Sunflower seed can be given to the larger species such as grosbeaks and cardinals. Seeding grasses, germinated seed and green food both collected and cultivated are avidly eaten by most buntings. I give adult birds commercial and home-bred live food on a regular basis, increasing the amount and supplementing with collected live food when the birds are breeding.

The word 'hardy' is often used about some birds in this

subfamily, but venturing the birds outside in winter is risky in most areas of Europe and impossible in the colder areas of North America. However, it all depends on variables such as area, type of accommodation, species, etc. I would certainly hesitate to keep many Central and South American species outside in the winter, without artificial heat and light, even in the comparatively mild winters of southern England.

## True Buntings

These birds are an Old World group with the exception of the Snow Bunting (*Plectrophenax*), and the Lapland Bunting and Longspurs (*Calcarius* spp.), which are circumpolar.

### Genus *Melophus*

CRESTED BUNTING *Melophus lathami* **Plate 6**
OTHER NAMES: Black-crested Bunting, Crested Black Bunting. In the earlier literature, it can be found recorded as *M. melanicterus*, *Emberiza erythroptera* and *E. lathami.*

The genus *Melophus* is monotypic and, since the species is a somewhat aberrant form, it has been suggested that its place in the Emberizinae is inappropriate. Importations of Crested Buntings into Britain have been small in number and erratic, the largest number occurring in the late 1960s. I obtained two pairs in 1967 which were in such poor condition, having been fed on a very basic seed diet and kept in cages which were too small, that I doubted they would ever attain breeding condition. However, three years later, one pair got as far as building nests. My hopes were dashed when I found the cock's decapitated body inside the aviary, the killer (probably a cat) having somehow managed to achieve this through 25 mm (½ in) wire. They were successfully bred in Sweden in 1983 and in the UK in 1990.

Description

150–165 mm (6–6½ in), sexually dimorphic.
COCK: Bill dark horn colour, fleshy at lower base; irides dark brown; plumage, including a pointed crest, is black, with the

exception of chestnut wings and tail; legs and feet light or greyish brown.
HEN: Smaller crest; upperparts dark brown; wings and tail brown, marked with cinnamon; underparts buffish, lighter near the throat, streaked with dark brown.

## Distribution and Habitat

Locally migratory, with a distribution from the Indian sub-continent to Upper Burma and southern China. In the outer Himalayas it is found up to elevations of 1500–1800 m (5000–6000 ft) on rocky hills or open cultivation on hillsides, favouring stony ground and scrub and, where present, walls and old buildings.

## Breeding

PERIOD: Captive breedings have commenced in May, June and July. Indian birds breed between April and August with local variation.
NEST: In the wild the site is low on the ground in a pocket of earth under a stone or grass tuft on the hillside, or in a hole in a bank or wall. I built a crude low wall in my aviary, leaving cavities of various sizes, and both nests were made in this wall some 30–60 cm (1–2 ft) from the ground. The second was made in a half-open nest box I had fixed in a gap between the bricks. Whistler (1963) records the nests are variable: some are deep well-made cups of grass lined with fine grasses, fibres, roots of moss and ferns or horse hair; others are loosely constructed, shallow saucers of grass roots without lining. The nests in my aviaries were made of dead convolvulus stems and grasses, lined with fine roots and stems. Both sexes take part in building the nest.
EGGS: The ground colour is pale greenish white, marked with spots and blotches of reddish brown, brown and purple, usually more dense at the larger end. They lack the hair lines and scribble markings of some true bunting species. Clutch size 3–4.
INCUBATION: The hen incubates for 12 days. Palmer (1990) records one period of 10 days.
CHICKS: The nestlings are covered in brownish black down;

the gape is red. They leave the nest at 12 to 14 days, at which stage they resemble the female. The adults feed the young largely on live food, although soft food is also taken. In captivity, and possibly in the wild, *M. lathami* is multi-brooded.

Behaviour

Very terrestrial, picking up seeds and live food from the aviary floor. Locomotion is a rapid walk, sometimes hopping for a short distance. On one occasion I saw the so-called 'peacock walk', the posture upright with crest erected and tail fanned out. They were very fond of rain-bathing, sitting near the top of a bush or shrub in the pouring rain, shaking their wings and preening themselves, the cock birds often singing. Live food of any type was eaten, including large earthworms which they managed after much billing and mangling. Copulation was seen on only one occasion; the cock chased the hen with crest erected and singing, and when she alighted on the ground copulation took place. Afterwards the cock gripped the base of the hen's tail with his bill, she broke away and flew into a shelter. They did not appear to be aggressive birds, but when Black-bellied Weavers (*Euplectes nigroventris*) alighted near them, they would give a forward open-bill threat and the weavers flew away.

## Genus *Emberiza*

### RED-HEADED BUNTING *Emberiza bruniceps*

OTHER NAMES: Brown-headed Bunting, Yellow Bunting.

This large bunting is a sibling species of the Black-headed Bunting (*E. melanocephala*). It has been considered a subspecies of *E. melanocephala* and they freely hybridise where their breeding ranges overlap. Once properly established in captivity the Red-headed Bunting is a hardy bird which, with adequate shelter, can be wintered outside in the UK. Although imported into Europe and to a lesser extent into North America in large numbers until the late 1970s, the first recorded breeding was in 1972. This breeding was at Chester Zoo in a very large, outside planted aviary. The lack of successful breeding is due to a number of factors: there was a low percentage of hen birds in shipments; the birds were cheap and readily available; and they were often recommended as suitable companions for budgerigars, which, although true to a certain extent, meant that the few true pairs were living in conditions totally unsuitable for breeding. In addition to these factors, the rare breeding attempts failed because insufficient live food was provided. In 1952 I had a pair in a planted aviary with some zebra finches, *Lonchura* mannikins and Java sparrows which, at the time, were of more interest to me. I gave the buntings to a friend who was very keen to have them and later in the year the pair nested and hatched three chicks, which, because of lack of live food, died three or four days later. Because my friend's aviary was very small and not planted, the birds even lacked the benefit of 'natural' live food in the aviary, and unfortunately he did not realise the amount of live food needed for the successful rearing of the chicks.

## Description

180–190 mm (7–7½ in), sexually dimorphic.
COCK: Bill pale fawn, the upper mandible somewhat darker; irides brown; head and large throat patch extending to the upper breast varies from chestnut to a light reddish brown; upperparts olive brown, streaked with black; underparts yellow, shading to pale on lower abdomen; legs and feet pale brown to flesh colour.
HEN: Upperparts brown, streaked with darker brown, lighter brown on the underparts; vent and undertail coverts yellowish.

## Distribution and Habitat

Breeding range from west central Asia to Baluchistan and Afghanistan. During migration and often in company with the Black-headed Bunting it is found in vast flocks in many areas of the Indian subcontinent, where it is responsible for much damage to growing grain crops. It has frequently been reported as a vagrant in western Europe, including the UK, however, in view of the large numbers formerly imported, I suspect that many of these 'records' are captive escapes. The habitat, which usually includes areas of water, is scrub, thickets, reedbeds, and steppes (orchards, open fields, gardens and hedges in cultivated areas).

## Breeding

PERIOD: The successful breeding at Chester Zoo took place in May and June, coinciding with the feral breeding period which begins in May. Possibly double-brooded.
NEST: A well-made cup of dried grasses and plant stems, lined with hair fibres and fine grasses. Usually 60–120 cm (2–4 ft) above ground level, in scrub, thickets, reedbeds, tall herbage or hedges. Both the nests at Chester were built in clumps of honeysuckle. The second was described as a untidy cup of grass mixed with dead leaves and Lucerne stems, lined with hair and fine grassy fibres and built by the hen.
EGGS: White and glossy, finely speckled and spotted with pale grey; purplish grey or brown usually concentrated at the larger end. Clutch size 3–5.
INCUBATION: Carried out by the hen, period 14 days.
CHICKS: Timmis describes the Chester nestlings as brownish above with streaks of blackish brown in parts. The throat was yellowish red, turning to whitish yellow on the chest and lower body. Both parents fed the young and for the first few days the food consisted of small insects and regurgitated soaked seed. Later mealworms, caterpillars, maggots and soaked seed were taken. The fledging period was 15 days and the young were fed by the parents for a further two weeks.

## Behaviour

It would appear that this bunting can be kept safely with the more robust unrelated species such as Java sparrows and *Lonchura* mannikins. However, the space available is important and the only detailed account of a breeding (at Chester) was in an aviary of approximately 15 × 3 × 2 m high (50 × 10 × 6 ft). Timmis reported that the buntings' first nest was deserted due to weavers taking the material. My overall impression, from the one pair and a few cock birds I have kept, is that in an aviary of reasonable size, say 3.5 × 2 × 2 m (12 × 6 × 6 ft), it would breed without displaying overt aggression and would probably be a victim rather than an aggressor. Rather a nervous bird, it is best kept in an aviary, although I once came across a cock bird kept as a pet 'canary' by an elderly lady in her living room, which was so tame it took tit-bits from her hand and responded to her voice with calls.

## BLACK-HEADED BUNTING *Emberiza melanocephala*

Not as often imported as its sibling species the Red-headed Bunting, shipments of the Black-headed Bunting rarely contained hens, although I have noticed that in the last few years, with shipments now much fewer and smaller, the percentage of hens has increased. At one time it was a common occurrence to find both species arriving in the same travelling cage. I can find no record of this species having been bred in captivity (although it has been said to have bred in Europe) and there is little doubt that the reasons for this lack of success are the same as those for the Red-headed Bunting. It shares many characteristics with the Red-headed, and it is hardly surprising that some taxonomists consider *E. bruniceps* a subspecies of *E. melanocephala*. Like *E. bruniceps* it is hardy, and long lived once established in captivity.

### Description

180–190 mm (7–7½ in), sexually dimorphic.
COCK: Bill greyish horn, upper mandible browner; irides dark brown; top and sides of head black; a yellowish collar on the hind neck is connected to the yellow of the entire underparts; rest of upper plumage chestnut with blackish streaks; uppertail coverts brown; legs and feet fleshy-brown. In autumn the colours are obscured with dark fringes to the feathers.
HEN: Upper plumage brown, streaked with darker brown; rump chestnut; uppertail coverts yellowish; underparts very pale yellow near lower abdomen.

### Distribution and Habitat

Breeding range from south-eastern Europe to Iran and the Caucasus. Winters in northern and central India. Breeding habitat is open country with patches of cover, and cultivated areas with gardens and plantations, sometimes in woods. In India it is found mainly in open cultivated areas, grain fields and scrub-jungle.

### Breeding

PERIOD: In south-eastern Europe breeding commences in May. Single-brooded.

NEST: An open cup of grasses, dead leaves and sometimes straw, lined with hair, fine grasses and roots. Usually built on or near the ground, in herbage, bush or vine, occasionally in a small tree.

EGGS: Glossy, the ground colour pale greenish blue, spotted and speckled with ashy-brown and grey, mainly at the larger end. Clutch size 4–5, rarely 6–7.

INCUBATION: Carried out by the hen. Period 14 days (Harrison).

CHICKS: No information, the immature bird is like the hen but the rump and uppertail coverts are sandy brown; breast buff, belly whitish, yellow on undertail coverts very pale (King *et al*).

## Behaviour

Over the years I have kept two cocks, at different times with weavers, Java sparrows, and *Lonchura* mannikins and munias. Neither showed any aggression, although one cock was bullied by an unmated cock Orange Weaver in nuptial plumage and later by a very pugnacious unmated cock Green Singing Finch.

## CINNAMON-BREASTED ROCK BUNTING *Emberiza tahapisi*

OTHER NAMES: African Rock Bunting, Seven-striped Bunting.

Five subspecies are recognised which show limited morphological variation. This species, although attractive and elegant, lacks bright colours and has not been popular in aviculture. Never imported into the UK in large numbers, a few small shipments are received most seasons, often as a 'replacement' for more colourful and popular species. It was first bred in the UK in 1937 and since then has been bred fairly frequently in Europe, but detailed breeding reports are rare. I obtained two pairs in 1969 and although the hens were fit the cocks looked below par. Only one cock achieved full breeding condition and, although often seen copulating, proved to be infertile. The hen of this pair laid and incubated 12 clutches of infertile eggs during the next two seasons. In 1971, I managed to purchase a really fit cock and mated him to the prolific but frustrated hen; they bred successfully. Even when established, I would not winter these buntings outside without adequate shelter and enough heat to keep the temperature above freezing point.

## Description

150–165 mm (6–6½ in), sexually dimorphic.

COCK: Bill horn coloured with a yellowish area on the lower mandible; irides brown; head and throat black with white stripes below and above eye; rest of upperparts pinkish cinnamon, flecked with brown; tail brown, flecked with cinnamon; underparts, breast, abdomen, flanks and undertail coverts cinnamon; legs and feet brown.

HEN: Paler coloured then cock; head brownish grey marked with black; throat brownish grey.

N.B. One of the cock birds I obtained in 1969 had a dark-blue throat blending into the black of the head and neck, this was retained through successive moults until its death five years later.

## Distribution and Habitat

Wide-ranging in Africa from southern Saudi Arabia and Ethiopia to the Cape. Throughout its range found mainly in open rocky and hilly country, although it will visit cornfields and fair-sized country towns. In some parts of its distribution it can also be seen in woodlands and orchard bushes.

## Breeding

PERIOD: My birds bred successfully during May — July although in earlier unsuccessful attempts, eggs were laid and incubated from June until September. In a recent report breeding commenced in May. With such a wide geographical distribution feral breeding periods include almost every month of the year, in some areas it would appear to coincide with the end of the rainy season. Two and possibly three broods can be reared in captivity.

NEST: A loosely built shallow cup of fine twigs, grass and rootlets, lined with fine dry grass, sometimes with fine rootlets. The nest is usually on the ground in a slight scrape (often made by the bird) and may be in full view, although near a tuft of grass or stone. Other sites are on a ledge in a wall of a dry ditch at the base of a rock-face; in a dead tree stump; on a rock under weeds (Skead 1960). With the exception of two nests, my hen used shallow seed dishes on a feeding platform about 90 cm (3 ft) high, in the aviary shelter. This was in spite of a wide variety of (I thought) suitable sites and receptacles provided. The shallow cup of dried grasses and weeds were usually built on top of a few twigs and lined with upholsterer's fibre and a few feathers. The cock sang and carried material to the hen when she was at the nest site and also away from the site. The successful breeding was in a nest built on a ledge I had made with a number of large stones and bricks, and was about 45 cm (18 in) above the aviary floor.

EGGS: The eggs were of a bluish-white ground colour (white and greenish white recorded), spotted and blotched with dark brown, usually forming a zone at the larger end. Clutch size 2–3, sometimes 4. Of the fourteen clutches laid by my birds, eleven consisted of 3 eggs and three of 4 eggs.

INCUBATION: Carried out by the hen alone, and usually commences with the last egg laid (sometimes the day after and on one occasion with the second egg laid). Both cocks were often seen sitting very close to the hen while she was incubating, but were never seen on the nest. I only saw the cock feed the hen twice while she was incubating. Incubation period 12–13 days; Skead gives one record of 14 days. Although the hen sat very close and was tolerant of my presence, she did leave the nest and it was some time before she returned, so I became more cautious in case the eggs became chilled.

CHICKS: The two chicks of the first brood I saw were dark grey with pink mouths and pale yellowish-white gape flanges. The hen brooded them very closely for about six days. Both parents fed the chicks on a wide variety of live food ranging from spiders and crane flies collected from nettle beds and bushes, to commercially bred mealworms. I did not see the chicks feed on soaked seed or on the fine-grade softbill mixture provided, which I could not get the adult birds to eat at any time. The cock was adept at catching flies in the aviary (which he usually ate himelf). The young left the nest some time during the morning of the 14th day after hatching and the hen commenced another clutch the following day in the same nest to which a few more feathers had been added. The cock continued to feed the young for about another ten days, and they were seen eating dry seed 15 days after leaving the nest. I then removed the chicks as they were being chased by a pair of Black-breasted Weavers.

Behaviour

These buntings are very terrestrial in the wild and in captivity; in warm weather spending lots of time sunbathing on the ground. With one exception, copulation took place on the ground after much excited chasing and singing by the cock. They are not aggressive birds but held their own in an aviary of 2.5× 1.8 × 2 m high (8 × 6 × 7 ft) with a pair of Black-bellied Weavers (*Euplectes nigroventris*) and four cock Chestnut Sparrows (*Sorella eminibey*). The two occasions when conflict occurred were when the hen bunting decided to adopt the feeding platform as a nest site; this was solved by establishing a second feeding station, and when the chicks of the first brood had left the nest and the cock 'defended' them when a weaver approached. Although these buntings have been recorded as breeding in loose colonies in the wild, one pair of buntings per aviary must be the rule. Once only I saw a 'butterfly' display flight, when the second pair was housed in a larger aviary. The cock was singing and began to fly up and down the aviary with measured wing beats, then perched near the hen still singing.

PALE ROCK BUNTING *Emberiza impetuani*

OTHER NAMES: Lark-like Bunting, Lark Bunting. Two subspecies are recognised: the nominate, *E.i. impetuani*, and *E.i. sloggetti*, which is paler in colour and slightly smaller.

This interesting little bunting is very terrestrial in its behaviour and resembles a lark 'in the way it runs and crouches' (Skead 1960). When a shipment is seen in a travelling cage the impression is of small pale birds appearing almost white underneath. Imports into the UK have been few and far between, but a number of small shipments arrived in 1987, probably more than arrived at any other time. Because it was formerly very rarely imported, there appears to be only one breeding record and that was in Bulawayo (Harrap 1970) in a mixed collection. From the little I know of this bird I would treat it as a delicate species, perhaps not easy to establish in captivity.

## Description

130–140 mm (5–5½ in), sexes alike, the hen is said to be slightly smaller.
Bill, upper mandible slate, lower mandible flesh colour; irides hazel; head buffy brown, streaked with olive brown on the crown and nape; rest of upperparts the same with buffy brown on the rump and olive-brown uppertail coverts; tail olive brown, finely edged with buff; throat pale pinkish buff; breast olive becoming pale pinkish buff on the abdomen; underwing coverts pinkish buff; legs and feet flesh colour.

## Distribution and Habitat

Angola, Namibia, Botswana and Cape Province and occasionally Zimbabwe. Usual habitat is drier areas, open rocky veld and hillsides but has been seen in bushed veld and frequently wanders into grass veld areas. Single birds or small parties; sometimes flocks of several hundred will move but there is no evidence to suggest any regularity in these incursions.

## Breeding

PERIOD: There are apparently no captive breeding records outside of Africa, the Bulawayo breeding commencing in August. The feral breeding period is a long one, starting in September or October, March–April depending on the area. Two broods, possibly three.
NEST: A loosely-placed mass of twigs and plant stems, surrounding a compact shallow cup lined with fine grass and rootlets, occasionally with thistledown. The nest is built on the ground among stunted bushes or weedy plants, or in a slight hollow against a small bush plant or tuft of grass. Sometimes in the open or on bare ground or under rocks, the hen building alone (one sex builds) (Skead 1960). Harrap reported that his birds built at the base of a large clump of bamboo. The nest was made of coarse grass, bent and small broken twigs, lined with fine down from pampas grasses and hessian taken from an old sack.
EGGS: Ground colour whitish pale blue or greenish white,

freckled, spotted and blotched with red-brown, ash brown and grey. The markings dispersed over the shell. Clutch size 3–4, sometimes 2.

INCUBATION: Carried out by the hen. Period 12 days (Harrap).

CHICKS: (Captive breeding) The two chicks were covered with white down, pin-feathers growing when one week old. Both left the nest at 14 days, their tails being half-grown. Both parents fed the chicks on the termites and live food they caught in the planted aviary; seed was not fed by the parents until the chicks were nine days old. The staple diet was mixed seed, and grit and rock salt was supplied. All the birds in the aviary were fond of the salt.

### Behaviour

The Bulawayo birds bred in a planted aviary of 6 × 5 m (20 × 16 ft) with other bunting species, finch-larks, quail finches, waxbills of several species and doves, apparently without conflict. The cock bird sang from a rock in the aviary, then chased the hen with drooped wings. In the wild, the butterfly-flight has been recorded on one occasion.

## GOLDEN-BREASTED BUNTING *Emberiza flaviventris* **Plate 7**

OTHER NAMES: Red-backed Yellow Bunting, Red-backed Bunting. Five subspecies are recognised.

The Golden-breasted Bunting has been imported in small numbers for many years and they were available in 1989–90. They have been bred in the UK on a number of occasions; the first record was in 1911. Once established in captivity, they can be wintered in an outside aviary, providing that they have access to a well-lit shelter, with moderate heat available in hard weather. In the wild, the usual bunting cup-shaped nest is built, 45 cm–1.5 m (18 in–5 ft) high.

The chicks appear to be fed almost entirely on insects (Skead 1960) and captive breeding reports indicate some live food is essential for success. The few non-breeding adults I have kept have taken insectivorous soft food and soaked seed. In captivity, they are not particularly aggressive to other species. However, the size of the aviary and the cover provided will obviously affect their behaviour. They should not be housed with related species, or those of a similar colour.

Description

150–165 mm (6–6.5 in), sexually dimorphic.
COCK: Bill horn coloured, sometimes darker on the upper mandible; crown and sides of face black, with a white stripe along the centre of the crown and two on the face; upperparts chestnut, with white margins and tips to feathers of wing coverts; throat and breast yellow (there is a reddish flush on the upper breast); legs and feet brown.
HEN: Stripes on head and face brown or very dull white; yellow breast is paler; upperparts brownish.

Distribution and Habitat

Mali eastwards to Ethiopia, Kenya south to the Cape. Habitat open grasslands, woodland, plantations, gardens and parks in small towns.

## New World Buntings

These buntings, which include the subfamily Cardinalinae, have a geographical range from Canada to southern Argentina. For the aviculturist the generalisations made for all the seed-eating species in the family Emberizidae apply. They need live food and a varied interesting diet and are best kept in aviaries or large cages. The temperament of the group (especially the Central and South American species) and individuals varies from the good mixer to the murderous when breeding, and few can be kept with conspecifics. Housing with unrelated species is a different matter, but a cock of a similar colour, or competition for nesting sites or food can result in a sudden attack without warning. A factor to remember is that, with all the many seed-eating birds which require live food for rearing their young, the amount of live food you must supply increases at an alarming rate for every pair of birds in the same aviary.

It is inevitable that one pair will be dominant, and although this may not result in conflict, the dominant pair will monopolise the live food unless the aviary is large enough for the birds to establish territories, and/or you increase the number of feeding stations and the amount of food. Many New World buntings, especially those from Central and South America have a more rapid reproduction rate than the Old World buntings. Many incubation and nesting periods are lower and their breeding appears opportunistic — 'breeding when breeding is possible'. In general they are very tolerant of nest inspection.

### Genus *Zonotrichia*

RUFOUS-COLLARED SPARROW *Zonotrichia capensis*

OTHER NAMES: Pileated Song Sparrow, Andean Sparrow.

This species was formerly known as *Z. pileata* but recently published checklists (Gruson 1976, Walters 1980, Howard and Moore 1980) all list it as *Z. capensis*. They have a vast geographical distribution and 25 subspecies are currently recognised. *Z. capensis* is a member of the American bunting group known as 'sparrows', 'song sparrows', etc. The majority of the species have been a rarity in aviculture and are expensive as they are found within the United States and are, therefore, protected. Only those whose range includes Mexico and, to a lesser extent, Central and South America are sometimes available. Although a few are attractive, they lack bright colour and tend to be ignored by the Mexican trappers and exporters who concentrate on the grosbeak-cardinal group which includes the colourful and popular *Passerina* buntings and red cardinals. The only species which, over the years, can be considered as a fairly regular import into Europe is *Z. capensis*, and a small number arrived in the UK in 1990. Currently, the most commonly imported subspecies is *Z.c. septentrionalis*, whose distribution includes southern Mexico. This species has been bred on a number of occasions, the most detailed report being that of Herbert Murray, 1966. Murray was of the opinion that once established in captivity, the birds were hardy enough to winter without heat, providing adequate shelter was provided. I have not owned the species myself, but have cared for two 'pairs' belonging to someone else. They thrived on a diet of mixed millet, canary seed, soaked seed, seeding grasses, green food and a little fruit. All types of live food offered were taken with the exception of white worms (*Enchytraeus*). Murray remarks that out of the breeding season their food consists largely of seed, but live food is appreciated and eaten. With the variety of commercially bred invertebrates available in the 1990s, provision of rearing food is easier.

## Description

140–150 mm (5½–6 in). There is variation in the size and plumage pattern of subspecies. The species is difficult, if not impossible to sex visually, hens are said to be somewhat smaller than cocks.

Bill greyish to greyish horn; irides dark brown; crown of head has a central grey or greyish white stripe bordered with black, the feathers of the crown are frequently erected to form a crest; face dusky; superciliaries grey or white; back and wings brown with dusky streaking; throat white (there is a rufous collar on hind neck sometimes extending to the sides of the breast); breast grey; rest of underparts greyish white; legs and feet flesh coloured.

## Distribution and Habitat

From southern Mexico to southern Argentina, embracing many areas of Central and South America. Mainly a bird of open country, grassy pineland, scrub fields, gardens and parks, in some areas inhabiting high country up to 3350 m (11,000 ft). It can be confiding and it can be seen in small towns and villages.

## Breeding

PERIOD: I can find no period for captive breeding but it is obvious from accounts that they will breed while the conditions are favourable. Like many subtropical and tropical species a plentiful supply of live food, suitable nesting sites and seclusion are probably more important than daylight length or temperature (to a limit which obviously can vary with different species and individuals). Two, possibly three or more broods, are reared.

NEST: In the wild a cup-shaped nest is built on or near the ground usually in a bush. Murray records the nest as a deep cup built of grass and roots, usually about 1.5 m (5 ft) above the ground. The same nest is used for successive broods.

EGGS: Greyish ground colour, heavily splotched with dark grey with a rusty ring at the larger end. Clutch size 1–3, rarely 4–5.

INCUBATION: Ten to twelve days by the hen only.

CHICKS: Covered in charcoal-grey, almost black down, with yellow gape flanges. Fed on live food and possibly regurgitated seed. Murray records that the period between the chicks hatching and flying, which is a good three to four weeks, is longer than that of any comparable bird. The immature plumage is duller, lacks the rufous collar and the underparts are heavily streaked.

Behaviour

Murray, who kept his birds in very large aviaries, found them shy and retiring from human presence. Unusually for American buntings, they resented having their nests looked at and Murray may have caused desertions because of this. When the young have left the nest, they are most carefully hidden and looked after by the parents, who will savagely attack and even kill any bird of about their size who comes too near.

**Genus *Coryphospingus***

The two species in this genus, the Red-crested Finch (*C. cucullatus*) and the Pileated Finch (*C. pileatus*), are among the 'rarer' neotropical buntings best known to aviculture. In most literature before the late 1960s it was usually stated that while *C. pileatus* was fairly frequently imported, *C. cucullatus* was a rarity. I have always found the reverse to be true, certainly as far as the UK was concerned and after the mid-1950s. This is possibly due to *C. cucullatus* having the greater geographical distribution.

RED-CRESTED FINCH *Coryphospingus cucullatus*
OTHER NAMES: Sometimes called Brazilian Crested Finch, etc, by importers. Formerly *C. cristatus*. Three subspecies are recognised, the nominate, *C. c. cucullatus*, is probably the commonest import currently.
This attractive and interesting bunting is fairly hardy once established, although I have never wintered them outside later than November. In common with many species in the family they are terrestrial in habit and like nothing better than searching over freshly dug soil for any live food. A basic diet of mixed millet and canary seed is regularly supplemented with maw, rape, niger, millet sprays and soaked seed. Fruit such as pear and apple is sometimes taken and they will eat any live food from spiders to earthworms with the exception of white worm.

This species has been bred on several occasions in the UK,

although the first captive breeding was in France (Decoux 1927). I first bred this species in 1965 and from two clutches of three and two eggs, four young were hatched, although only one was reared to independence. This was due to the bulk of the live food lacking variety (mealworms) and competition for the food from other birds in the aviary. For example, quail monopolise any food on the floor. Next season I managed to get the adults taking soft bill mixture on a regular basis and supplied large amounts of collected live food. The quail were removed and two broods were successfully reared.

### Description

140 mm (5½ in), sexually dimorphic.

COCK: Bill, upper mandible dark grey, lower mandible light grey; irides brown; orbital skin around eyes pale yellowish to almost white; the head crest (which is erected vertically and laterally) carmine, edged with black; wings black; tail dark or reddish brown; rump vinous; chin whitish; breast and most of underparts vinous; legs and feet light grey.

HEN: Most of plumage light brown; vinous on breast, rump and vent. Although it has been stated frequently in avicultural literature that the hen has no crest, this is not so, the crest is smaller than the cock's and of the same light brown colour as most of the plumage. I have seen a hen which had the crest partly vinous. The bill, irides, orbital skin, feet and legs are the same as the cock's.

### Distribution and Habitat

Includes areas of Guyana, Brazil, Bolivia, Uruguay, Paraguay and Argentina. Usual habitat is scrub, pasture, cleared land, also gardens and in Brazil 'cerrado', a specialised growth on Brazil's tableland, a thick tangled vegetation of semideciduous low trees, sometimes fairly open and carpeted with coarse grass (De Schauensee 1970).

### Breeding

PERIOD: In captivity the breeding period is usually from about the end of May to August (Europe). Two or three broods.

NEST: Captive birds usually nest between 1–2.5 m (3–8 ft) up in a bush or clump of cut branches hung up in the aviary. The majority of nests are built in the lower sites even if higher ones are available. The receptacles used in my aviaries have in-

cluded plastic canary nest pans, and nest cups made of small-mesh wire and clumps of gorse (*Ulex*). The nests are a neat cup made of fine grasses lined with fine roots. Upholsterer's fibre, horse hair, coconut fibres and fine grasses have also been used for lining. The same nest is used for successive broods, usually after a limited re-lining with fresh material.
EGGS: Unmarked white, appearing bluish white when freshly laid. Clutch size 1–3. I can find no record for a clutch size of more than 3.
INCUBATION: Carried out by the hen, who although fed by the cock while incubating, frequently leaves the nest to feed, bathe and chase other birds away from the site. Period, usually 11 days, there is one record for 12 days. Incubation commences with the second or sometimes the third egg laid. The parents were tolerant of nest inspection, although I usually waited until the hen was off for a feed before looking.
CHICKS: The young nestlings are dark grey in colour, with traces of greyish-white down, mouth pinkish red, gape flanges yellow (Trollope 1966). In common with many neotropical buntings, they leave the nest at a young age — well before they can fly, i.e. nine to ten days after hatching or even before this if disturbed, as they are active with quill and feather growth at about eight days. They are fed and guarded with enormous zeal and care by both parents, the cock taking over completely when the hen commences a second clutch, which is usually within seven or eight days, sometimes two or three. The parents feed the chicks almost entirely on live food and I have not seen seed given until they are about 20 days plus. The young become independent at about 28–30 days and if the second clutch is hatched by this time it is wise to remove them to separate accommodation. The immature plumage is like the hen's but with very little vinous on the breast. Once chicks are out of the nest, the parents become very bold and defensive, often diving at me and flying around my head.

## Behaviour

They are active birds with a strong flight and although somewhat territorial and aggressive, chasing away other birds from the nest site, the pursuit is short lived. I have never known them to make a serious attack on another bird even when breeding. In my aviaries they have been housed with

*Lonchura* mannikins and munias, parrot-finches (*Erythrura*), quail finches (*Ortygospiza*), quail (*Coturnix*) and doves (*Columbina* and *Oena*). A good deal of time is spent on or near the ground and when live food is taken, such as flies which they catch with ease, the insect is taken to a low perch in cover to be eaten. The tail is frequently cocked when alighting on the ground or a perch. The nuptial display of the cock bird is vigorous, perhaps explosive might be more accurate. The objective seems to be to get the hen bird on the ground by driving and chasing and often she is struck by the cock during the chase. When the hen reaches (or is knocked) to the ground she faces the cock as he alights. His crest is erected vertically and laterally, the body posture is erect and the head and neck are swung from side to side with a rhythmic motion. During the chase and display the cock sings with great intensity. If copulation does not take place the hen flies off immediately and the chase is resumed. Copulation takes place on the ground and when perched. These birds are inveterate sunbathers, lying prone with the wings opened so that the dorsal surfaces are exposed, water bathing is also frequently observed.

## PILEATED FINCH *Coryphospingus pileatus*

OTHER NAMES: No English names that are valid, but like *C. cucullatus* it is often called after its supposed or real country of origin ('Colombian', 'Brazilian' Crested Finch, etc) by importers. In the past this has led to confusion of the two species. There are three subspecies, the nominate, *C. p. pileatus*, having a distribution in Brazil.

The first breeding record for this species was in 1905, and there have been a few other records. Comments made in avicultural literature usually imply that this species and *C. cucullatus* have good breeding results, although I do not think this can be substantiated. Both are very willing to go to nest, but most breeding reports record the problems of supplying enough of the right sort of live food, or substitutes the parents will accept to rear the chicks. The management for this species is the same as for *C. cucullatus* and even when established I personally would not winter them outside without shelter, and enough heat to prevent water from freezing and/or artificial lighting to shorten the long winter nights. The only pair I have kept were successfully established, although they seemed more difficult than *C. cucullatus*. After some 18 months a nest was built, but then the hen died, and I tried for some years afterwards to obtain another hen without success.

## Description

140 mm (5½ in), sexually dimorphic.

COCK: Bill greyish horn or horn colour; irides dark brown; orbital skin around eyes greyish white; head crest scarlet, edged with black, erected vertically and laterally; lores whitish, rest of upperparts grey or slate grey; tail black; throat, abdomen and undertail coverts greyish white; breast and sides light grey; legs and feet light grey.

HEN: The hen has a smaller crest which is blackish; upperparts sandy grey; like the cock below but the breast is streaked with blackish brown; bill, irides, orbital skin, legs and feet as for the cock.

## Distribution and Habitat

Colombia, northern Venezuela, eastern central Brazil. Habitat dry scrub and thickets.

## Breeding

Not enough detailed captive breeding reports, but it would appear that they will breed in outside avaries from about May to July. Two broods?

NEST: Usually a site below about 1.8 m (6 ft) from the ground in captivity, but obviously the aviary height and sites available control selection. In a shrub, bush or cup-type receptacle. Dried grasses lined with finer grasses, rootlets, animal hairs and feathers. Sometimes the nests are very frail and lack both strength and lining.

EGGS: Unmarked white or bluish white. Clutch size usually 3.

INCUBATION: Eleven days, by the hen alone who is fed on the nest by the cock.

CHICKS: Fed by both parents and leave the nest at about ten days, Thomasset (1931) says they resemble the hen at this age.

Behaviour

Terrestrial in behaviour, seeking food on the ground but less inclined to fly to low cover than the Red-crested Finch. My pair showed no aggression when housed with other birds. Reports suggest they are not overtly aggressive when breeding.

**Genus *Rhodospingus***

CRIMSON FINCH *Rhodospingus cruentus*
OTHER NAMES: Rhodospingus Finch.

This elegant and attractive little neotropical bunting is separated in its own genus, and there are no subspecies. Walters (1980) remarks that some consider this species should be placed in the Thraupidae (tanagers), which he has given family status, removing it from the Emberizidae. Certainly my purely avicultural impression is that these birds (in captivity) are more arboreal than the *Coryphospingus* and therefore that the two genera are not as closely related as many believe. The first time I saw them they reminded me of a *Euphonia* species and after keeping them for some years, to me they were still a smaller tanager. There is apparently no record of a captive breeding in the UK although they have possibly been bred in the USA and in Europe. Three factors account for the apparent lack of breeding reports. The first factor is that importations into the UK were very rare (or unknown) until the mid-1960s; they were not represented in the London Zoo collection between 1828 and 1927. It appears that the species was also little known in the United States; the National Zoological Park received one cock bird in 1965, which was not identified until later when twenty *R. cruentus* were obtained in Ecuador (Muller 1967). A few small shipments arrived in the UK the same year and I obtained two 'pairs' in December, however, one of the hens in these pairs proved to be a cock in immature plumage and this is the second factor concerning poor breeding results: many 'hens' are, in fact, immature cocks. The third factor affecting the apparent lack of breeding results is that many aviculturists when buying a 'finch' are inclined to assume that the birds will be easy to establish, will be hardy and that a diet of seed and green food will suffice. This attitude was often re-enforced by some importers, especially if the birds were difficult to establish and losses were likely. My birds were in reasonable condition when purchased, although both the adult cocks were slightly fluffed out showing signs of feeling cold. I therefore placed them in a hospital cage at 28°C (85°F) for 48 hours, then released them with the 'hens' in an isolation cage for a period of two weeks, the temperature being slowly reduced during this period. They thrived on a diet of mixed millets, maw, small canary seed, green food, fruit, meal-worms and maggots. Later I managed to get them to eat fine-grade softbill mixture. From later experience I would class this species as fairly difficult to establish, but with good management they adjust well to captivity. When established (in southern England), I wintered them with moderate heat 8–10°C (45–50°F), and extended the day length with artificial light. Since the late 1960s, importations have been small and scarce; they were available in 1990.

## Description

115–130 mm (4½–5 in), sexually dimorphic.

COCK: Bill narrow and pointed, greyish horn; irides horn-coloured; orbital skin light buffish; head crest bright red; head, back, wings and tail dull black; underparts crimson; legs and feet grey.

HEN: Head crest yellowish or golden buff; remaining plumage varies from dark brown to olive brown; bill, irides, orbital skin, legs and feet as for the cock.

## Distribution and Habitat

The arid tropical zone from western Ecuador to north-western Peru. Habitat dry scrub, bushes.

## Breeding

PERIOD: My birds did not get past the nest building stage as the only hen died of egg-binding. Marchant (1960) records the breeding in south-western Ecuador for this species. In common with many neotropical buntings and other passerines they have a short incubation and nestling period. The species was absent from the area during the dry season, their return coinciding with the onset of heavy rain. The birds are common in the area within a week and they start breeding in a burst some 10–14 days after arrival, with the first flush of vegetation. The whole nesting cycle is probably completed in 22–26 days, two or three broods are reared.

NEST: The nest in my aviaries was built in a wicker nest basket fixed in a clump of gorse, about 1.2 m (4 ft) high. It was a flimsy cup of grasses lined with finer grasses and kapok. The nests in Ecuador were rather bulky and untidy on the outside and made of dead grass and plant stems, lined with finer material, with lumps of wild cotton on the outside.

EGGS: Ground colour very pale blue, marked with black spots, blotches and scrawls mainly in a zone around the larger end, with fine underlying spots and smears of brown or mauve.

INCUBATION: By the hen alone. Period approximately 11 days. Marchant (1960) remarks that the hens were not as shy as comparable species in the same area and could be observed while incubating.

CHICKS: Blind and naked at hatching, developing a sparse down at about four days, quickly developing quills and feathers. In Ecuador their crops were not filled with grass seeds and Marchant presumed they were fed on animal matter (insects, etc) which, from collected specimens, is known to be the adult diet.

## Behaviour

In Ecuador, territories were held and vigorously defended without any striking song or display flight. My birds lived amicably in an aviary 4.3 × 2.4 × 2.4 m high (14 × 8 × ×8 ft) with two pairs of waxbills (*Estrilda* spp) and two pairs of munias (*Lonchura* spp). Apart from some chasing away from their nest site, the Crimson Finches displayed no aggression. However, as breeding did not occur this may give a false impression; Kerry Muller also found that this species (unlike *Coryphospingus*) displayed no aggression, but at the time the birds had not bred.

## Genus *Lophospingus*

### BLACK-CRESTED FINCH *Lophospingus pusillus*

OTHER NAMES: There are no valid alternative English names, although the species is called the Pygmy Cardinal by importers. No subspecies are recognised and the only other species in the genus, the Grey-crested Finch (*L. griseocristatus*) is unknown in aviculture.

This species has been fairly frequently imported into the UK over the last 15 to 20 years, although shipments are usually small in number. They are occasionally still available and have been imported in 1989–90. It was first bred by Amsler in 1939, and since then has been bred fairly frequently. Like the *Coryphospingus* species, successful breeding is dependent on providing enough live food and substitute rearing food that the parents will feed to their young. Miss Leitch achieved this in 1970 in an inside flight and her birds reared six healthy young in three broods. Basic care is the same as for *Coryphospingus*. I have only kept two cocks but from the experience of others, I would not winter them outside without adequate protection and moderate heat in hard weather.

### Description

130 mm (5 in), visually sexable.
COCK: Bill greyish or greyish horn, lower mandible lighter; irides dark brown; long black head crest; top and sides of head dark brown; sides of crown black; white eye stripe; back greyish brown; rump grey; throat black; breast and sides ashy grey; centre of abdomen white; wings ashy grey; wing coverts tipped white; tail blackish, tipped white; legs and feet flesh colour or greyish flesh.
HEN: Generally paler than cock; throat whitish.

### Distribution and Habitat

Southern Bolivia, Paraguay and Argentina. Habitat open shrubby plains.

### Breeding

PERIOD: In outside aviaries nesting begins in May/June, two broods and attempts to rear a third have occured. Three broods have been successfully reared in inside accommodation.
NEST: The sites in captivity have included bushes and artificial sites created by fixing clumps of twigs and branches in the enclosure. Sites chosen by the birds have usually been well

screened. Nesting receptacles used have varied from canary nest pans, baskets and nest boxes to old wild birds' nests. The often flimsy nests have varied from cups of twigs, grasses and rootlets, lined with hair, feathers or wool, to a few feathers in an old bird's nest. The hen builds.
EGGS: Ground colour bluish green, greyish green or white, spotted and speckled with brown and sometimes blackish. Clutch size 2–3.
INCUBATION: Carried out by the hen who is fed on the nest by the cock. They are close sitters and usually tolerant of nest inspection. Incubation period 12 days.
CHICKS: Like other neotropical buntings the chicks have a rapid growth rate, and show downy growth soon after hatching. They are fed by both parents and the main rearing food in successful breedings has been live food, proprietary insectivorous mixtures, other rearing foods and soaked seeds. Chicks leave the nest at 12 days, the cock continuing to feed them when the hen starts the next clutch. The cock must be watched at this stage and the young removed as soon as they can feed themselves, as the cock has been known to attack and kill young birds. The main cause of breeding failure, as with other related species, would appear to be the young age of the chicks when leaving the nest. Often they cannot fly, or can only just perch above ground. During wet weather in an outside aviary, they can rapidly become soaked and chilled. It should be noted that probably the most successful breeding of this species (Leitch) took place in an inside aviary. The second cause of breeding failure is the lack of enough live food and other animal protein foods.

### Behaviour

The best results are obtained when a pair are given an aviary to themselves. There is considerable evidence that in mixed aviaries disruption and serious aggression will occur. If other birds are housed with them, the others should be fairly robust species, certainly not waxbills, which have been found dead when housed with breeding *L. pusillus*.

## Genus *Poospiza* (Warbling Finches)

The warbling finches are acrobatic and rather tit-like members of the bunting family, with a South American distribution. *Poospiza* appears to be a homogenous genus with attractive but quietly coloured plumage. Most species are predominantly black, white, grey and brown. They are elegant birds with slender bills which, in some species, appear quite long compared to their size. It is doubtful if more than 6 of the 16 species in the genus have been imported into Europe. Most years however, a few small shipments arrive in the UK.

There are records for two species being bred in captivity, the Pretty Warbling Finch (*P. ornata*) by Zackrisson in Sweden (1972), previously bred at Keston in 1960, and the Collared Warbling Finch (*P. hispaniolensis*) (Trollope 1984). From the limited details available, there are three main factors to be considered with the breeding and care of *Poospiza*. They are insectivorous and live food or soft food substitutes must be provided for rearing and the maintenance of adults in good condition. They can be aggressive when breeding and like many bunting species are best housed on their own or with a pair of small doves or quail. Finally they cannot be considered hardy, and in many areas of Europe and in the USA should be provided with moderate heat during the winter months.

## PRETTY WARBLING FINCH *Poospiza ornata*

OTHER NAMES: Cinnamon Warbling Finch. There are no subspecies.

In spite of its name, Boosey (1962) considered this species to be one of the least attractive of four *Poospiza* species. The bird reminded him 'of a small biscuit-coloured chaffinch'. He was also of the opinion that *P. ornata* was the only member of the genus which deserved the misnomer of 'finch.' The other three species kept at Keston he thought of as being something between a tit and warbler.

### Description

130 mm (5 in), sexually dimorphic.

COCK: Bill horn coloured, upper mandible darker near base; irides brown; crown and uppertail coverts dark ashy grey; eye stripe light chestnut, bordered above by a blackish colour; rest of upperparts grey with white bar on the wings; underparts cinnamon, darker on the throat and breast, pale on undertail

coverts; legs and feet fleshy colour.
HEN: Much paler than the cock.

## Distribution and Habitat

North-western Argentina. Habitat bushes and low trees in pastures.

## Breeding

PERIOD: From the limited information on the genus in outside aviaries nesting would commence in May. Two broods, possibly three could be reared in a season.
NEST: Zackrisson describes a deep cup-shaped nest, of grass blades and moss lined with horse-hair. Aviary sites have included pine thickets, bushes and clumps of twigs hung up under cover. The cock bird collects material and also plays a small part in building the nest.
EGGS: Ground colour white, marked with irregular brown or black spots mostly at the larger end. Clutch size 3.
INCUBATION: Carried out by the hen, who is fed on the nest by the cock, she is a close sitter. Incubation period 12–13 days.
CHICKS: The nestlings are greyish with grey down, they are fed by both parents. They demonstrate the usual rapid development of neotropical bunting chicks and leave the nest early at about 12 days. The immature plumage is like that of the hen, with a white eye stripe, and the breast is streaked with greyish and white. The parents fed the chicks largely on live food, fresh ant pupae, mealworms and, if spiders are provided, little else. Soaked sponge cake was also fed to the chicks and a variety of collected insects.

## Behaviour

In Sweden the breeding took place in a planted aviary of 5 × 3 × 2 m high (17 × 10 × 7 ft), in the company of waxbills, (*Estrilda, Uraeginthus*) and social weavers (*Pseudonigrita*). The cock bird was very aggressive to birds of a similar colour and a second cock bird attacked and badly injured a Violet-eared Waxbill (*U. granatina*).

At Keston one nesting came to an abrupt end when the cock killed the hen — this occurred during a period when she came off the nest while brooding a chick.

Wild birds are said to feed on the gound. This is also true of birds in aviaries (given the opportunity).

## COLLARED WARBLING FINCH *Poospiza hispaniolensis*

**Plate 9**

OTHER NAMES: Has also been known as Bonaparte's Warbling Finch.

The Collared Warbling Finch, like its congenerics, has been imported fairly frequently, but in small numbers, for many years. My experience with a breeding pair differs from that of Zachrisson (1972), with *P. ornata.* Although the pair chased other species from their nesting site, they did not attack the birds housed with them, or inhibit their visits to the feeding stations.

### Description

130 mm (5 in), sexually dimorphic.

COCK: Bill blackish and glossy; irides brownish, lower eyelid white, long eybrow stripe surmounted by narrow dark line; side of head black; upperparts grey; wing coverts with a buff wash; tail black with inner webs of outer feathers whitish; underparts white; side of breast and body grey; centre of breast black; sides of vent chestnut; legs and feet light brown.
HEN: Bill greyish brown; eyebrow stripe greyish white; upperparts brown streaked with dusky; tail greyish brown; underparts greyish; the hen lacks the black on the sides of head and centre of breast.

### Distribution and Habitat

South-west Ecuador and coastal Peru. Found in cactus, scrub and cultivation.

### Breeding

PERIOD: In contrast to other breeding reports on *Poospiza* in outside aviaries, my birds commenced the first of three broods in August. The last bird left the nest in November and was successfully reared. This is yet another indication that, in

areas like Northern Europe, reproduction is not apparently inhibited by declining photoperiod and temperature.
NEST: The same nest was used for three clutches, a deep cup of dried grasses and straw, lined with finer grass stems and built in a fork of cut conifer branches. The hen alone built the nest.
EGGS: Very pale blue ovates, marked at the larger end with small blackish and dark ash spots. Clutch size 3.
INCUBATION: Like other neotropical buntings, the hen is a close sitter and tolerant of nest inspection. The incubation period is 13 days, carried out entirely by the hen; the cock occasionally feeds her while she is incubating, although she leaves the nest to feed herself and exercise.
CHICKS: The nestling has dark greyish skin, with greyish brown down; the gape is pinkish with whitish gape flanges, darker near the bill tip. Both parents feed the chicks, the cock brooding them when the hen comes off to feed. In common with other neotropical bunting species, the chicks leave the nest at an early age (in my experience at 10 and 9 days respectively); neither the primaries nor tail feathers are fully developed and they cannot fly effectively for another 4 to 5 days.

At 26 days the young have the bill dark horn in colour, the irides are light brown and the forehead, crown and nape are greyish brown with a pronounced greyish white eyebrow stripe. The area from the bill across the upper face to the nape is brownish grey; the throat and lower cheeks are greyish white. Breast and abdomen are light grey, heavily streaked with dark brown; the upper surface is greyish brown, streaked with darker brown; wings and tail brown, with a few feathers tipped with light grey; legs and feet light flesh colour.

The parents feed the chicks almost entirely on live food, collected from nettle beds and bushes and supplemented with mealworms. Insectivorous softbill mixture provided has not been fed to the chicks, although the young eat soft food when they are fledged. They become independent of their parents at about 24 days, eating hard seed and other foods.

## Behaviour

*P. hispaniolensis* is an active fast-flying species, constantly flirting their wings and tail and perching on the sides of the aviary and plant growth, acrobatic and effective at catching flying insects. Pair bonding and pre-copulatory display consists of bill touching: the birds will fly towards each other then briefly touch bills while hovering, and when perched they move rapidly towards each other along the perch and touch bills. Bill touching is often followed by copulatory chasing, the cock chasing the hen until she perches. The soliciting posture consists of the hen raising her head, flirting the wings and tail, then the tail is moved to one side and raised; the cock then mounts with rapid wing beats. There is often an element of aggression in this display, usually from the hen, who will jab at the cock after bill touching.

### Genus *Sicalis* (Saffron Finches)

The saffron finches (with the *Paroaria* cardinals) are probably better known in aviculture than any other neotropical buntings. The species *S. flaveola* was first imported into Europe in the 1860s and it has been regularly imported ever since, sometimes in large numbers. Some species in the genus are often listed as grass finches or grassland finches and are not to be confused with the Australian grassfinches (*Poephila*). There are 11 species in the genus, all of which have yellow, or yellowish, in their plumage to some extent. They are small to medium-sized birds, ranging from about 115–165 mm (4½–6½ in). Apart from *S. flaveola* a few other species have occasionally been imported, and the current situation is that importations of all species, including *S. flaveola*, are limited. Small shipments arrived in the UK in 1989–90.

SAFFRON FINCH *Sicalis flaveola* **Plate 3**

OTHER NAMES: Brazilian Saffron Finch. Four subspecies are recognised, the most distinctive of which is Pelzeln's Saffron Finch (*S. f. pelzelni*), which is slightly smaller, with dark streaking on the flanks.

The Saffron Finch is fairly hardy once established, aggressive in mixed company and willing to breed. From the limited details available, I would think this also applies to its most frequently imported congeneric, *S. luteola*, the Yellow Grass Finch. The first breeding of the Saffron Finch in the UK was probably c1904, and the most detailed account is that of C J O Harrison (1973).

## Description

140–150 mm (5½–6 in), sexually dimorphic.
COCK: Bill short and blunt, horn-coloured, lower mandible pale; irides dark brown; forehead and crown orange; sides of head yellow; rest of upperparts greenish or olive green with darker streaking on the back, wings and tail; underparts yellow; legs and feet dark flesh colour.
HEN: Olive green above, with dark streaking on the mantle and back, finer streaks on the head; sometimes an orange tint on the forehead; wings and tail dark with greenish-yellow feather edges.

N.B. Breeding can occur in immature plumage, which is sometimes not obtained until the second or third year.

## Distribution and Habitat

Widespread in the lowlands of tropical South America, introduced into Panama and Jamaica. Found in the semi-arid area of the lower tropical zone, in open bush, river valleys, grasslands, parks, gardens, villages and towns.

## Breeding

PERIOD: In natural habitat the breeding season varies throughout its vast distribution and is doubtless controlled by the wet and dry seasons. Captive birds in outside aviaries start nesting in April/May, two or three broods are often reared.
NEST: The Saffron Finch and, possibly, other *Sicalis* are probably the only members of the bunting family to frequently nest in holes and crevices in trees, walls or rocks. The old nests of other birds are also used. Bond (1960) records that in the West Indies the usual sites are cavities in trees, the base of a palm frond or under the eaves of a house. Their favourite nesting receptacle in captivity is a nesting box, either half open or the budgerigar type with a hole. Nests have also been built in clumps of branches and twigs hung up in the aviary. It is usually a rather untidy cup of grasses and roots, lined with hair and feathers and almost any other material provided. The cock plays little or no part in building the nest.
EGGS: Ground colour white, heavily marked with spots and specks of purplish brown, sometimes blackish grey, often

forming a zone at the larger end. Clutch size 3–4, sometimes 5.

INCUBATION: Carried out by the hen, although I have been told the cock will sometimes cover the eggs for brief periods. There is no indication that the cock feeds the hen on the nest. Incubation period 13–14 days.

CHICKS: Harrison describes the nestlings as virtually naked, dull purplish pink in colour with sparse tufts of down. The mouth is orange and the gape flanges very pale yellow. The young are fed by both parents and leave the nest at 14–16 days, the cock will continue to feed them when the hen commences a second clutch which can occur within a few days. The young are fed on live food, semi-ripe and unripe grass and weed seeds and soaked seed. Commercial insectivorous rearing food is a great asset if the parents will feed it, and it should be made available to the adults before breeding. When the young become independent, which is between 10 to 14 days, the cock must be watched in case he begins to harass them.

### Behaviour

Some authors have remarked that Saffron Finches 'are not aggressive to other birds' and are 'tolerant'. However, the majority of reported breedings, and the aviculturists I have spoken to, consider them very disruptive in a mixed collection. For breeding it is best to keep one pair in a small aviary or perhaps a large cage. Having the advantages of being visually sexable and willing breeders, and having colourful plumage, they would be an ideal species for establishment in aviculture. Alan Silver suggested this many years ago, and I can only conclude that their rather aggressive behaviour is the reason for the apparent lack of interest in his proposal. The courtship behaviour of the cock is vigorous, chasing the hen with neck and head feathers erect, wings drooped and tail cocked. Aggression to other birds is shown with a forward threat posture with the bill open.

## Genus *Piezorhina* (Cinereous Finch) Plate 2

This finch is a monotypic form, probably most closely related to the Inca finches, *Incapiza.* I have included it in this edition as they have been imported fairly frequently in small numbers in recent years. This availability could come to an abrupt end and, as there seems to be little recorded on their breeding, feeding and general habits, this is an opportunity for the aviculturist to provide this information.

CINEREOUS FINCH *Piezorhina cinerea*

The Cinereous Finch was available in the UK during 1989–90; I have at present a pair? of these robust-looking finches, which I have found easy to feed. They have taken all the seed offered, with a preference for canary and millet, except sunflower, also mealworms, house crickets, soft food and greenfood.

Description (from captive birds)

165 mm (6.5 in), sexes alike?
Bill bright yellow and large; irides dark brown, with a narrow margin of white, above and below the eye; lores black, upperparts grey to dark grey, with darker streaks on secondaries and primaries; throat dull white; underparts pale grey, shading to white on the belly; legs and feet very strong and yellow.

NB: One of the birds described is much paler on the upperparts, the bill is pale yellow with indistinct greyish streaking on the upper and lower mandible. This bird is probably an immature, but it is possible that this species is sexually dimorphic. I await this bird's moult with interest.

Distribution and Habitat

Coastal north-west Peru from Tumbes south to La Libertad up to elevations of 300 m (1000 ft). Common on open desert-like plains with scattered shrubs and low trees. Ridgely and Tudor (1989) record that it is a conspicuous bird often perching fully in the open on the ground, regularly at roadsides. Usually single birds or pairs are seen, at most small loose groups.

**Genus *Sporophila* (Seed-eaters)**

*Sporophila* is a large New World genus of 31 species including *S. collaris* (**Plate 4**) with a distribution mainly in Central and South America. One species, the White-collared Seed-eater

(*S. torqueola*) has a range which extends into the United States.

These birds are generally small, 100–130 mm (4–5 in), and compact in build, with stubby conical bills, which have a slight curve in some species and can be large in proportion to their body size. Most, if not all, of the species are sexually dimorphic, the cocks having grey, black, white, brown and (rarely) yellow or chestnut in their plumage. The hens are usually brown, olive, grey or yellowish. As their name suggests, these birds live largely on seed in the wild, and much is made of this in some avicultural literature, with the implication that a seed diet would suffice not only for adult maintenance but also for breeding. However, it must be remembered that in captivity, the variety of grass and other seeds available to these birds in the wild is difficult if not impossible to supply. Certainly the cocks of three or four species I have kept over the years have eagerly taken live food of all types when offered, including maggots and mealworms, and some have also taken softbill mixtures of various types. With such supplements, soaked and germinated seed and a wide variety of seeding grasses a good rearing diet is achieved.

The major drawback to the breeding of this genus in captivity is the usual one: the rarity or absence of hens in shipments. Other factors are the sober colouring of the cocks and the fact that they are usually more expensive than other more freely imported species, so unless an aviculturist is a *Sporophila* enthusiast, the importer finds demand is limited. Over the years probably some 10 or 12 species have been imported into Europe. During 1989–90 there have been a few small shipments into the UK of the White-collared Seed-eater (*S. torqueola*), the Lined Seed-eater (*S. lineola*), the Parrot-billed Seed-eater (*S. peruviana*) (**Plate 1**) and the Chestnut Throated Seed-eater (*S. telesco*) (**Plate 5**).

Once established, seed-eaters are fairly hardy birds, but I do not winter them outside at temperatures below freezing, and provide heating at a temperature of about 8°C (45°F). When breeding, these birds should never be housed with related species, and one pair per small aviary will save a lot of disruption and possibly injured birds. With unrelated species, again one must be cautious; certainly I would never house them with waxbills, but would house them with the more robust and phlegmatic species such as Java sparrows and

*Lonchura* mannikins. Single cocks housed with most other species will create no problems, but as with many birds, a breeding pair can change a situation very rapidly.

It should be noted that 'seed-eaters' is a name also used for some species of Ethiopian region serins.

CAYENNE SEED-EATER *Sporophila frontalis*

OTHER NAMES: Buffy-throated Seed-eater, Buffy-fronted Seed-eater. There are no subspecies.

This species was first bred by W R Partridge in 1962, in a large planted aviary they shared only with a pair of Imperial Fruit Pigeons.

## Description

130 mm (5 in), sexually dimorphic.

COCK: Bill dark horn brown, short and thick, with a deeply curved culmen; irides dark brown; upperparts olive brown; narrow white stripe behind eye; underparts white, from throat to abdomen, with a broad greyish-brown band across the breast; centre of abdomen and flanks greyish or buffy brown; legs and feet brown.

HEN: Plumage olive green; chin yellow, shading to greenish yellow from throat to breast.

## Distribution and Habitat

South-eastern Brazil to north-eastern Argentina. Habitat shrubbery.

## Breeding

PERIOD: In captivity, breeding in outside aviaries has commenced as early as the end of March and continued until September. Two or three broods are reared.

NEST: A fairly deep cup of twigs and feathers in low bushes, the cock takes part in nest building, and on one occasion made the entire nest.

EGGS: White ground colour, the markings are variable, heavily blotched with dark brown at the larger end, or covered with indistinct sandy spots.

INCUBATION: Carried out by the hen, period approximately 12–13 days.
CHICKS: Leave the nest at 14 days then spend the next two to three days on the ground or in low bushes. The chicks are fed by the hen almost entirely on insects, very little seed being given. The immature plumage is like that of the hen, with a more yellowish tinge on the underparts.

## Behaviour

No information. An interesting point is that the breeding by W R Partridge was with two hens and a cock; there was no conflict but the aviary was large.

## LINED SEED-EATER *Sporophila lineola*

OTHER NAMES: Lined Finch. There are three subspecies.

This species has been bred on several occasions on the European continent, the first was in 1933. I know of one successful breeding in the UK, which was not published. From all accounts it would be an ideal subject for establishment in captivity.

## Description

100 mm (4 in), sexually dimorphic.
COCK: Bill black, not so heavy and stout as those of many other *Sporophila* spp; irides blackish brown; upperparts bluish black, with a white band extending from back of bill, over the crown and ending in a point at the neck; sometimes a white area on the cheeks; underparts white; legs and feet blackish.
HEN: Bill yellowish; irides brown; upperparts yellowish grey, darkest on back, wings and tail; underparts paler; legs and feet yellowish.

## Distribution and Habitat

North-western and central South America to Argentina, Trinidad and Tobago. Inhabits grasslands, shrubbery, the outskirts of plantations and edges of marshy areas and swamps.

## Breeding

PERIOD: Variable throughout its range, in Trinidad and Tobago it extends from April until September/October (Herklots). In outside aviaries nesting commences April/May, two broods are reared and attempts at a third have been recorded.
NEST: A nest cup of fine root fibres and grass stems lined with finer material, usually low in a small shrub, sometimes in a tree. In captivity, the nests have been made of grasses lined with finer grass stems and feathers. The nests have been made in bushes, and in cut branches hung up in the aviary.
EGGS: Ground colour greyish to greenish white, heavily marked with brown, olive brown and ash grey. Clutch size 2–3.
INCUBATION: Carried out by the hen, who is sometimes fed on the nest by the cock. Incubation period 12 days.
CHICKS: The chicks are fed by both parents when in the nest, the cock feeding them when they leave the nest, which is at 14–16 days. Albrecht-Moller records 18–26 days.

## Behaviour

No information. A single cock I had chased other birds and was rather assertive.

### Grassquits

This group of small, seed-eating birds, consisting of the genera *Volatinia* and *Tiaris*, has a distribution in South and Central America. The only species formerly frequently imported were two in the genus *Tiaris*, (*T. canora* and *T. olivacea*), and the Jacarini Finch (*Volatinia jacarini*). The Cuban Finch (*T. canora*) has not been imported from Cuba for many years now, although some arrived in the UK in 1990 which had been bred on the European continent. A small shipment of Olive Finches (*T. olivacea*) also arrived in that year. The Jacarini is currently more often imported than *Tiaris* species, which is a reversal of the former situation.

Grassquits have been wintered outside in the UK without heat, but this has resulted in losses in hard weather, and moderate heat should be provided. I also consider electric light, for an extended day of 14 hours, to be essential.

## Genus *Volatinia*

### JACARINI FINCH *Volatinia jacarini*

OTHER NAMES: Glossy Grassquit, Blue-black Grassquit. *Volatinia* is a monotypic genus, three subspecies of the single species, *V. jacarini*, are recognised.

This grassquit was first bred in the UK in 1910 and has frequently been bred since. Australian aviculturists have been particularly successful. In the wild the diet appears to be mainly of grass and other seeds, but in captivity live food is the main diet fed to the chicks, and the adults will successfully hawk for flying insects in an aviary. In cold climates grassquits are best kept in a shelter during hard weather, with moderate heat, 8°C (45°F). The Jacarini differs from the *Tiaris* grassquits in that it builds an open, cup-shaped nest instead of a domed structure.

#### Description

100–115 mm (4–4½ in), sexually dimorphic.
COCK: Bill pointed, colour very dark greyish, the lower mandible lighter; irides blackish; entire plumage of adult glossy blue black, with the exception of white underwing axillaries; immature cocks show varying amounts of brown and pale brown; legs and feet very dark grey or blackish.
HEN: Brown above; ashy on the head; underparts pale brown.

#### Distribution and Habitat

Lowlands of Mexico, Central and South America to northern Chile and Argentina. Inhabits grasslands, the edges of swamps, marshy country and cultivated areas.

#### Breeding

PERIOD: In many parts of its distribution it breeds practically throughout the year, in Trinidad and Tobago the main breeding season is June to September. In the UK in outside aviaries breeding usually commences in late April/May. All the indications are that in the wild two broods are reared. Aviary birds will rear two or three broods. Rutgers states that as many as six to eight broods have been reared in a season.

NEST: A shallow cup of dead grasses, lined with finer grasses or rootlets and plant down, usually built low, in small shrubs and other herbage and well hidden. In captivity the preferred site is also shrub, and even in a small planted aviary the nest can be difficult to find. Nest cups made of wicker and wire are sometimes used, as are clumps of cut branches and twigs. The materials are grasses, twigs and stems, lined with finer grasses and other materials provided, cotton wool, kapok or feathers.
EGGS: The ground colour varies from pale greenish to pale green or bluish green, marked with spots and blotches of reddish brown, often concentrated at the larger end. Clutch size 2–3.
INCUBATION: The main incubation is carried out by the hen, although the cock has been seen covering the eggs for brief periods. Incubation commences with the last egg laid. The period is 12 days.
CHICKS: Fed by both parents on live food, seeding grasses, chickweed and insectivorous softbill mixture. Ant pupae is excellent food for the young chicks if obtainable, but not all the adults will feed them to the chicks. Soaked and germinated seed and, later in the chicks' life, hard seed is used. The young will leave the nest at about 10–12 days, and the usual problems presented by chicks on the aviary floor or in low herbage in possibly wet and cold weather arise (as with so many Central and South American species). They are fed by the cock when the hen starts the next clutch and should be removed when independent (at about 16–18 days), to avoid harassment by the cock.

## Behaviour

The cock has a display flight which consists of flying up from a perch vertically for about 60 cm (2 ft) and returning to the same spot, singing as he flies. Because of this behaviour, the species is called 'Johnny-jump-up' in the West Indies. These grassquits are not considered aggressive birds to unrelated species, but two pairs should never be housed together. In Australia some breeders tried housing two hens with one cock, but the results were not particularly successful. Cocks in immature plumage will sing and are also capable of breeding, although it is advisable to delay pairing until they are fully mature.

## Genus *Tiaris*

### CUBAN FINCH *Tiaris canora*

OTHER NAMES: Cuban Grassquit, Melodious Grassquit.

Prior to the ban on the export of these birds by the Cuban Government, this species was the most frequently imported grassquit. Although a free-breeding species in captivity, it is apparent that aviary stocks were inadequate for it to become established. They are still bred on the European continent and aviculturists in the UK are maintaining breeding groups.

#### Description

100 mm (4 in), sexually dimorphic.

COCK: Bill rather stubby and blackish in colour; irides brown; forehead black; crown grey; yellow band below throat extends to sides of neck and above eyes; rest of upperparts olive green; wings and tail brownish grey; underparts dark grey; centre of breast ashy; abdomen whitish grey; legs and feet brownish grey.

HEN: The plumage of the hen is duller, the yellow areas on the cock are replaced with very pale yellow or rusty brown.

#### Distribution and Habitat

Cuba and the Isle of Pines. Inhabits trees and bushes in grasslands and cultivated areas.

#### Breeding

PERIOD: In outside aviaries breeding will begin in April/May. Two broods, sometimes more, are reared in a season.

NEST: A substantial domed structure of grasses, plant fibres and roots, lined with feathers and hairs, with an entrance hole low down at the side, usually built in bushes and trees. In captivity, domed nests are built in natural sites such as bushes. When waxbill-type wicker baskets and similar receptacles are used, the nest is usually small. Dried grasses lined with finer material and feathers. In mixed aviaries Cuban finches will take over the nest of other pairs, evicting the rightful owners unless the owners can resist them.

EGGS: Ground colour pale bluish green speckled with reddish

brown, sometimes white and unmarked. Clutch size 2–3, sometimes 4.

INCUBATION: The hen incubates for about 12 days, usually commencing with the last egg laid.

CHICKS: The young nestlings have greyish-white down. Rearing food can consist of ant pupae, various fine-grade softbill mixtures, soaked and germinated seed, seeding grasses and green foods. Some aviculturists have also supplied maggots, mealworms, larvae, and collected natural live food. Broods have been reared with very little live food, the bulk of the rearing food consisting of soaked and germinated seed and softfood mixtures. The chicks leave the nest at between 13–16 days and are fed mainly by the cock for a further 10–14 days. When the young become independent they should be removed as the cock will harass them, especially if the hen commences another brood.

Behaviour

This lively and self-assertive bird should be housed one pair per aviary for successful breeding. They have been bred in cages. It is the general opinion of most aviculturists that the cocks are belligerent to conspecifics and other species, and that even housing two pairs in adjoining aviaries will result in them indulging in competitive singing and chasing up and down the dividing wire, instead of settling down to breed. This behaviour is common in other self-assertive species, and I have had the same problem with *Serinus* spp. However, individuals vary, I have heard of breeders having no problems housing more than one pair together with other birds. The size of the aviary and the cover provided is obviously the crucial factor. There is no indication that breeding results with mixed and multi-pair housing are particularly successful. An aviculturist who bred Cuban finches for many years found that while the disruption in a mixed collection of unrelated species was tolerable, but undesirable, the housing together of more than one pair led to disaster, as occasionally the cock or a single pair would harass the cock's hen. I have not bred these birds myself; the few I have kept have given every indication that they could be very disruptive in a mixed collection when breeding.

They have been bred on a colony system in Australia, the

theory being that with several pairs of birds the aggression becomes 'diluted' and one pair is not victimised by a dominant cock. However, the general disruption reduces successful breeding and in practice the results are rather poor.

OLIVE FINCH *Tiaris olivacea*

OTHER NAMES: Yellow-faced Grassquit, often listed by importers as Cuban Olive Finch. Five subspecies are recognised.

Although this species has a wider distribution than the Cuban Finch, shipments of the Olive Finch were fewer than those of the Cuban Finch, in the days of uninhibited bird importation, because the Olive Finch's duller plumage was less popular in aviculture. Now, of the two species, *T. olivacea* is obviously the one more likely to be imported from its countries of origin. Like *T. canora* it has proved to be free breeding in captivity.

Description

115 mm (4½ in), sexually dimorphic.

COCK: Bill dark grey to blackish grey; irides dark brown or blackish; upperparts greyish green, with a bold orange-yellow stripe above eye, and small stripe below; chin and throat yellow; black on foreneck and chest; rest of underparts greyish or greyish olive; legs and feet greyish or brownish grey.

N.B. The amount of black in the plumage has considerable subspecific variation.

HEN: Paler than cock with less orange-yellow marking; no black on underparts.

Distribution and Habitat

The Atlantic slope of Mexico through Central America to western Venezuela and the Greater Antilles. Usual habitat grasslands, pastures and cultivated land.

Breeding

PERIOD: In outside aviaries breeding commences in April/May, sometimes March. Two broods, sometimes three.

NEST: A similar structure to that of *T. canora*, domed with an entrance hole low on the side. The usual site is low in a shrub or small tree. Aviary nests are usually built in bushes and clumps of cut branches; nesting baskets and half-opened boxes have been used. I had a pair nest in a budgerigar nest box with one side removed. The materials favoured are grasses and stems, with feathers, cotton wool or sometimes fibres and hair for lining. Like the Cuban Finch, in a mixed aviary they will often evict the rightful owner of a nesting receptacle if they can bully them into deserting.

EGGS: The usual ground colour is pale greenish, spotted with brown; eggs with a whitish ground colour, both marked and immaculate are sometimes laid. Clutch size usually 2–3, but 4 and 5 have been recorded.

INCUBATION: Carried out by the hen and usually commencing with the last egg laid. Period 12–14 days.

CHICKS: There is little if any difference between the Olive Finch and the Cuban Finch in the nestling period, age of reaching independence and rearing foods are the same. The young birds must be isolated from the cock when they can feed themselves.

### Behaviour

Accounts of their breeding behaviour in captivity have varied from 'several pairs can be safely kept together and bred on the colony system' to reports of murderous and fatal attacks, on unrelated species, let alone conspecifics. I have only bred this bird on one occasion and that was in 1952, when two broods were reared in a small planted aviary. They shared the aviary with a pair of Grenadier Weavers (which, like many species of the Ploceidae family are seldom the losers in aviary conflicts). The Olive Finches more than held their own and were first at the food pots.

## Genus *Gubernatrix*

This is a monotypic genus, the only species being a large neotropical bunting, the Green Cardinal. Both this genus and the genus *Paroaria* (five species) have been listed in the subfamily Cardinalinae (cardinal-grosbeaks) by Howard and Moore (1980), but Walters (1980) has listed the two subfamilies as families, i.e. Emberizidae and Cardinalidae, including both genera in the former. As most (if not all) aviculturists will look for them under Emberizinae, that is where I have left them. Sensible people try to avoid taxonomic controversy (just as they try to avoid pestilence, poverty and death).

## GREEN CARDINAL *Gubernatrix cristata*

OTHER NAMES: In most ornithological literature this species is called the Yellow Cardinal.

Because of its crest and rather heavy bill this species resembles the 'true' Red Cardinals of the genus *Cardinalis*. The plumage of this species, however, is mainly olive green with yellow. It is a hardy bird once established and has long been known in aviculture. The first captive breeding was in 1863 in the Zoological Gardens of Cologne. They are considered the easiest cardinal to breed in captivity, but plenty of live food to rear the young is essential for the first crucial five to seven days at least. Live house crickets, which can be obtained in many sizes, can make up the bulk of live food needs. If the adults can be accustomed to take insectivorous softfood before breeding, the rearing of the young will be easier. They should be housed in an aviary on their own.

### Description

180–190 mm (7–7½ in), sexually dimorphic.
COCK: Bill grey or brownish grey, stouter than the bills of the *Paroaria* cardinals; irides dark brown; black head crest; stripe above eye yellow; upperparts olive green, streaked with blackish on back and shoulders; tail yellow with centre feathers black; chin and centre of throat black, sides of throat yellow; breast greenish yellow; rest of underparts yellow; legs and feet blackish grey.
HEN: The plumage is greyer; sides of the head, stripe above eye and sides of throat off-white; upper breast brownish grey.

### Distribution and Habitat

South-eastern Brazil, Uruguay, Argentina. Inhabits scrub country and woodlands.

### Breeding

PERIOD: No information for the breeding season in the wild, probably controlled to some extent by rainfall like many neotropical species. In outside aviaries, breeding commences in April/May two or three broods are reared.

NEST: Usually in low thick bushes, a loosely made cup of twigs, grasses and fibres. In aviaries the birds will nest in bushes, on clumps of cut branches hung up in the aviary, wire and wicker nest baskets, and old wild birds' nests. The nest is built by both sexes. Materials used are grasses, sometimes hair. Feathers are rarely used.
EGGS: Ground colour pale greenish blue, sometimes whitish, spotted with blackish colour and purplish black. Clutch size 3–4, rarely 5 or 6.
INCUBATION: The hen carries out most of the incubation, the cock covering the nest for brief periods. Period 13–14 days.
CHICKS: Fed by both parents, small live food for first few days. Collected live food, with variety, i.e. spiders, caterpillars etc, can supplement small mealworms, house crickets, maggots and their pupae. Seeding grasses, chickweed, and soaked and germinated seeds should also be provided. The young leave the nest at about 12–14 days, and are fed entirely by the cock when the hen starts the next brood. Once the young are independent separate them from the cock, or you can leave them until the next brood hatches, but keep a careful watch in case the cock starts to harass them.

## Behaviour

In the wild, as for the majority of species in the bunting family, most food seeking takes place on the ground. They usually remain in cover and seldom fly across open country. Although somewhat aggressive when breeding in captivity, they can be kept with robust unrelated species of different plumage colours in a large aviary.

### Genus *Paroaria* (Red-headed Cardinals)

This is a genus of five neotropical buntings, which are fairly homogenous in behaviour, breeding biology and appearance. Only one of the species is sexually dimorphic, the Yellow-billed Cardinal (*P. capitata*). In size they range from 165 mm (6½ in) to about 190 mm (7½ in) and their heads are all some shade of red. Of the five species, four are known in aviculture and have been bred. The fifth, the little known Crimson-fronted Cardinal (*P. baeri*), has probably been imported, but was possibly identified as the Red-capped Cardinal (*P. gularis*) which it closely resembles. The Red-crested (*P. coronata*) and the Pope (*P. dominicana*) were, and still are, the most frequently imported. The Yellow-billed (*P. capitata*) is also brought in occasionally. The Red-crested and the Pope are fairly hardy birds once established, but the other two species known in aviculture are, in my experience, more difficult to establish. The Yellow-billed and the Red-capped are also insectivorous, their bills being rather more pointed than the other species, which could be an indication of different feeding habits in the wild.

With the exception of the Yellow-billed Cardinal, the major drawback to the breeding of these species in captivity is that the sexes are alike. It is generally accepted that they can be sexed by various minor plumage differences such as the depth of colour and extent of the red plumage and, in the case of the Red-crested, the length of the head crest. Comparison of body size and bill shape is also among the many methods advocated, but they are only of use if you have at least three or four birds to select from. The singing of the cock is a more reliable indication. However, true pairs can be selected as proven by the quite considerable number of breeding results, but I personally would not select a cock or hen visually with any confidence. For successful breeding, live food is essential, and if problems arise with collecting wild live food, commercially-bred house crickets, which can be purchased in a wide range of sizes, are ideal food. It is also a good idea to supply mealworms and small maggots for variety. As with all birds with some red plumage, the red colour fades in captivity, but this is not as pronounced as in some other species.

### RED-CRESTED CARDINAL *Paroaria coronata*

OTHER NAMES: No other valid English names. Synonym *P. cucullata*.

These birds are lively, active and best kept in an aviary. They are long established in aviculture, the first captive breedings being by Passerini in 1837–9. Occasionally imported into the UK, small shipments still arrive, and they were available in 1988–9. The most effective breeding method is to keep one pair in a planted aviary or an enclosure, with cover and nesting sites provided by cut branches of conifers, gorse, clumps of twigs and similar material.

These birds are lively, active and best kept in an aviary. They are long established in aviculture, the first captive breedings being by Passerini in 1837–1839. Frequently imported into the UK, small shipments still arrive, and were available in 1980-1981. The most effective breeding method is to keep one pair in a planted aviary or an enclosure, with cover and nesting sites provided by cut branches of conifers, gorse, clumps of twigs and similar material.

## Description

190 mm (7½ in), sexes alike.
Bill light horn colour, greyish towards the tip; irides dark brown; head red with pointed crest; upperparts grey; feathers are edged black on back wing coverts and primaries; throat and front of neck red; sides of neck and rest of underparts white, turning to greyish white at the flanks; legs and feet grey to dark grey. The hen has paler red on the head and throat and some authors say the hen is slightly smaller.

## Distribution and Habitat

South-eastern Brazil, eastern Bolivia, Paraguay, Uruguay and northern Argentina, introduced into Hawaii. Frequents trees and bushes, often near river banks and wet scrubland, and often seen in the vicinity of villages.

## Breeding

PERIOD: No information on a breeding period in the wild, probably varies throughout its wide distribution. Breeding in aviaries commences in April/May, two or three broods are reared.
NEST: The usual bunting cup-shape of twigs, grass stems and fibres, lined with finer grasses and soft material such as hair. The site is most often in a bush or thicket, seldom at any height. Aviary nests are made in bushes and clumps of material hung up in the aviary under cover. Wire and wicker nest cups and old wild birds' nests are also used. They are built of twigs, grasses, roots and plant stems, lined with finer grasses and rootlets. Sometimes material such as kapok,

cotton wool, hair and feathers will be used if available. The nest is built mainly by the hen but the cock will also collect material and assist.

EGGS: Ground colour whitish, sometimes pale greenish or greenish blue, spotted with grey and olive often concentrated at the larger end. Sometimes so heavily marked, the ground colour is almost obscured. Clutch size 3–4, rarely more.

INCUBATION: Carried out mainly by the hen, but some evidence the cock will sit for brief periods, difficult to ascertain with sexes alike even with coloured identification rings, unless one actually sees the change over. Incubation period 13–14 days.

CHICKS: Skin colour of nestlings dark purplish, down greyish white, they are fed by both parents, mainly on live food, for the first six to seven days. They leave the nest at about 14 days, and are fed by the cock, as by this time the hen has usually commenced a second brood. The young become independent at approximately 28–30 days and it is advisable to separate them from the cock, especially if the second brood has hatched.

## Behaviour

Imported birds are rather nervous but in a stable environment they settle down and, except when breeding, are not concerned about showing themselves. They are not only self assertive, they are also capable even when not breeding, of making murderous attacks on other birds. The victims can be an unrelated species and have totally different plumage colour to the cardinals. Some authors say that these birds can be housed in a mixed aviary with the more robust species such as weavers, except perhaps when breeding. This has not been my experience, and unless it is a very large aviary, Red-crested Cardinals are best kept on their own. Doves and quails are the only birds I have kept with them who have not been harassed or attacked, and I always keep a wary eye on the aviary in case the doves become victims. This aggression may not occur for many months and in the past I have been misled by the peace, only to find that, without warning, the cardinals cause disruption or injury to another bird. Copulation is preceded by a nuptial display which consists of the cock approaching the hen with his crest raised, bill pointed up exposing the throat, and wings lowered slightly and tail cocked.

POPE CARDINAL *Paroaria dominicana*
OTHER NAMES: Dominican Cardinal, Red-headed or Red-cowled Cardinal. Synonym *P. larvata*.

This species has also been a frequent import, and has been known in aviculture for many years, the first breeding in the UK being in 1912. Currently it is not as frequently available as *P. coronata*, due to its more limited distribution. It resembles *P. coronata* in appearance (apart from a crest), and also in behaviour and breeding biology.

Description

180–190 mm (7–7½ in), sexes alike.
Like *P. coronata*, but lacks crest; head and throat are a deeper red, and the back is darker grey. The hen bird is slightly smaller than the cock; visual sexing very difficult.

Distribution and Habitat

North-eastern Brazil. Inhabits the edges of forests, open areas of woodland and scrub, also frequently found in the vicinity of human habitation.

Breeding

PERIOD: No information for country of origin. In captivity the few breeding reports indicate nesting commencing in early April/May, two or three broods are reared in captivity.
NEST: The usual bunting open cup of twigs, grass, plant stems and roots, lined with finer and softer material, usually set low in a bush or thicket. In captivity, a bush or other plant providing cover is chosen, also nest baskets and old wild birds' nests, the materials are similar to those used by *P. coronata*. When a basket or other receptacle is used the nest is often rudimentary. The cock may assist in the building and has been seen carrying material.

EGGS: Ground colour usually whitish, pale greenish or greenish blue, heavily spotted with olive or olive brown. Clutch size 3–4.
INCUBATION: Carried out by the hen. It is possible that the cock may cover the eggs for brief periods, incubation can commence with the second or third egg laid. Period 13–14 days.
CHICKS: The nestlings have dark purplish skin, dark grey and whitish down. They are fed by both parents, but the cock plays a small part in rearing until the young leave the nest, at 11 to 14 days. They become independent some 14 days later. Chicks should be removed as soon as they can feed themselves, or as soon as the next brood is hatched, otherwise they will be harassed or attacked by the parents.

### Behaviour

This species is said by some authors to be less aggressive than *P. coronata*. It is also said that if kept, even in a moderately sized aviary, with weavers and other robust species, no trouble will arise. I disagree. I have found it very aggressive, and non-breeding birds have killed weavers, even in an enclosure of some size. The cock's display is like that of *P. coronata*, bill raised, wings drooped and tail cocked.

## Subfamily Cardinalinae

This New World subfamily was formerly known as Pyrrhuloxiinae based on the generic name *Pyrrhuloxia*. Currently most taxonomists include in this subfamily the true cardinals (*Cardinalis* and *Pyrrhuloxia*), the grosbeaks (five genera), the Dickcissel (*Spiza*), the *Passerina* buntings and grosbeaks, and the saltators (*Saltator*). Many of these genera are virtually unknown in aviculture and are seldom imported. I have, therefore, only included those which are currently available: *Cardinalis*, *Passerina*, and *Guiraca*. These are, for the most part, colourful birds which are sexually dimorphic, and some have large, strong bills, which in a few species are decurved. The cock birds in many species have quite a good song. They are active, lively birds which should be housed in aviaries and, for isolation or winter quarters, inside flights or large cages. Besides the usual bunting foods, the larger species will take sunflower seed, wheat and oats, and I find that most will eat many of the seeds supplied for doves, when they are housed together.

Live food is essential for the rearing of young and for the maintenance of adults in good health. For adults, a few mealworms and house crickets fed live two or three times a week will suffice. In winter, with the exception of the Virginian Cardinal (*Cardinalis cardinalis*), they should be accommodated in a minimum temperature of 8°C (45°F).

### Genus *Cardinalis* (True Cardinals)

This is a small genus of three species (or one species depending upon which checklist you consult) and includes the Virginian Cardinal (*Cardinalis cardinalis*) which is probably the best known of any New World passerine species.

VIRGINIAN CARDINAL *Cardinalis cardinalis*

OTHER NAMES: Cardinal, under which name it is listed in most ornithological literature and field guides. It has been pointed out that the name 'Virginian' is inappropriate and can be equated with referring to the Chaffinch (*Fringilla coelebs*) as the *Oxford* Chaffinch. It is also known as Red Cardinal, Common Cardinal, Scarlet Cardinal, Crimson Cardinal and Redbird. Synonym *Richmondena cardinalis*. There are 18 subspecies recognised.

This species, for me, has all the avicultural virtues: beauty, a good song, is a willing breeder and can be sexed visually. The only disadvantages are the fading of the cock's brilliant red plumage in captivity and the fact that it is best housed one pair to an aviary. Although not particularly aggressive, when rearing young, competition for live food if housed in a mixed aviary will increase the difficulties of supplying the large amounts needed. The species has for many years been increasing its range in America, steadily northwards. It is a ubiquitous and popular bird in many areas and I have seen the flash of its red plumage disappearing into an evergreen bush in an Ontario garden and watched it in Central Park, New York.

This cardinal is a hardy bird once established, and one of

the very few New World species I have wintered outside without heat, in an aviary with a weatherproof shelter. The fading of the plumage is certainly less noticeable if they are housed outside and are given a varied and good quality diet. The worst example of plumage fading I have come across was when I bought a single cock bird from someone who had kept it in an inside flight with budgerigars on a diet of canary seed, millet and green food. The brilliant red of the cock's plumage had become a light straw colour. When this bird was housed outside in a planted flight and fed on a varied seed diet, live food, fruit, green food and seeding grasses, the colour improved to a light red in two years. Although a very long way from the striking colour of the newly imported bird, this and similar cases indicate that the colour of a very faded bird can be improved. The fading of a fresh import can also be reduced, both in the time factor and loss of colour. The use of proprietary colour food preparations is another and possibly more effective method, but one I have not tried. This species has been bred in captivity on many occasions and has been imported into Europe fairly frequently for many years. It was available in the UK in 1988, although it seems unlikely to be imported in the future.

## Description

200–230 mm (8–9 in), sexually dimorphic.
COCK: Bill large, red in colour; irides dark brown; head crest well developed; the entire plumage is red, except for a black patch at the base of the bill; legs and feet brown or dark brown.
HEN: Bill a paler shade of red than the cock's; plumage light brown or yellowish brown, paler below; faint flush of red on the head, wings, tail, and sometimes the undertail coverts.

## Distribution and Habitat

Canada, central and eastern United States, Mexico, south to Guatemala. Inhabits woods, parks, gardens, cultivated areas, swamps and cane brakes, and semi-desert regions in south-western United States.

## Breeding

PERIOD: In the USA nesting begins in late March/April, in aviaries, the end of May is usual. A breeding pair I had built their nest and laid in late May for five consecutive seasons. Captive birds will rear three broods, sometimes three or four will be reared in the wild.

NEST: A cup of thin twigs, weed stems, grasses, bark fibres, vines and rootlets, sometimes paper and rags etc, lined with rootlets, fine grasses and hair. The site is variable, but usually in a shrub or vine tangle. The nests built by my birds were deep cups made of a few twigs, dried grasses and stems, lined with finer grasses, and once a small amount of dried moss. The site was always in a clump of cut gorse hung up in the aviary. The same nest was relined and used again for the next brood on most occasions. Other captive breeding accounts have listed a canary wire nest-cup fixed in a small tree and 'natural' nests in shrubs. The hen plays the main role in building but I have often seen the cock carrying material to the site.

EGGS: Ground colour white or slightly greenish; speckled and spotted, and with small blotches of medium to dark brown, rarely reddish brown and paler purple or grey. The many clutches laid by one hen in my aviaries were consistent, a very pale bluish colour, sparsely spotted with brown and ashy brown concentrated at the larger end. Clutch size 3–4, rarely 2 or 5.

INCUBATION: Carried out by the hen, but the cock has been seen covering the eggs for brief periods, when the hen is off the nest feeding or bathing. Period 12–13 days.

CHICKS: The nestlings have orange skin and blackish-grey down. Mouth is red, the gape flanges cream coloured (Harrison). The hen broods the chicks very closely for the first five to six days. The young are fed by both parents. The chicks will leave the nest as early as ten days, and at this stage have little or no tail feather growth but have short crests. The chicks can reach the top perches in an aviary, but their flight is limited and perching uncoordinated. The hen will lay the next clutch within eight to ten days, sometimes less, and then the cock will carry out most of the feeding of the first brood. The hen has been seen to feed them when she leaves the nest and the young will roost near the nest while she is incubating. On several occasions I have seen the chicks sitting and standing on her back while she is sitting. Both the hen and cock will feed the first brood at the nest during incubation of the second clutch. The young can feed themselves at about 14–16 days from leaving the nest. The young can be left in the aviary until the second brood has hatched, then the cock will sometimes begin to harass them.

The young are fed almost exclusively on live food for the first eight to nine days at least. I give them a mixture of mealworms and pupae, house crickets and stick insects of various sizes, as well as the usual seed mixtures, soaked seed and green food. The 'commercial' live food is supplemented with collected live food to give the essential variety. The adults will sometimes feed the young on soft food mixture and they are very fond of tomatoes, apples, peas and leaf buds. I am sure parts of these items are fed to the young. For example, I have watched adults carefully pick out the seeds from a cut tomato and fly to the nest. The adults hawk for flies in the aviary and in spite of their size and large bills, are adept at catching them. There is one published account recording that the young were reared largely on egg food with addition of small amounts of mealworms and ant pupae.

## Behaviour

Nesting and copulation are preceded by courtship feeding, the cock approaching the hen with an insect or some other choice morsel which she often solicits with a begging posture with shivering wings. Sometimes the pair will just touch bills before courtship feeding, and the hen having accepted the offering, will feed it back to the cock. The nuptial display consists of the cock chasing after the hen singing loudly. When she perches, he approaches her with crest erect, the head and neck is swung from side to side (the cock still singing), and the head is sometimes lowered then raised. This display is similar to that of the Red-crested Finch (*Coryphospingus cucullatus*), but not so 'explosive'.

These cardinals are avid sunbathers and rain bathers. During heavy rain I have seen them perched near the top of a heavy leafed shrub, singing loudly, preening themselves and rubbing their plumage on the leaves. When I put ant pupae collections in the aviary they will 'ant' for some time, rubbing the adult insect in their plumage and often eating the ants as well as the pupae. They are not aggressive birds and provided they are housed with unrelated birds which favour different nesting sites (and have no red in their plumage) no serious conflict should occur. I have bred them in the company of hole-nesting bush petronias (*Petronia dentata*) who also bred successfully. However, I did not repeat this the next season as the amount of live food needed to ensure that was no competition for it was considerable.

PHOENIX CARDINAL *Cardinalis phoeniceus*
OTHER NAMES: Venezuelan Cardinal, Vermilion Cardinal. Recorded as *Pyrrhuloxia phoeniceus* in some checklists. No subspecies are recognised.

This species has occasionally been imported into the UK, and small shipments sometimes arrive in Europe. I have had two cocks only, as the percentage of hens imported is low. These birds are more difficult to establish than *C. cardinalis* and should not be wintered outside without a minimum heat of 8–10°C (45–50°F). I can find no record of this species being bred in captivity but from the limited information available captive care and breeding would seem to be the same as for *C. cardinalis*.

## Description

200 mm (8 in), sexually dimorphic.
COCK: Bill large and decurved, colour a very pale bluish white; irides dark brown; head, crest and underparts rosy scarlet; back, wings and tail vermilion: legs and feet brownish or dark brown.
HEN: Crest rosy scarlet; front and sides of crown grey; back sandy grey; wings brown, tinged vermilion; tail dull vermilion; chin blackish; rest of underparts buffish.

## Distribution and Habitat

The arid tropical zone of Venezuela and Colombia. Habitat thorny scrub, cacti and thickets.

**Genus *Guiraca***

This monotypic genus consists of a single species, the Blue Grosbeak, *G. caerulea* which is now merged with *Passerina* in some taxonomic checklists.

BLUE GROSBEAK *Guiraca caerulea*

OTHER NAMES: Chestnut-shouldered Blue Grosbeak, Northern Blue Grosbeak. Synonym *Passerina caerulea*. Seven subspecies are recognised.

This beautiful bird resembles two other New World species with blue plumage which are imported, the Ultramarine (Brazilian) Grosbeak (*Cyanocompsa* [=*Passerina*] *brissonii*) and the Indigo Bunting (*Passerina cyanea*). At one time the Ultramarine Grosbeak was imported more frequently into Europe than the Blue Grosbeak, but currently the situation is reversed. The Indigo Bunting is still available occasionally, and mainly differs from the Blue Grosbeak by its smaller size and bill.

Although the Blue Grosbeak has been bred (the first in the UK was in 1921), its captive breeding is a rare event. I have had a pair nest and lay eggs on two occasions but the eggs did not hatch. As is usual with many colourful, sexually dimorphic species exported from Mexico, hens are always in short supply and obtaining a pair can be difficult. This species should not be wintered outside in colder areas without heat; a temperature of approximately 8°C (45°F) is satisfactory.

Description

165–190 mm (6½ –7½ in), sexually dimorphic.

COCK: Bill large, usually pale grey or whitish grey, darker on the upper mandible; irides dark brown or blackish; plumage blue to purplish blue; chin is black which sometimes extends around the base of the bill; wings have two rusty-brown bars, occasionally there are brown flecks on the back; legs and feet brownish grey or grey. In winter, areas of blue are obscured with brown, and often the feathers are edged with rusty brown, giving a scalloped effect.

HEN: Bill light brown or brownish; upperparts brown, paler below; there are two buffy wing bars.

Distribution and Habitat

Southern United States through Mexico to Costa Rica. Found in the edges of woodlands, hedgerows, gardens, orchards, thickets and other cover bordering fields and streams.

Breeding

PERIOD: Wild birds begin nesting from mid April, in the southern part of their range, to early June in the north. The information on captive breeding is very limited. My birds commenced breeding in early May. Two broods can be reared.
NEST: A cup of stems, thin twigs, rootlets, bark strips, dead leaves, corn husks, sometimes paper and cotton, lined with fine rootlets, tendrils, hair and fine grass. The site is in a shrub, thicket, vine or low tree. Captive nests have been made of twigs, grasses lined with finer grasses and, on one occasion, feathers. The sites chosen by my birds were in clumps of cut gorse hung up in the aviary. The nest was built by the hen, but I have seen the cock carrying material, so it is possible he plays some part in the building.
EGGS: Very pale blue, unmarked. Clutch size usually 4, can be 2–5.
INCUBATION: Carried out by the hen. Period 11 days.
CHICKS: The young are fed by both parents and leave the nest at nine to thirteen days. If the hen commences a second clutch, the cock will feed the young. The nestlings are fed largely on insects and other live food, and for successful breeding in captivity live foods should be supplied in variety, especially for the first six to seven days after hatching.

Behaviour

Avicultural literature suggests that this bird is not aggressive in a mixed collection, however, the information on breeding pairs is so limited that I would suggest caution and keep one pair to an aviary, or house them with a pair of doves. Nesting is preceded by courtship feeding, and many aspects of their behaviour appear similar to that of *C. cardinalis*, including rain and sun bathing.

**Genus *Passerina* (Passerina Buntings)**

This is a genus of sexually dimorphic New World buntings

which in many ways are homogenous. Indeed two species, and sometimes three, have been considered to be conspecific. The cocks are for the most part colourful, and cheerful, but not particularly talented singers. These species differ from the grosbeaks and cardinals by virtue of their smaller size and 'normal' bunting-type bills. There are six species in the genus, whose collective distribution is from southern Canada, the USA, Mexico and Central America to Colombia and Venezuela. Although some avicultural literature suggests that some species are fairly hardy, they should not be housed outside in hard weather without heat, which need not be more than 8–10°C (45–50°F). To some extent live food is essential for rearing young of all the species. The basic diet is the same as for other species in the Cardinalinae, but they cannot manage the harder and larger seeds such as wheat and sunflower.

With the exception of the little-known Rosita or Rose-bellied Bunting (*P. rositae*) all the species have been imported into Europe and the UK, and have been bred in captivity, although breeding records are few and far between. This, I suspect, is for two reasons: the first is the very small percentage of hens in the shipments, and the second is that many aviculturists do not supply the quantity and variety of live food needed for rearing. Insectivorous softbill mixtures, egg food and other rearing foods are adequate substitutes, *if* the parents will accept them to rear their young. Currently two species are imported into Europe on rare occasions: the Painted Bunting (*P. ciris*) and the Rainbow Bunting (*P. leclancheri*), which is also known as the Orange-breasted Bunting.

PAINTED BUNTING *Passerina ciris*

OTHER NAMES: Nonpareil Bunting. Two subspecies are recognised.

This attractive little bunting is considered by many to be one of the most colourful of the New World seed-eating birds. The first breeding in the UK was in 1898 and it has been bred on a few occasions since. Imported birds are not easy to establish and those acquired from an importer should not be exposed to any stress until they have become adjusted to their new environment. The red in the cock's plumage always fades to some extent, but given a varied diet and housed in an aviary, the fading is minimal.

## Description

130 mm (5 in), sexually dimorphic.
COCK: Bill greyish or pale horn; irides dark brown; head, nape and sides of neck blue; back, wings and tail yellowish green; rump red; throat and underparts red; legs and feet greyish horn.
HEN: Dull greenish above; underparts olive yellowish, fading to a dull yellow on the abdomen.

## Distribution and Habitat

The southern United States through Mexico to Panama. Inhabits scrub and grasslands.

## Breeding

PERIOD: From late March in the south-west United States, to early and mid May in other parts of its breeding range. In aviaries, nesting begins from the end of April or early May. Double brooded, sometimes three or four broods have been reared.
NEST: A neat deep cup of grasses, weed stems and leaves, lined with hair and fine grasses. The sites are in scrubby growth, hedgerows and rank herbage. In aviaries the nests have been built of grasses, stems and moss, lined with finer grasses and soft material supplied. Sites have been in shrubs and clumps of cut branches. Half-open nest boxes have been used. The nest is built by the hen.
EGGS: Ground colour white, finely speckled with chestnut red and purple, often with a wreath or cap of heavier spotting at the larger end. Clutch size usually 3–4, sometimes 5 (Harrison).
INCUBATION: Carried out by the hen. I was told by an aviculturist who bred Painted Buntings that the cock was seen to feed the hen on the nest occasionally. The incubation period is 11–13 days.
CHICKS: There is some doubt that the nestlings are fed by the cock. When they leave the nest, at 9–12 days, they are fed by both parents and the cock takes over the feeding completely when the hen starts another clutch. Live food is essential,

especially if the parents will not use any insectivorous softfood or other substitutes provided, which can act as a supplement to some extent.

## Behaviour

I have only kept single cocks, as the only pair I obtained turned out to be an adult and an immature cock, which closely resembles the hen. They were fairly assertive but not aggressive in a mixed collection aviary, but a breeding pair should be housed on the their own.

# 6
# Fringillidae — Finches

This family is divided into two subfamilies, the Fringillinae (consisting of one genus with three species, the chaffinches [*Fringilla coelebs* and *F. teydea*] and the brambling [*F. montifringilla*]) being separated from the second subfamily, the Carduelinae, for anatomical and behavioural differences — the absence of a crop in the Fringillinae being the major difference. This subfamily have a Eurasian distribution and, with the exception of *F. teydea* are 'British birds' and are therefore not covered in this book.

The majority of finch species inhabit the temperate regions of Eurasia, the Americas and Africa, others are found in the Arctic, sub Arctic, deserts, and tropical and sub-tropical regions. The family, especially the subfamily Fringillinae, has been the subject of controversy with regard to their taxonomic position. The family *per se* has been divided into various subfamilies, and some authors have included the Cardinalinae (cardinal-grosbeaks) and the Emberizinae (buntings). The current position is that only two subfamilies are recognised, the Cardinalinae and Emberizinae being retained within the bunting family. It should be noted that some species in the Estrildidae (waxbills, munias *et al*) are often called 'finches' or collectively 'weaver-finches' in some ornithological works and in European avicultural literature. Finches are, in the main, arboreal, living and nesting in trees, shrubs and hedges, although many species will feed and a few will sometimes nest, on the ground. Finches range in size from the hawfinches (*Coccothraustes* spp) at 175–250 mm (7–10 in) to some species of serins (*Serinus* spp) and siskins (*Carduelis* spp) measuring 100–115 mm (4–4½ in).

Although seed-eating birds, the variety of seeds and other food taken by finches is demonstrated by the diversity in the functional size and shape of their bills. These vary from the massive fruit-stone cracking bills of the hawfinches to the attenuated and pointed bills of the goldfinches. In the crossbills (*Loxia* spp), the tips of the bill are crossed at an oblique angle to extract seeds from the cones of conifers.

## Subfamily Carduelinae

### Accommodation and Breeding

Finches build cup-shaped nests which, generally, are neater and more compactly built than those of the buntings. The nest is built by the hen, although the cock may collect material. The nests are made of grasses, roots, twigs, mosses and lichens, lined with fine grasses, rootlets, feathers, wool and down, depending on the habitat and the species. The site is usually in a bush, hedge or tree, at a height from about 1.2 m (4 ft) to as high as 25 m (80 ft), although certain species will occasionally nest close to, or on the ground. In some areas this is due to lack of tall plant growth, for example the Arctic Redpoll (*Acanthis hornemani*) nests in dwarf willows and crevices in rocks. Finch eggs vary from blue or bluish to olive brown or olive ground colour, spotted and streaked with black, brown and reddish. The clutch size can range from 3–7, more usually 4–6. Incubation is carried out by the hen, the cock playing a small part in some species. The period varies from 10–14 days, in most species it is 12–13 days. In captivity the favoured nesting receptacles are canary nest pans, and wire and wicker baskets. Old wild birds' nests and half-open nest boxes are sometimes used. The sites are usually bushes and clumps of cut branches of gorse, conifer, and other cover-providing material, hung up in the aviary at various heights. Some finch species nest in loose colonies and generally speaking, the territories held are small in area and the 'boundaries' nebulous. In spite of this, species in some genera display aggression in captivity, the size of the aviary being the important factor, especially for birds such as serins. Closely related species should not be housed together, and unrelated species should preferably have a different plumage colour and breeding behaviour. For smaller species which display aggression, a roomy box cage with nesting receptacles screened with branches is a viable alternative, if enough of the correct rearing food for the chicks can be provided.

## Food and Care

The basic diet, in my aviaries, consists of mixed millet, with approximately 40% canary seed. For Ethiopian region species such as the African serins, the nutritional value of this diet is enhanced with the addition of maw, rape, linseed and other 'oily' seeds. For other species, a canary mixture which includes additional seeds such as hemp is always available. Birds such as hawfinches are also given sunflower seed, oats, peas, cherries and fruit tree buds. Softbill insectivorous mixture, coarse or fine grade depending on the species, is also offered, with seeding grasses and other collected plant foods being given as available. Sprouted and germinated seed, millet sprays and cultivated green foods are made available on a regular basis. Commercial live food such as mealworms are given regularly; in the breeding period the amounts are increased and, with collected live food, are always available when the birds are breeding. Various fruits are taken by some species.

The majority of finches are fairly hardy once properly established which, to me, means once they have been in the owner's aviaries for at least a year and have had a summer in an outside aviary. Some finches can then be wintered outside without heat, providing shelter is available which is dry and free of draughts, and that adequate natural or artificial light is provided. If the larger and active species such as hawfinches are wintered inside, the cage provided should have a minimum size of 1.8 m × 45 cm × 60 cm high (6 × 1½ × 2 ft) or better still an inside flight or aviary.

### Genus *Serinus* (Serins)

The serins have long been represented in aviculture by the domestic canary. Some African species are among the foreign birds still regularly imported into the UK. Their virtues for the aviculturist include their singing ability, they are also reasonably hardy, long lived, the majority are good breeders, and a few species are attractively coloured. As a generalisation, their disadvantages are aggression to conspecifics and unrelated birds when breeding, and the fact that some species are virtually impossible to sex visually. When breeding, they are not so insectivorous as other finch genera, especially if you can get adults to take insectivorous softbill mixture or canary rearing food. However, I have not been successful in breeding serins without supplying live food.

### GREEN SINGING FINCH *Serinus mozambicus* **Plate 10**

OTHER NAMES: Yellow-fronted Canary, Yellow-eye Canary, Icterine Canary. Eleven subspecies are recognised.

This attractive serin is probably imported into the UK more frequently than any other species in the genus. Their song is cheerful and vigorous and matches their behaviour, and once established they are hardy and long lived. I know of at least one record of a cock living for over 20 years, and several others between 15 and 18 years. These birds, which can be sexed visually, would make an excellent subject for establishment in captivity as a species. The only avicultural disadvantage they have is their energetic aggression. I have never known them to make a prolonged attack or kill another bird, but their continuous territorial 'defence' causes disruption and tension in a mixed collection. Comments in avicultural literature imply that aggression will only be a problem in overcrowded aviaries, but this has not been the case in my experience. I have bred *S. mozambicus* to the fourth generation, and have found them consistent but not prolific breeders. Ideally, a small aviary to themselves, or perhaps housed only with a pair of the smaller species of doves or quail would produce the best results. The other alternative would be a roomy cage with screened nest sites, and they have been bred in these conditions.

#### Description

115–130 mm (4½–5 in), adults visually sexable.
COCK: Bill light or greyish horn, upper mandible darker; irides dark brown or blackish; forehead and wide stripe above eyes and cheeks bright lemon yellow; ear coverts and sides of neck light greyish; crown and nape olive, streaked with dusky drab; hind neck, mantle and back olive-khaki, marked with dusky drab; tail sooty brown; rump lemon yellow; underparts, chin, throat, breast and abdomen lemon yellow, turning pale at the vent and on undertail coverts; legs and feet dark brown or greyish brown.

HEN: Similar to cock, except for a necklace of olive markings across the throat, which are often ill defined; the yellow of the forehead and eye stripe is paler, as is the yellow of the underparts.

## Distribution and Habitat

Wide distribution in Africa south of the Sahara. Habitat varies from bushveld to cultivated areas and open woodland.

## Breeding

PERIOD: The breeding period of the majority of imported birds remains synchronised with the feral breeding period, with nesting usually commencing in August/September and continuing into November, December and January. I have frequently had to remove birds to winter quarters in late November, to prevent them from trying to rear chicks during the short day length of the cold winter months. Some third and fourth generation captive-bred birds are beginning to nest in April and May; two or three broods can be reared in captivity.

NEST: An open, usually neatly made, deep cup, built in three parts; basal mass, central lining and upper lining. The base is made of tendrils, dead grasses, string, rootlets, seed heads, twigs; the central lining of dead grass, seed heads, fine grass and plant fibres, and occasionally a few feathers; the upper lining is thinly laid with cow or horse tail hair. The cup and exterior of the nest is bound with coarse cobweb. The nests are usually sited in small shrubs, trees, and thickets in the bushveld, and in street trees in towns. They are usually built in horizontal forks near the ends of branches and in upright forks, the height above ground varying from 1–6.2 m (3–20 ft), usually between 2–3 m (7–10 ft). In captivity the site is usually in a fork of a bush, tree or clump of cut branches, the receptacles favoured are canary and wicker nest cups. These nests are made of coarse grasses, a few twigs lined with finer grasses and rootlets, and this is covered with feathers or kapok. It is interesting to note that the exterior of the whole nest is often bound with kapok wadding, 'teased out' by the birds like the cobweb 'binding' for feral nests. There is limited evidence that both sexes take part in building in the wild, as identification of the sexes in the field is virtually impossible, however, in captivity my cock birds collect a good deal of the material and have been seen building. The same nest is usually relined and used again for the next brood.

EGGS: Ground colour white, sometimes pale blue, spotted and blotched with reddish brown, brown, pinkish, grey and black. Unmarked eggs are sometimes laid. Clutch size 3–4.

INCUBATION: The hen bird incubates, however, the cock bird will sometimes cover the eggs while the hen is off the nest feeding and the cock seems to play a small but regular part in incubation within the pair bond in captivity. The cock will also feed the hen while she is incubating, and will sing at a nearby vantage point. Some hens sit very closely, others will leave the nest when approached. Incubation can commence with the last but one egg of the clutch but more often when the clutch is complete. The incubation period is 13–14 days.

CHICKS: The nestlings are dark-skinned with sparse greyish down, mouth dark pink, gape flanges pale yellowish. The hen broods the young very closely for the first five or six days, and the cock passes food to the hen who feeds the chicks. Later both parents take food to the chicks, who give audible hunger calls, 'see-see-see'. In captivity the young leave the nest at 13–17 days, in the colder months of October/November, they rarely leave the nest before 15 days. The plumage at this stage is duller than the adults, with grey-speckled areas on the throat, breast and flanks, the yellow eye stripe is well defined. The hen will often commence a second clutch shortly after the young leave the nest; on one occasion it was the following day. I have known the fledged young to sit alongside, and sometimes on the back of the hen while she is incubating the second clutch. The cock continues to feed and protect the young until the next clutch is hatched. Some chivvying of the young usually begins at this stage and as they can feed themselves I remove them. On several occasions broods have been reared with limited live food, usually because the adults were reluctant to feed them. (Maggots and mealworms are not suitable for young chicks.) Late in the year (October/November) collected live food can be difficult to obtain in sufficient amounts, so, after the first crucial five to seven days, the live food for these broods has been supplemented with germinated soaked seed.

## Behaviour

In the wild and in captivity this species demonstrates some terrestrial behaviour. In an aviary when identical food items are placed on the ground and up on a feeding platform, they take the food on the ground first. The bulk of the nesting material is also collected from the ground. Pre-nesting behaviour consists of frequent chasing, singing and courtship feeding, the hen soliciting food from the cock with the wing-quivering soliciting posture of the fledgling. Courtship feeding is often followed by copulation. I have seen what can be described as a butterfly flight on a few occasions, the cock flying up and down the aviary with a slower wing-beat than in 'normal' flight, hovering briefly.

YELLOW-RUMPED SERIN *Serinus atrogularis*
OTHER NAMES: Black-throated Canary, Yellow-rumped Seedeater. Nine subspecies are recognised. These vary mainly in the shading of the black marking on chin and throat, and in other minor plumage differences.

This species is obtainable occasionally, and importers have periods of calling them Yellow-rumped Serins or Black-throated Canaries; currently we are back in the 'yellow-rumped' phase.

This little serin, like many of its congenerics, is lively, active and a good singer. Although lacking the brighter colours of other species, the flash of the bright yellow rump when it flies is as pleasing as a brief sunny spell on a dull day. They are impossible to sex visually, but when a true pair is obtained they are willing breeders. Their care and breeding in captivity is the same as for *S. mozambicus*, although I have found them less aggressive in a mixed collection.

## Description

115 mm (4½ in), sexes alike.
Bill horn or greyish horn; irides dark brown; upperparts greyish or light drab, heavily streaked with blackish brown; rump bright lemon yellow; tail blackish brown, edged white, tipped white; underparts, chin and throat greyish, marked with blackish brown; breast drab or greyish, streaked blackish

brown; belly and flanks greyish buff, not heavily streaked; legs and feet fleshy colour or light greyish. The notion that the hen is less heavily marked with blackish brown on the chin and throat has little support in fact, due to subspecific, intermediate and individual variation. Proven true pairs in my aviaries show no sexual dimorphism.

### Distribution and Habitat

Irregular but widespread distribution, southern Arabia, eastern and southern Africa from Ethiopia to Angola and the Cape. Main habitat dry country in bush and trees along water courses. In some areas of its distribution it can be found in farm gardens and towns.

### Breeding

PERIOD: In the wild, the breeding season is long, in many areas of its distribution. In my aviaries, unlike *S. mozambicus*, imported birds will breed from April/May onwards. However, my numbers are too small for me to make any significant judgement and it is probably a chance factor associated with the achievement of breeding condition in captivity. Two or three broods can be reared.

NEST: A neat cup very like that of *S. mozambicus*, the favoured sites are usually forks in trees or bushes. In captivity, the sites and nest materials chosen are also the same as for *S. mozambicus*, both sexes build the nest but the hen does most of the building.

EGGS: Ground colour white or pale greenish blue, spotted and speckled with black, brown and purple, usually more heavily at the larger end. Unmarked eggs are common in both the wild and in captivity. Clutch size usually 3, rarely 4 or 5.

INCUBATION: Carried out by the hen who is fed by the cock on the nest. In captivity I have seen the cock playing a small part in incubation, covering the eggs while the hen is off the nest feeding (like *S. mozambicus*). Incubation usually starts with the last egg laid, occasionally with the last but one. Period 13–14 days.

CHICKS: Nestlings' skin very dark greyish, with sparse greyish down, mouth pinkish, gape flanges very pale yellow. The hen broods the chicks closely for the first few days, and both parents feed them with insects and later seeds, especially seeding grasses such as *Poa annua*. The young leave the nest at 14–15 days, the cock feeding them and the hen commencing a second clutch, usually within two or three days. The same nest is relined and used again on most occasions. On leaving the nest, the young resemble the adults, but look light in colour as they are less streaked with blackish brown. They have the yellow rump but the coloured area is smaller and of a paler yellow.

### Behaviour

In captivity and in the wild behaviour is very like that of *S. mozambicus*. Captive birds when nesting will guard and chase away other birds from the nest site, however, once the intruder leaves the immediate vicinity, the chase is usually over and persistent aggression is rare.

## GREY SINGING FINCH *Serinus leucopygius*

OTHER NAMES: White-rumped Seed-eater. Three subspecies are recognised.

The Grey Singing Finch has been a commonly imported species. These finches are aptly named, being rather drab little birds, but excellent singers. Their care and breeding in captivity is the same as for the two preceding species. I have found imported *S. leucopygius* to be more difficult to establish than *S. mozambicus* and *S. atrogularis*. However, once this is achieved they are long lived and reasonably hardy, but I would not winter them outside in hard weather without moderate heat. The main problem with breeding them is trying to find a true pair, as the sexes are alike.

### Description

100 mm (4 in), sexes alike.
Bill light horn colour; irides brown; head light grey; rest of upperparts greyish brown or ash grey, streaked with dusky brown; rump white; underparts, chin, throat and breast grey; abdomen and undertail coverts white; legs and feet fleshy coloured or very light brown.

## Distribution and Habitat

Senegal, northern Nigeria, Chad, the Sudan and Ethiopia. Inhabits open bush, cultivated areas, often near water, but also arid and desert regions. Small flights are commonly observed in bushes and trees near settlements.

## Breeding

PERIOD: In the wild, the breeding season varies throughout their distribution. Captive birds in the UK breed from April/May until late in the year. I know one case of a pair of these birds hatching chicks outside in late December, the hen covering the chicks with snow on the nest, not surprisingly the nestlings died. Allowing birds to nest in hard weather with short day length is seldom successful or warranted. In captivity two or three broods are reared in a season.

NEST: A very neat cup made of fibres, plant stems and hair, lined with feathers or vegetable down. The site is in a fork of a bush or tree. In captivity the nest is made of dried grasses and fibres, lined with finer grasses, feathers or hair. Kapok, if available, will be used in the main structure and sometimes as lining. Canary nest pans, wicker and wire nest pans and half-open nest boxes are the usual receptacles. As in the wild the captive nest should be built in a natural site, such as a fork in a bush, between upright stems or in a clump of twigs. The main part of building the nest is carried out by the hen, the cock collects material.

EGGS: Ground colour pale bluish, greenish or white, spotted with brown and black. Unmarked eggs are sometimes laid. Clutch size 3–4.

INCUBATION: The hen incubates and is fed by the cock. I have not seen the cock cover the eggs when the hen comes off to feed and bath but, like his congenerics, he will stand guard and sing from a nearby perch. True incubation usually commences with the last egg laid, but the eggs are often covered before this and therefore the start of incubation is sometimes difficult to ascertain. Period 13–14 days.

CHICKS: When the chicks hatch, they are brooded very closely by the hen for a few days, the cock bringing food which is fed to the chicks by the hen. She will leave the nest to collect food for the chicks, but the time period is very short. The young leave the nest at 13–14 days and are then fed by the cock and the hen, unless a second clutch is commenced, which often occurs within a few days. With this species a new nest is often built, the occasions when the original nest is used again are fewer than with *S. mozambicus* and *S. atrogularis*. For some unexplained reason, they seem more willing to feed commercial rearing foods to their chicks than their congenerics, although live food appears to be essential for the chicks for the first few days of their life. When the young leave the nest they are more heavily streaked on the upperparts and breast than the adults. Unless a second clutch is commenced, the cock is usually tolerant of the young after they can feed themselves, but the cock must be watched in case he starts to chivvy the chicks.

### Behaviour

In an aviary of any size, the butterfly display flight is often seen, accompanied by song. Like its congenerics, courtship feeding is a prelude to nesting and will sometimes continue into the incubation period. The cock feeds the hen when she comes off the nest for food or exercise. Generally speaking, I have found this species, like *S. atrogularis*, less aggressive in a mixed collection than *S. mozambicus*. However, like most serins I have kept, they are 'bossy' and can be disruptive to other birds.

## ST HELENA SEED-EATER *Serinus flaviventris*

OTHER NAMES: Yellow Canary, Yellow-bellied Seed-eater. Often called Giant Green Singing Finch by importers. Seven subspecies are recognised.

Not so often imported as the preceding species, small shipments of these attractive birds arrive in the UK in most years and they were available in 1989–90. I have found them easy to establish and breed; they appear to be less aggressive than their congenerics. The hens are close sitters when incubating or brooding young chicks. One female would allow me to gently stroke her back with a finger while she was sitting. Like *S. mozambicus*, they have the advantage, for the aviculturist, of being able to be visually sexed.

## Description

140 mm (5½ in), sexually dimorphic.

COCK: Bill horn colour; irides dark brown; forehead, stripe above the eye and cheeks rich yellow; crown olive green, streaked with drab; rest of upperparts olive green flecked with drab; rump and uppertail coverts yellowish; underparts yellow; flanks grey; underwing coverts grey, fringed with yellow; legs and feet dusky brown.

HEN: Greyish olive above, streaked with drab; underparts buffy, streaked with drab on breast and flanks.

## Distribution and Habitat

East and southern Africa, from Ethiopia to Angola and the Cape, introduced into St Helena. Habitat scrub, scrubby veld, bushy areas along water courses. Also low scrub and weedy growth on mountainsides in some areas.

## Breeding

PERIOD: Variable throughout its distribution in southern Africa, Skead records July/October, September/March for the Cape and the Karoo. The few captive breeding reports indicate a period from May until September. Two broods can be reared in captivity, rarely three.

NEST: In the wild the nests are variable in construction, some are loose and ragged, others neat and compact. The materials are dry stalks, rootlets, weeds or dry grass, lined with plant down or other soft material. The site is usually low in a shrub or small tree, sometimes on the ground. In captivity the nest is made of dried grasses or any similar materials provided, and will be lined with finer grasses, feathers, etc. The sites have included privet bushes and small trees. I have known of one nest made in a clump of cut conifer branches fixed in an aviary shelter and they have bred in cages. The nest is built by the hen, although the cock will collect material.

EGGS: Ground colour usually white, sometimes pale blue or greenish, sparsely marked with spots and small lines of red, brown, purple and black. Unmarked eggs are sometimes laid. Clutch size 2–5, usually 3 or 4.

1

2

3

4

**1.** Parrot-billed Seedeaters ♀ above, and ♂ *Sporophila peruviana*
**2.** Cinereous Finch *Piezorhina Cinerea*
**3.** Saffron Finch ♀ *Sicalis flaveola*
**4.** Collared Finch ♀ *Sporophila collaris*

5

6

7

8

**5.** Chestnut-throated Sporophila ♂ *Sporophila telasco*
**6.** Crested Bunting ♂ *Melophus lathami*
**7.** Golden-breasted Bunting ♂ *Emberiza flaviventris*
**8.** Black-tailed Hawfinch ♂ *Coccothraustes migratorius*

9

10

11

12

13

14

**9.** Collared Warbling Finch ♂ *Poospiza hispaniolensis*, immature
**10.** Green Singing Finch ♂, left, and ♀ *Serinus mozambicus*
**11.** Himalayan Greenfinch *Carduelis spinoides*
**12.** Yellow-winged Pytilia ♀ left, and ♂ *Pytilia hypogrammica*
**13.** Red-cheeked Cordon Bleu ♀, left, and ♂ *Uraeginthus bengalus*
**14.** Red-billed Fire-finch ♂ *Lagonostica senegala*

15

16

**15.** Red-winged Pytilia ♂ *Pytilia phoenicoptera*
**16.** Blue-headed Waxbill ♂ *Uraeginthus cyanocephala*

17

18

19

20

21

22

**17.** Red Avadavat ♂ *Amandava amandava*
**18.** Red Avadavat ♂ melanistic *Amandava amandava*
**19.** Green Avadavat *Amandava formosa*
**20.** Golden-breasted Waxbill ♂ *Amandava subflava*
**21.** Orange-cheeked Waxbill *Estrilda melpoda*
**22.** Red-eared Waxbill *Estrilda troglodytes*

23

24

**23.** Rosy-rumped Waxbill *Estrilda rhodopyga*

**24.** Red-faced Crimson-wing ♂ *Cryptospiza reichenovii*

25

26

27

28

**25.** Cut-throat Finch ♂ *Amadina fasciata*
**26.** Red-headed Finch ♂ *Amadina erythrocephala*
**27.** Diamond Firetail Finch *Emblema guttata*
**28.** Star Finch *Poephila ruficauda*

29

30

31

**29.** Zebra Finch ♂
**30.** Long-tailed Grass Finch (subspecies *hecki*) *Poephila acuticauda*
**31.** Cherry Finch ♂ *Aidemosyne modesta*

32

33

**32.** African Silverbill *Lonchura malabarica cantans*
**33.** Black and White Mannikin (subspecies *nigriceps*) *Lonchura bicolor*

34

35

36

**34.** Chestnut Munia *Lonchura malacca*, pair (sexes alike)
**35.** Chestnut and White Munia *Lonchura quinticolor*
**36.** Java Sparrow *Lonchura oryzivora*

37

38

39

**37.** Senegal Indigo Bird ♂ *Vidua chalybeata*
**38.** Fischer's Whydah ♂ *Vidua fischeri*
**39.** Pin-tailed Whydah ♀, left, and ♂ *Vidua macroura*

40

41

42

**40.** Orange Weaver ♂ *Euplectes orix franciscana*
**41.** Red-shouldered Whydah ♂ *Euplectes axillaris*
**42.** Gambel's Quail (juvenile) *Lophortyx gambelii*

43

4

3. Harlequin Quail ♂ *Coturnix delegorguei*
4. Japanese Quail *Coturnix japonica*

45

46

**45.** Chinese Painted Quail ♂ *Excalfactoria chinensis*
**46.** Green-spotted Wood Dove *Turtur chalcospilos*

47

48

**47.** Tambourine Dove ♂ *Turtur tympanistria*
**48.** Masked Dove ♂ *Oena capensis*

49

50

**49.** Emerald Dove ♀ *Chalcophaps indica*
**50.** Diamond Dove *Geopelia cuneata*

INCUBATION: The hen incubates. Like most serins she is usually a close sitter, but, as with all birds, some individuals will readily leave the nest, even desert, if disturbed. The incubation period is 12–14 days, commencing with the last but one egg of the clutch or when the clutch is complete.
CHICKS: Like its congenerics the hen broods the chicks closely for the first few days. From the information available, the cock plays a limited role in rearing the chicks, however, he will feed and guard them if the hen commences a second brood. Either the chicks shoud be removed as soon as they are independent, or else a careful watch should be kept on the cock. The young resemble the hen when fledged, the young cocks beginning to show adult colour about three weeks after this. An aviculturist who has bred these birds told me that his chicks had been reared mainly on soaked seed and commercial rearing food, live food was limited to small maggots.

### Behaviour

In the wild, the butterfly flight has been frequently recorded, but in captivity it has probably been overlooked, or the aviaries have been too small. Courtship feeding of the hen and nuptial chasing by the cock are regular features of captive breeding behaviour. Shore-Bailey, who was the first aviculturist to breed the species in the UK, found that they 'were not quarrelsome with other birds', however, the other birds in his aviary were not named, except for the largest, which were South American thrushes. I have found them less aggressive than *S. mozambicus* and have bred them when housed with mannikins, Java Sparrows and Red-headed Finches, without serious conflict or disruption.

### **Genus** ***Carduelis***

Goldfinches, siskins and greenfinches are currently placed in this genus, although formerly each group had the status of its own genus. The birds in this group are best known to those aviculturists who keep British birds, as importations of foreign species into the UK have never been regular or large in number. The Hooded Siskin (Red Siskin) (*C. cucullata*), which has red in its plumage, was sought after by canary breeders to produce a red canary by crossing with siskin cocks. Considering the taxonomic positions of the two species, I would have thought that this aspiration would be difficult to achieve. Currently only two species appear to be imported annually into the UK, and shipments are small in number and erratic.

As a general rule, most species in this genus are not delicate, although some Central and South American species are not easy to establish and I would not winter them outside without moderate heat. A wide variety of seeds (with the addition of commercial insectivorous mixtures), green food such as seeding grasses, chickweed, germinated and sprouted seed constitute a good diet. Some species are very insectivorous when breeding, and probably will not maintain top condition in the long term without live food or adequate substitutes.

DARK-BACKED GOLDFINCH *Carduelis psaltria*
OTHER NAMES: Lesser Goldfinch, Green-backed Goldfinch. Howard and Moore list it as the Dark-backed Greenfinch. Five subspecies are recognised.

This species was formerly included with other siskins in the genus *Spinus*. It is an attractive little bird which becomes confiding and tame in captivity. Importations are erratic and shipments small, the species was imported into the UK in 1989. I obtained four birds some 18 years ago, two of which were in immature plumage and I suspected that they were all cocks, which turned out to be the case. They were in poor condition, having been kept in a crowded stock cage with only millet seed for food. After they had been kept in a hospital cage and fed on a variety of seeds and live food, they were released into a small inside aviary and became fit and active. They always went for mineralised grit before taking food and, like many other seed-eating passerines, these birds probably have a need for minerals which is seldom satisfied in captivity. Mealworms were rationed because they ate them so voraciously that I became rather worried and gave them collected live food in the warmer weather instead. They ate everything from spiders to caterpillars. Later I persuaded them to take commercial insectivorous mixture by sprinkling a little maw seed and small maggots on top of the mixture. For many years afterwards I tried to obtain some hens, without success as the only establishment within reasonable distance which had these birds could only offer cocks. The one breeding record I can find for this species took place in Europe. They are delightful little birds and once properly established I feel they would prove willing breeders, the main problem is obtaining a true pair.

## Description

100 mm (4 in), sexually dimorphic.
COCK: Bill light horn, darker on the upper mandible; irides brown; top of head bluish black; sides of head, back and rump olive green; wings and tail bluish black, the wings have a conspicuous white bar; underparts bright lemon yellow; legs and feet light grey; the entire upperparts can be bluish black, with the yellow underparts and white wing bar retained.
HEN: Dull olive green or greyish olive, the underparts paler; wings and tail dusky brown, the wing having a smaller area of white.

## Distribution and Habitat

From western United States and Mexico, through Central America to northern Venezuela and north-western Peru. Habitat arid open country and scrub, also plantations and fields in some areas.

## Breeding

PERIOD: In North America breeding commences in late March in the south to early May in the north (Harrison). No date for captive breeding period.
NEST: The sites are in twig forks, usually well hidden in the foliage of trees and shrubs close to water. In larger trees the nest can be well out in the canopy. The height above ground can vary from 6–10.5 m (2–30 ft) usually between 1.5–3 m (5–10 ft). The nest is built by the hen and is a compact cup of fine grass stems, plant and bark fibre, moss or wool, lined with fine fibre or plant down.
EGGS: Ground colour pale blue or greenish blue, unmarked. Clutch size usually 4–5, sometimes 3 or 6.

INCUBATION: Carried out by the hen who is fed by the cock. Period 12 days.
CHICKS: The young are downy, fed by regurgitation, and tended by both parents. The immature bird is like the hen, but duller, the upperparts are tinged with buff and the wing bar is buff.

## Behaviour

In a planted aviary my birds were very active and acrobatic, seldom alighting on the ground. Housed with Java sparrows and parrot finches they displayed no aggression; a breeding pair could be a different matter.

HIMALAYAN GREENFINCH *Carduelis spinoides* **Plate 11**
OTHER NAMES: Yellow-breasted Greenfinch, Himalayan Siskin, Black-headed Greenfinch. Three subspecies are recognised.

This attractive finch is still occasionally imported into the UK and has been bred on a number of occasions. The first in the UK was by Teschemaker in 1914. They were also successfully bred at Keston in the 1960s and Cummings (1964) records that they were suggested as potential foster parents for Hooded Siskins (*C. cucullata*). However, because the eggs did not hatch, their abilities as foster parents remain untried. This species has been considered a siskin, and was placed in the genus *Hypacanthis*, not with other greenfinches in *Chloris*. Once recovered from the stresses of importation Himalayan greenfinches adjust well to captivity and thrive on a good seed mixture, live food, green food (such as chickweed), seeding grasses, and sprouted and germinated seed.

## Description

130 mm (5 in), sexually dimorphic.
COCK: Bill fleshy horn, tipped dusky; irides brown; upperparts greenish brown to black, darkest on head, with broad yellow line over eye and indistinct collar around neck. Wings dark brown, variegated with yellow, black and a little white; tail dark brown; whole of underparts bright yellow, legs and feet brownish flesh.

HEN: Duller than the cock with less yellow on the wings.

## Distribution and Habitat

From Pakistan across the Himalayas to Assam and Burma. A bird of the high country, breeding at elevations of 1200–2700 m (4000–9000 ft) occasionally up to 3300 m (11,000 ft). In winter it leaves the mountains and lives in the foothills and plains.

## Breeding

PERIOD: In India the breeding season is from July until early October. From the few captive breeding reports, they commence to nest from late May/early June and finish about the end of September. Two broods have been reared.
NEST: A neatly constructed cup of fine grass roots, lined with hair which is interwoven with the interior; the exterior often includes moss which blends with the surroundings. The site is usually in a coniferous tree at considerable height from the ground, in a fork, close to the trunk or on top of a vertical bough near its extremity. In aviaries, the favoured site is a bush, although open-fronted nest boxes have been used. In a recent breeding report, Beckett (1980), the two nests were neat cups made entirely of coconut fibre. Materials used in other captive breedings have been dried grasses and moss, lined with hair and a few feathers.
EGGS: The ground colour is pale green, bluish or bluish white, spotted with reddish brown or black, the spotting often confined to the larger end. Clutch size 3–4.
INCUBATION: Carried out entirely by the hen. The cock does not appear to feed the hen on the nest. Incubation usually commences with the third egg laid. Period 13–14 days.
CHICKS: The hen broods the chicks very closely for about the first week. Although, from the limited information available it seems that the cock plays no part in the feeding of the hen or the young until they have left the nest (this is unlike the behaviour of the European greenfinch, *C. chloris*, where pre-nesting courtship feeding is extended into the incubation period, the cock feeding the hen and later bringing food for the chicks.) I feel certain that more detailed observation will

reveal that *C. spinoides* has similar breeding behaviour. The young leave the nest at about 14 days, the immature plumage is like the hen's, but much paler with heavy flecking on the breast. In captivity the young have been reared on commercial soft food, seeding sow thistle, chickweed, bread and milk and maggots. The Keston breedings took place in one of the large planted aviaries for which the establishment was famous, so plenty of natural live food must have been available. The provision of suitable rearing food should now be much easier, with the variety of commercially bred live food now available.

### Behaviour

From observations on wild birds, and from limited avicultural reports, the behaviour of this species is very similar to *C. chloris*. The main display flight is the same, and during nuptial chasing the cock has been observed to adopt one of the postures of *C. chloris*; the bill pointed upwards and the wings lowered. In the wild, there is some evidence that this bird will occasionally breed in loose colonies like *C. chloris*. From the very limited information available, *C. spinoides* does not appear to be aggressive in a mixed collection.

## Genus *Carpodacus* (Rosefinches)

There are 21 species of rosefinch, 18 of which have a Eurasian distribution, the remainder being found in North America. Some of the Eurasian species are fairly large birds and if housed in small cages will develop behavioural stereotypes, such as tilting back the head when alighting on a perch. This can be a problem with other large active passerines and I have known hawfinches to develop stereotyped behaviour when closely confined. Rosefinches are attractive birds, and the plumage of the cock birds is red, the extent of which depends on the species. Unfortunately, as with many diverse bird groups with red in their plumage, this colour fades in captivity, although, if the birds are housed outside and given a varied diet, the fading is reduced. Feeding with various commercial 'colour food' preparations will also retard the fading to some extent. Rosefinches adjust well to captivity once established, and some of the few species imported have been bred occasionally.

## HOUSE FINCH *Carpodacus mexicanus*

OTHER NAMES: Mexican House Finch, also Linnet in the USA. There are 11 subspecies.

This attractive North American finch, which is a good songster, is still occasionally imported into the UK. It has been bred on a few occasions. The first breeding in the UK was by Teschemaker in 1910. Successful breedings also took place at the London Zoo in 1912–1913 and 1915. As with many species which have colourful cock birds, the trappers concentrate on these, and hens are seldom shipped. This, along with the fading of the red plumage, is the main reason for the lack of captive breeding records for this bird and for other *Carpodacus* species. I have kept a few cocks but have never been lucky enough to obtain a hen.

### Description

140 mm (5½ in), sexually dimorphic.
COCK: Bill brownish or horn, large and stout; irides brown; forehead, stripe over eye and rump bright red; rest of upperparts brown; breast bright red, fading to pinkish white on the sides and flanks; abdomen white, streaked with brown; legs and feet brown or light brown. The red areas are variable in shade, some individuals are almost orange.
HEN: Upperparts greyish brown, streaked with darker brown; underparts whitish, streaked dusky.

### Distribution and Habitat

South-western Canada, western United States and Mexico. Habitat desert scrub, mountain areas, cultivated land and the vicinity of buildings.

### Breeding

PERIOD: In the wild the breeding season begins late February in the south of its range, to mid or late April in the north of its range. The few reports indicate captive breeding to occur from May until August, two broods sometimes three are reared.
NEST: The sites are varied in the wild. A raised ledge or cavity, the branch of a tree or shrub, on cacti, or in the old

nests of other birds, from grosbeaks to swallows. The nest is a cup of fine weed and grass stems, leaves, rootlets, thin twigs, string, wool and feathers, with similar but finer material as lining (Harrison). Aviary nests have been made of dried grasses, roots and moss, lined with finer grasses and feathers. Sites have included bushes, small trees and an open cage hung on an aviary wall.

EGGS: Very pale blue or bluish green, unmarked, or sparsely spotted with black and pale purple, with a few fine scrawls around the larger end. Clutch size 4–5, sometimes 2–6.

INCUBATION: By the hen alone, who is fed on the nest by the cock. Period 12–14 days.

CHICKS: The nestlings have long greyish-white down and are tended by both parents. The brooding is carried out mainly by the hen. Shore-Bailey records that his birds fed the chicks mainly on seed, but as the breeding was in a planted aviary, some live food must have been available. Lynch bred them in 1956 and the young were reared on mixed seeds, soaked teazle and maggots. The young leave the nest at 14–16 days, and they resemble the hen but are more heavily streaked.

## Behaviour

In the wild this bird is sparrow-like in behaviour. It is often seen in small towns feeding on the ground. In some parts of its distribution it is regarded as a pest owing to the damage it causes to fruit tree buds. In captivity, it would appear that the House Finch can become quite tame and confiding, and in mixed collections it has not been proven aggressive, but the details are limited.

### PURPLE FINCH *Carpodacus purpureus*

OTHER NAMES: Purple Rosefinch. Two subspecies are recognised.

This species has been imported occasionally but not as often as *C. mexicanus*. The first breeding in the UK was by G Lynch in 1958. I have not kept this species myself, but have seen a few cocks in mixed-species shipments from Europe on rare occasions. In common with other New World species and imported birds in general, the future availability of these birds is uncertain.

## Description

140 mm (5½ in), sexually dimorphic.
COCK: Bill large and stout, brownish or darkish horn; irides brown; on the plumage colour Peterson (1941) remarks, 'Purple is hardly the word; old rose is more like it'; upperparts rosy red, brightest on the head; back and scapulars streaked with brown; throat and breast bright red or purplish red, fading on the flanks; abdomen white; legs and feet brown or light brown.
HEN: Upperparts olive greenish, streaked with darker olive or brownish; underparts white, heavily streaked with dusky olive.

## Distribution and Habitat

Canada, north-eastern to south-eastern and south-western United States, Baja California. Inhabits woods, parkland, cultivated areas and shrubby growth, also mountain areas in some parts of its distribution.

## Breeding

PERIOD: Breeding in the wild begins early to mid May. In captivity, nesting commences at the end of April continuing until July; information is very limited. Two broods can be reared.
NEST: The commonest site in the wild is a tree, and when a conifer is chosen the nest is usually built high up. Lower sites are sometimes used. The nest is a cup of fine twigs, grasses and rootlets, lined with moss, hair or wool. In an aviary an open wooden box has been used, as has a privet bush. The nests were made of dried grasses, bents and tow. The cock bird was not seen to take part in the building, or in the collecting of material.
EGGS: Ground colour pale blue. Finely speckled, spotted and sometimes scrawled with black and purple, often concentrated at larger end. Clutch size 4–5, sometimes 3 or 6.
INCUBATION: The hen incubates and is fed by the cock. Period 13 days.

CHICKS: Fed by both parents, a captive-breeding report records that the young were fed on egg rearing food, soaked seed and chickweed. The young leave the nest at about 14 days. The immature plumage is like the hen's plumage but paler.

## Behaviour

In the wild, like *C. mexicanus*, it is a wanderer out of breeding season and will invade areas of cultivation. In captivity the indications are that it adjusts well once established and is not aggressive in a mixed collection even when breeding.

## COMMON ROSEFINCH *Carpodacus erythrinus*

OTHER NAMES: Rose-breasted Finch, Scarlet Grosbeak and, as the Indian subspecies of the bird is imported, Indian Rosefinch. Five subspecies are recognised.

This species is the one representative of the Old World rosefinches frequently imported. They are active, restless birds which are best kept in an aviary. Once established they can be wintered outside with adequate shelter. I have had a few 'pairs' over the years in which, unfortunately but predictably, the 'hens' turned out to be immature cocks. This bird has never been popular in aviculture because of its restless behaviour and the rapidly fading red in its plumage. It has been bred in captivity in Europe, and by G De Pass in the UK in 1955.

## Description

150 mm (6 in), sexually dimorphic.

COCK: Bill horn brown, rather heavy and conical; irides dark brown; entire body plumage dull crimson, brightest on the chin, throat, breast and rump, mixed with brown on the back and flanks; underparts grow paler until they are whitish under the tail; wings and tail brownish, edged with rufous; legs and feet dusky brown or brown.

HEN: Whole plumage olive brown, streaked with brown; double whitish bar across the wing coverts.

## Distribution and Habitat

From Eastern Europe over much of Asia, including India,

Tibet and China. Habitat varies throughout its wide distribution and includes swampy woodland with undergrowth, copses, scrub-thickets, cultivated areas, bushy cover and grasslands. In the Himalayas it breeds at heights of 3000 m 10,000 ft) upwards. Whistler (1963) records that Indian birds, during migration and in the winter, feed in flocks on millet and similar crops, also entering gardens and villages.

## Breeding

PERIOD: The breeding season begins in mid May in Europe, and in June until August in India. Captive-breeding reports suggest that, in aviaries, nesting will commence in June, although sometimes as late as August. Wild birds are single-brooded. There is no evidence that more than one brood has been reared in captivity.

NEST: A shallow cup of twigs and dried grass, lined with finer roots, stems and hair. Usually low in a bush or a tree, from ground level up to a height of about 3 m (9 ft). In aviaries, recorded nests have been built in low bushes, in a box tree and in a half-open nest box. These nests have been made of dried grasses, lined with finer stems and hair. G De Pass described a nest as being 'not unlike that of a Bullfinch' so one can assume twigs were used.

EGGS: Ground colour light or deep blue, marked at the larger end with spots, streaks or small blotches of black or purplish black. Clutch size usually 5, rarely 3–6.

INCUBATION: Carried out by the hen who is a close sitter, 'allowing herself almost to be caught rather than leave the nest' (Whistler). Period 12–14 days.

CHICKS: The nestlings have a pinkish skin with very dark grey down, the mouth is pink and the gape flanges whitish yellow. The young are fed by both parents and leave the nest at between 11–17 days. Immature birds resemble the hen but are more heavily streaked. In captivity the young have been reared on paddy rice, chickweed and mealworms, also on insectivorous mixture and egg rearing food.

## Behaviour

In captivity they seldom alight on the ground and they are

somewhat acrobatic in spite of a rather heavy sparrow-like build. In one nesting in captivity, the nesting was preceded by nuptial chasing by the cock and courtship feeding. The cock did not attack the other birds in the medium-sized aviary, but once the young had left the nest and become independent he became aggressive and began to chivvy his young and the other birds in the aviary.

**Genus** ***Coccothraustes*** **(Hawfinches)**

The hawfinches are represented in aviculture by the European Hawfinch (*C. coccothraustes*) which is well distributed in the UK, although the populations are very local. Apart from the European Hawfinch which has been bred in captivity fairly frequently over the years, I can find records of only three other species being bred; these are the Evening Grosbeak (*C. vespertinus*), the Black and Yellow (*C. icterioides*) and the Black-tailed (*C. migratorius*). Of the nine species in the genus only three have been imported over the years with any kind of regularity: two Old World species, *C. migratorius* and *C. personatus* (the Japanese Hawfinch), and the New World *C. vespertinus*. Currently, only the Black-tailed is imported annually, the Japanese rarely.

BLACK-TAILED HAWFINCH *Coccothraustes migratorius*
**Plate 8**

OTHER NAMES: Black-headed Hawfinch, Yellow-billed Grosbeak, Chinese Hawfinch. It is also erroneously called the Japanese Hawfinch. Two subspecies are recognised.

This species was formerly placed in the genus *Eophona*, with the closely related Japanese Hawfinch. This large, attractive and interesting finch, which is still imported into the UK, was on the lists in 1990. Hens, unfortunately, are few in most of the small shipments that arrive. They are often confused with the Japanese Hawfinch (*C. personatus*), especially as both are sometimes called Black-headed Hawfinches. The two major differences are size — *C. migratorius* is about 190 mm (7½ in) and *C. personatus* 215–230 mm (8½–9 in) — and head colour–the entire head of *C. migratorius* is black, and *C. personatus* has the crown, lores, base of cheeks and chin black. The hens of these species lack black on the heads, but both sexes in *C. migratorius* have a rufous wash, on the flanks and sides of breast, which is lacking in *C. personatus*. *C. migratorius* has apparently yet to be bred successfully in the UK, although there have been a number of unsuccessful nestings. As there seems to be a lack of information about these birds, brief details are recorded here:

1962 (published) V Whittaker Carr. Inside flight 1.2 m × 1.2 m × 91 cm (4 × 4 × 3 ft), housed on their own. Eggs incubated but did not hatch.

1962 (published) C D Beckett. Outside aviary 1.8 × 1.8 × 1.8 m (6 × 6 × 6 ft), housed alone. Three young hatched, two left nest but were neglected and died as the cock was driving the hen to nest again.

1975 (unpublished) J Trollope. Outside aviary, 3 × 1 × 2.5 m (10 × 3½ × 8 ft), housed with other birds. Three clutches laid and incubated, one hatched but the young were dead at approximately three days. The hen was found dead on her nest; a *post mortem* revealing no cause for death.

Apart from these nestings I know of three other unsuccessful attempts in which young were hatched but not reared. In all cases the cock displayed aggression to the hen and other birds.

They have been bred in Europe and have been imported fairly frequently in recent years. However, the future availability of imported birds is very uncertain, so the owners of these birds should make every effort to breed them.

## Description

190 mm (7½ in), sexually dimorphic.

COCK: Bill massive and stout, yellow with bluish grey at base and slight marking of ashy grey at tip; irides very dark brown, with an outer zone of light reddish brown; entire head black; upperparts greyish brown; uppertail coverts white; wings black, tipped white; tail black; underparts greyish white with a rufous wash on the flanks and sides of breast; legs and feet flesh colour.

HEN: Lacks black on the head; upperparts greyish brown; light below; the wash on flanks and sides of breast is paler.

## Distribution and Habitat

East Asia from Amur to China. Inhabits forests, scrub, bamboo and cultivated areas.

## Breeding

PERIOD: Captive nestings in outside aviaries have commenced in April/May in the UK. There is evidence that like the European Hawfinch, two broods are sometimes reared.
NEST: Aviary nests have varied from almost typical Hawfinch structures, a cup of twigs, roots, lined with rootlets, grasses and fibres, to a few leaves placed in an old blackbird's nest. My birds built two quite substantial structures of twigs and grasses, lined with finer grasses and feathers. The sites have varied from bushes and creepers to a window ledge. The cock collects material and I have seen him sitting in the nest and arranging material on one occasion.
EGGS: Descriptions in avicultural literature are few and vague. The following details are given from eggs laid in my aviaries. Sub-elliptical, slightly glossy, ground colour pale bluish, spotted, blotched with dark and ashy brown, with a few blackish scribblings at the larger end. The two eggs measured were 22.2 × 15.8 mm and 22.8 × 16.2 mm (⅞ × ⅝ in). Clutch size 3–4.
INCUBATION: Carried out by the hen, but I have seen the cock covering the eggs while the hen is off the nest for a brief period. The hen is also frequently fed by the cock while on the nest. Period 14 days.
CHICKS: Fed by both parents, and brooded closely by the hen for the first five or six days. The food fed to the chicks has included; seeds, maggots, mealworms, collected live food, commercial insectivorous mixture and egg food.

## Behaviour

Like the European Hawfinch, the nesting of this bird is preceded by a period of courtship; this is needed to break down the barriers of tension between such powerful birds, which, in confinement, are considerable. In my aviary the cock bird approached the hen to courtship feed her, hopping along a perch and alternately presenting one side then the other. When about 15 cm (6 in) apart, they stretched out their necks and touched bills, the hen jabbing at the cock with her bill. He retreated, the same performance being repeated many times, until she took the food offered. The hen occasionally fed him, returning the same food. The cock then began to sit in various potential nest sites around the aviary, often taking a twig or grass stem, and holding the material crossways in his bill, making movements as if he was placing material in a nest. Copulation, which took place on the ground, was preceded by courtship feeding and was often followed by both birds jabbing at each other with their bills. During incubation the cock would sometimes fly to the nest with material, such as a feather or small twig, which the hen would sometimes take from him.

From the limited information available, the main reasons for the captive-breeding failures of this species appear to be the aggressive behaviour of the cock towards other birds, causing disruption, and, perhaps more importantly, the driving of the hen to nest before the chicks are reared. The solutions are to house the birds on their own, giving them as much space and cover as possible, to remove some of the pressure from the hen.

# 7
# Estrildidae — Waxbills, Mannikins, Munias and Allied Species

This family of Old World seed-eating birds includes many species well known in aviculture. Delacour (1943) divided them into three tribes: the waxbills, *Estrildini*, the grass and parrot finches, *Erythrurini*, and the mannikins and munias, *Amadini*. These three groups have been variously combined by other authors, sometimes as subfamilies. However, in current checklists, such subfamilies and other divisions are not recognised within the family. However, the captive care and breeding of these groups differs enough to warrant the retention of these divisions in a practical avicultural book. The members of this family are often called weaver-finches; this name was used to differentiate them from the weavers when they were previously placed in the Ploceidae as a subfamily.

The Estrildidae share a number of reproductive and ethological characteristics. For example, they build domed nests (which they do not weave) with a side entrance, and the eggs are white and unmarked. Both parents play a part in nest building, incubation and feeding the young, though the involvement of both sexes seems to vary to a certain extent between different genera and, in some cases, species. The food soliciting posture of young estrildines differs from other 'finch-like' forms. Instead of the neck-stretched gape presented to the parents of most passerines, the young crouch with the head lowered and twisted around and up towards the parent.

Many species in the family are called 'finches' and this can cause confusion to beginners in aviculture, especially as waxbills, munias *et al* are often the first foreign birds a beginner will keep. The Estrildidae probably have more species imported, either from the countries of origin or bred elsewhere, than any other passerine family.

## Waxbills

Many waxbill species have short conical bills which are red or pinkish red in colour, and the resemblance of waxbill red to the red of sealing wax gave the group its popular name. The bills are of different colours in some genera, a few of the bills are rather long and pointed and some are quite large compared to the size of the bird. The waxbills are an entirely African group, with the exception of two Asiatic *Amandava* species, and the Australian Sydney or Red-browed Waxbill (*Aegintha temporalis*); this bird is a problematic species as it has affinities with both the waxbills and the grass finches.

The pair bond has proved to be strong in those species studied, and there is evidence that, in some species, it could be for life. Waxbills are sociable birds, and the pair bond is initiated and sustained by mutual preening, vocalisations and displays. They will 'clump up' (sit closely side by side) to roost, or to have a nap on a warm afternoon. In the wild they are usually seen in pairs or small groups (or flocks in some species). Most species feed on the ground or in low herbage.

In many species the courtship display of the cock bird consists, mainly, of a stem display, in which the bird picks up a stem, which is held by the stiff end in the bill tip. He then flies to a perch and commences to jerk, or throw, the head upwards, the body jerking up at each throw and the stem moving in an arc from low to high. The extent to which the head is thrown back varies from species to species, depending on what areas of conspicuous plumage they wish to display. In some species the jerking results in the feet *just* leaving the perch, so the movement becomes a bounce or jump. The head can be held in direct line with the body, or swung from side to side. Hens will sometimes stem display, presumably in an attempt to arouse an unresponsive mate. This display is sometimes performed on the ground. I have often seen cock Melba Finches (*Pytilia melba*) display vigorously on a perch, to a hen who is on the ground and apparently indifferent. The cock will then fly down and often pick up a fresh stem and start all over again. If the stem is a long one, it often becomes caught and even without this hazard, ground stem displays are never an elegant performance.

The tail-twist posture (or display) is common to all waxbills, and to some other estrildines. One bird hops or sidles along a perch towards another, with its head turned and its tail twisted towards the other bird. The feathers of areas of conspicuous plumage will be raised.

## Accommodation and Breeding

Waxbills, like all captive birds, are best accommodated in aviaries. If the aviary has adequate areas of shelter, then the birds can benefit from sun and rain when *they* choose. In a planted aviary, the number of insects the birds can find will assist in the rearing of chicks, and they can seek food in a natural manner. The main problem with aviary housing for waxbills is the danger presented by cats and rodents. However, I have kept and bred many species in protected aviaries of reasonable size. The ideal, I think, would be a conservatory or spare room converted to house birds. These birds can be kept in cages, and have been bred; the results with most species are improving.

In the wild, waxbills build domed nests which, in some cases, have a tubular projecting entrance, and a 'cock's' nest usually built on top. This is not for the cock to roost in, but is generally accepted to be an anti-predator device. This false nest is sometimes more conspicuous then the real nest and has an obvious entrance. I once had a pair of St Helena Waxbills (*Estrilda astrild*) which built three nests in a row with a cock's nest on top. The real nest was difficult to see and unlike the others was lined with feathers.

In the wild, the nest site is usually low down in a bush, tree or herbage. Some species will nest in outhouses and in other human or domestic-animal accommodation. Bizarre sites are sometimes selected, both in the wild and in captivity. In captivity the favoured nesting receptacle is the domed wicker-type nesting basket, and the majority of nests in my aviaries are made either in these or in clumps of branches of cut gorse. Half-open nest boxes are sometimes used, and wire tubes of various sizes, open at one end with dried grasses pushed in, will be used. 'Natural' nests are also built in bushes, vines and other plants. Materials provided should include dried grasses, plant stems, coconut fibres and feathers.

Waxbills are, generally speaking, amiable little birds and should not be housed with aggressive or large species. The larger birds may not harm the waxbills, but they will be a source of disruption and fright. Too many pairs of waxbills housed together will lead to bickering and squabbling, which is hardly conducive for successful breeding. This can be reduced by using cover in an aviary: the practice of 'out of sight, out of mind' will often reduce conflict in a mixed collection. Unrelated species to be housed with waxbills can include silverbills and some other *Lonchura* species such as spice birds, and White-headed and Black-headed munias, and small pairs of doves, such as the Diamond (*Geopelia cuneata*) and the Cape (*Oena capensis*).

### Food and Care

Small mixed millets, with the addition of small canary seed, give the basic diet. This can be improved with a number of smaller seeds, such as maw and niger, which are best provided with one of the 'tonic' or special foreign bird seed mixtures. Soaked and germinated seed and millet sprays are a useful stand-by when the seeding grasses waxbills prefer (such as *Poa annua*, and other wild grasses) are out of season. Chickweed, dandelion, sow thistles, and many other wild green foods are picked over, and they obviously provide small insects, which are taken. As pointed out by Goodwin, green food is taken by the birds seizing a piece in their bill and tearing it off with a sharp backward jerk, and the birds cannot do this if it is lying loose on the floor of an aviary or cage. So green food must be fixed, by placing a heavy stone over the clump of food and allowing leaves to stick out, so that the birds can work on it. Turves of grass, complete with roots and soil, are always received with enthusiasm, and when the birds have had a chance to work on the grass section, I turn the turves over to the soil side.

Live food is essential to keep waxbills fit, not just when they are breeding (or one hopes they are breeding); small meal-worms and larvae are the live food favoured. A white worm (*Enchytraeus*) culture is always worth keeping, as are fruit-flies in warmer weather. In every aviary I keep a large tin of rotting fruit, covered with layers of fine-mesh wire, and placed in the warmest and most sheltered position. The waxbills spend a long time perched on this tin picking off the flies, which at times group like a cloud around the tin. If you can 'train' your birds to take fine-grade insectivorous soft food, egg food or other rearing foods, this will supplement and, to a certain extent, replace the live food needed for rearing the young.

Waxbills, like many other birds, show a need for minerals. These must be supplied regularly and with as much variety as possible. Mineralised grit, powdered cuttle fish, commercial bird sand and Kilpatrick's pigeon minerals should be given daily. Eggshells heated in an oven to sterilise them, and then broken up into tiny pieces, are another source of minerals.

Like many other foreign birds, the term 'hardy' (and currently, 'half-hardy') is applied to some waxbill species. This is misleading, especially for people keeping birds for the first time. Although I keep established and aviary-bred birds in outside aviaries between April and November, I work by the British weather, not the month, and bring the birds in if hard weather occurs. During periods of short day length, combined with low temperatures, these birds should be housed in protected and heated accommodation with the day length extended by artificial lighting. The ideal outside accommodation is a flight with a shelter attached, which is provided with heat and electric light. The environmental temperature need not be high and my birds seem to winter well with a *minimum* temperature of 8–10°C (45–50°F), and extended lighting until about 20.00 hours.

### Genus *Pytilia* (Pytilias)

The pytilias are a genus of four species which, morphologically, do not resemble closely the typical waxbills (*Estrilda*). The pytilias are larger, 115–130 mm (4½–5 in), and are all sexually dimorphic. Although not suitable for a beginner, they adjust well to captivity once properly established.

The four species of this genus fall into two ecologically distinct superspecies. The Melba Finch (*P. melba*) and the Yellow-winged Pytilia (*P. hypogrammica*) are birds of bush and scrub in open country, while the Orange-winged Pytilia (*P. afra*) and the Red-winged Pytilia (*P. phoenicoptera*) live mainly in trees, except when feeding. *P. afra* is considered to be the link between *P. melba* and *P. hypogrammica*, with *P. phoenicoptera* the most distinct. However, anyone who has seen *P. hypogrammica* and *P. phoenicoptera* living together in the same aviary, would, I think, agree that morphologically they are similar in size and shape of body, bill and some plumage areas. They respond to the call notes of each other, and an unmated *P. hypogrammica* cock housed with a widowed *P. phoenicoptera* hen for company went to nest. I had to cut short their possible breeding as it was mid November, and they were therefore removed to winter housing. Although the cross-breeding of congenerics is hardly unexpected or desirable, it would have proved interesting in this case.

The four *Pytilia* species are parasitised by the Paradise Whydah group. *P. melba* is host to *Vidua paradisea* and three *V. orientalis* subspecies, *P. afra* is host to the Broad-tailed Paradise Whydah (*V. orientalis obtusa*), and *P. hypogrammica* and *P. phoenicoptera* are hosts to two other subspecies of *V. orientalis*, *V.o. togoensis* and *V.o. interjecta*. It should be noted that these whydahs were in the genus *Steganora*, now merged with *Vidua*.

RED-WINGED PYTILIA *Pytilia phoenicoptera* **Plate 15**

OTHER NAMES: Crimson-winged Waxbill, Crimson-winged Pytilia, Aurora Finch. There are three subspecies; *P.p. lineata* has a red bill and is sometimes called the Red-billed Aurora Finch.

This species is one of the most delightful in the family. It is not as frequently imported as many species in the *Estrilda* and other waxbill genera, but small shipments usually arrive in the UK in most years. This is the ideal subject for establishment in captivity; attractive, visually sexable and a willing breeder. I have bred them to the fourth generation and have had 22 young from two pairs in a season. I have heard of another aviculturist who had even better results. The subspecies usually imported is the West African, *P.p. phoenicoptera*.

Description

115 mm (4½ in), sexually dimorphic.

COCK: Bill dark steel grey or blackish; irides reddish brown; head, back and rest of upperparts grey; underparts grey, barred with white from the lower breast to the undertail coverts; wings darker grey, with variable area of crimson,

usually from the lesser coverts and scapulars to the primaries, which are edged with dark brown; uppertail coverts and tail feathers crimson; legs and feet flesh colour.
HEN: Plumage browner; white barring on the underparts less defined; crimson areas paler and smaller.

## Distribution and Habitat

The semi-arid zone from Gambia to the northern Congo, Uganda and southern Sudan. Frequents dry karoo and shrub clearings in dry forests, dense brushwood and agricultural land.

## Breeding

PERIOD: For wild birds, the only information I have is that nesting begins at the end of the rainy season. In captivity they will breed from April to November. When I first kept this species, the imported birds would commence nesting in July. Now my aviary bred birds begin in early April, as soon as they are released in outside aviaries. Three or four broods are usual, rarely five.
NEST: In the wild the nest is a loosely-made domed structure, of grass stems and heads, lined with feathers, with an entrance hole at the side. The site is in a tree or bush, usually between 0.9–1.8 m (3–6 ft) above the ground. Aviary nests are built, for preference, in domed wicker nest baskets, the type with a large entrance hole is preferred. They will also use a clump of cut gorse branches, hung up under shelter in the aviary. Dried grass stems are the usual nest material, lined with a few finer grasses and feathers. Both sexes collect material and build the nest, one partner usually sitting inside.
EGGS: White and rather large for the size of bird. Clutch size 3–4.
INCUBATION: Carried out by both sexes, the cock's share appears to be a brief period in the morning and a longer period in the afternoon. The cock will often sit in the nest with the hen and roost with her at night. Period 12–13 days.
CHICKS: The nestlings are dark skinned and have reddish mouths, showing two rather inconspicuous violet spots inside gape, and a greyish white tubercle on each corner of the gape; these are often retained for a few days when the chicks leave

the nest. The chicks leave the nest between 18–20 days and are fed by both parents, by the cock alone when the hen starts a second clutch. They become independent at 14–16 days. The immature plumage is like the hen's, but the chicks' bills are a light grey, and the crimson areas are very pale and indistinct. I have not known the cock to harass the young, and at one time I had two independent previous broods in with parents who had chicks in the nest. The only reason you may have to move them, is to prevent overcrowding and competition for live food. In the summer months, broods have been reared almost completely on fruit-flies, small maggots and seeding grasses. The independent young of previous broods will feed the nestlings of later broods. As all my birds are ringed with coloured identification rings as soon as they leave the nest, I have no doubts that this helping occurs. Once, the adult hen died when the nestlings were about seven days old, and the three young of the previous brood played the major role in rearing them, which was carried out successfully.

## Behaviour

The stem display is performed on a perch; at least, I have never seen it performed on the ground. The cock jerks his head and body upwards, to the left and right, so the stem is swung up and down to each side and not in line with his body. As the feet do not leave the perch this is a jerky bobbing movement and not a jump. These pytilias are not aggressive birds, and I have kept them with other waxbill species (which had little or no red in the plumage), and with *Lonchura* munias. I have never seen these birds attack another bird. They will sometimes threaten other birds at the feeding station, but overt aggression has not been observed.

When frightened, for example, if someone makes a sudden movement in the bird room, this pytilia will, in one movement, turn its body so the tail is directed to the source of the fright, the head facing away. The tail is cocked and the body is held in line so the area visible to the 'enemy' is reduced. The bird will stay 'frozen' in this position until the offender leaves the bird room. This position ensures that the red areas of its plumage are hidden. It is a reasonable assumption that this behaviour is *contra-predator* in function, however, I have not seen it in other *Pytilia* species, and it occurs less often with established and aviary-bred birds.

## YELLOW-WINGED PYTILIA *Pytilia hypogrammica* **Plate 12**

OTHER NAMES: Red-faced Pytilia.

This species is not well known and, to my knowledge, was not imported into the UK until about twelve years ago, although it could have arrived in shipments of *P. afra* and not been recognised. Since then, a few small shipments have arrived in the UK in most years, including 1990. It has been imported into Europe on a few occasions, and was bred by M Arbeiter sometime in the 1960s. There was a report of a successful breeding in the UK in 1980, but unfortunately the details were limited, so I will supplement them with details from several unsuccessful attempts by my own birds. They are rather delicate birds until established, and even then should not be wintered outside without heat. I have kept established birds at a temperature of 8–10°C (46–50°F) between November and March during a hard winter. With artificial light until 20.00 hours and the essential varied diet, including live food, they winter well.

### Description

115 mm (4½ in), sexually dimorphic.
COCK: Bill black; irides reddish brown; face, ear coverts, rump, uppertail coverts and tail red; rest of upperparts brownish grey; wings brownish with yellow edges; tail red; throat red; rest of underparts grey, with whitish barring on abdomen; legs and feet flesh coloured.
HEN: Lacks the red on the head; underparts brownish grey.

### Distribution and Habitat

Sierra Leone to Cameroon. Inhabits dry grasslands in the vicinity of bushes and trees.

### Breeding

PERIOD: No information from the natural habitat; probably immediately following the rainy season. In outside aviaries in the UK they have commenced nesting in April. They are probably multi-brooded like *P. phoenicoptera*. Attempts to rear two and three broods have occurred, but only one has been successfully reared.

NEST: A domed structure, with an entrance hole at the side. Built of grass stems lined with finer grasses and feathers, sometimes built on a base of leaves. In the wild, the site is in a thicket or shrub, usually fairly low down. Aviary nests are mainly built of grasses lined with finer grasses and feathers. Dead leaves were used in the construction of one nest. My birds built in clumps of gorse, and there is a report that a nest was made in a log-type nesting box, with an entrance hole. Both sexes collect material and build the nest, the hen playing the major role.

EGG: White, more oval than those of *P. phoenicoptera*. Very large for the size of the bird. Clutch size 3–4.

INCUBATION: Carried out by both sexes. Period is not known.

CHICKS: The only information on the nestlings is that they are very dark in colour. The young are fed by both parents, the cock doing most of the feeding once the chicks have left the nest. The successful breeding report stated that one brood was lost due to the lack of live food.

## Behaviour

The cocks have given stem displays on a few occasions, these were of the same 'type' as the stem display of *P. phoenicoptera*; the feet not leaving the perch, the stem lifted and lowered to the left and right. These birds seem to do well in a mixed collection of waxbills and munias, provided that the other birds have no red in their plumage, although this probably depends on where the area of red plumage is situated, as they have been kept with Lavender waxbills, *Estrilda caerulescens*, (who have red on the rump, uppertail coverts and tail feathers) without conflict. I would certainly not keep them with their 'red-faced' congenerics.

## MELBA FINCH *Pytilia melba*

OTHER NAMES: Green-winged Pytilia. Eight subspecies are recognised. These vary largely in the amount of red in their plumage, and some are paler.

This pytilia has long been known in aviculture. It was first imported into Europe in 1874. Shipments are fairly frequent, and it is still available. The first captive breeding was in the UK in 1936. It has been bred on quite a few occasions since. Unsuccessful attempts, due to the parents deserting and the chicks dying because insufficient live food was provided, are more common than successes. The birds are attractive and have a natural 'steadiness' which is appealing, even imported birds soon adjust to their new environment.

Because pytilias are larger than many other 'waxbills' (and the Melba is the largest pytilia), it leads people to assume that they are hardier, sometimes with fatal results. Once established, the Melba can be kept outside between April and October, but this bird is certainly less resistant to cold and to wet weather than *P. phoenicoptera*.

## Description

130 mm (5 in), sexually dimorphic.
COCK: Bill longer and more pointed than the bills of preceding *Pytilia* species, colour pale or pinkish red; irides reddish brown; forehead and cheeks red; rest of head grey; upperparts olive green; lower rump, uppertail coverts and tail crimson; throat red; upper breast yellowish; lower breast and flanks light grey, barred with white; legs and feet brownish grey.
HEN: The hen has no red on the head, and the olive-green upperparts are paler; underparts pale grey, spotted with white.

## Distribution and Habitat

Wide distribution south of the Sahara. Habitat varies throughout its distribution, but is mainly denser thickets, in thorn scrub in dry semi-arid regions. In southern Africa it is found in the Kalahari.

## Breeding

PERIOD: Varies throughout the vast area of its distribution. February to June in the southern region. In the UK captive birds will commence nesting outside in April. Two broods have been reared, possibly three attempted.

NEST: Usually low down in a shrub or thicket. In some areas of its distribution a tree is the favoured site. The nest is a thin walled, domed structure of grass stems; the ends of these protrude all round like bristles. The entrance is on the side. Grass heads are the only lining material recorded. Most nests built by my birds have been typical thin walled, unlined grass structures. Some have been so flimsy, that a sitting bird is plainly visible, especially the red-faced cock. Aviary birds have sometimes chosen somewhat bizarre sites, apart from the usual nesting baskets and gorse clumps, one nest was woven into the aviary wire and, nesting on a batten adjoining a safety porch, the sitting bird looked at me every time I entered the porch and passed within inches of the nest. The building and collection of material is carried out by both sexes, one partner sitting inside and arranging the stems. One nest was a very large, substantial structure about 125 mm across and 190 mm high (5 × 8 in), lined with feathers.
EGGS: White. Clutch size 3–4, sometimes 5.
INCUBATION: Carried out by both sexes. The cock incubated during the day, with, it would appear, no regular pattern. He would often cover the eggs when the hen left the nest to feed. Both sexes were sometimes seen in the nest and on several occasions the cock roosted in the nest. Incubation period 12–13 days.
CHICKS: Fed by both parents, almost entirely on live food for the first ten days. My adults eat fruit-flies and white worms, and these, with the addition of small maggots, mealworms, pupae and soft food (if the birds will take it), should be sufficient to rear the chicks. Collected live foods, with its variety, is obviously important. If not possible, very small stick insects and the smaller house crickets should be given. The young birds leave the nest at about 20 days and are fed by both parents.

## Behaviour

The stem display is given from both perch and ground. The 'type' of display is like that of the other *Pytilia* species, the stem swung up and down to the left and right of the body. I have seen a cock display to a hen sitting on eggs, it was the usual flimsy nest and she was plainly visible.

The bill of the Melba Finch is a formidable weapon, and these birds are best kept on their own when breeding, although I have kept them with species which have different nesting behaviour, such as sparrows of the genus *Petronia*, without trouble. The Melbas are dominant and if another bird is at the feeding site, a fast jab of the Melba's bill will ensure that the other bird leaves. This jab is not delivered with any posture or threat movements. The Melba looks completely relaxed, then the fast jab, then relaxed again. Threat displays are poorly developed in most Estrildinae, usually consisting of the bird crouching with lowered head and open bill. They very seldom bother to pursue another bird which ventures too near their nest, the cock 'sees them off' with minimal effort.

ORANGE-WINGED PYTILIA *Pytilia afra*

OTHER NAMES: Golden-backed Pytilia. In earlier avicultural literature it will be found as Wiener's Finch (*Pytilia wieneri*), also as the Red-faced Finch. No subspecies are recognised.

This pytilia, although considered an intermediate form between *P. melba* and *P. hypogrammica*, resembles the Melba more closely than the other pytilias, in my eyes. At one time they were imported into the UK fairly frequently, but they are seldom available now. In the curious vagaries of bird importation, their place has been taken by the once rare *P. hypogrammica*.

These birds have been bred quite often, and the successful breedings have probably been more frequent than those of *P. melba*. From the information available their behaviour, care and breeding in captivity is very similar to that described for *P. melba*.

## Description

115–130 mm (4½–5 in), sexually dimorphic.

COCK: Bill red; irides reddish brown; forehead, area around eyes and sides of head red; rest of upperparts olive grey; wings have an olive suffusion, with the greater wing coverts and primaries orange; tail and uppertail coverts crimson; underparts grey, barred with off-white; legs and feet flesh-coloured.

HEN: Has no red on the head and is greyer and generally paler.

Distribution and Habitat

East and central Africa, from Ethiopia to Angola, Tanzania and Mozambique. Frequents tangled thorn-brakes near water, also bush and semi-arid country.

**Twin-spots**

The systematic position and relationships of these attractive African estrildines are somewhat problematic. Currently most taxonomists recognise four genera comprising six species: in the genus *Clytospiza* the Brown Twin-spot (*C. monteiri*); two species in the genus *Hypargos*, the Rosy and Peters's Twin-spot (*H. margaritatus* and *H. niveoguttatus*); two species in *Euschistospiza*, Dybowski's and the Dusky Twin-spot (*E. dybowskii* and *E. cinereovinacea*); and in the genus *Mandingoa* the Green-backed Twin-spot (*M. nitidula*), formerly often united with *Hypargos*. The *Euschistospiza* species have been variously placed with *Clytospiza*, *Lagonosticta* (the fire-finches) and *Cryptospiza* (the crimson-wings).

The twin-spots, like the pytilias, are somewhat larger than many 'typical' waxbill species of the genus *Estrilda*, measuring approximately 114–127 mm (4½–5 in). Of the six species in the well differentiated genera only two are available to aviculturists on anything like a regular basis: Peters' Twin-spot (*Hypargos niveoguttatus*) and the Green-backed (*Mandingoa nitidula*), both of which have been imported into Europe and the USA fairly often over the years. They have been bred on several occasions in Europe and the USA, and aviculturists in South Africa have been particularly successful with Peters's Twin-spot breedings.

Twin-spots are not suitable birds for the beginner and imported birds must be established in captivity with care. If obtained in regions with low winter temperatures such as many areas of Europe and the USA, they are best acclimatised in roomy box cages in a heated bird room, or preferably, an inside aviary. They can be housed in outside planted aviaries during the summer and after a first season in captivity in these conditions I winter these established birds with a minimum temperature of 8–10°C (45–50°F). They thrive on a varied seed diet and my birds seem to take more small canary seed than many other African estrildines. This basic diet is supplemented with seeding grasses, a fine-grade commercial insectivorous mixture and live food such as white worms, mealworms and fruit-flies. Twin-spots are very adept at catching flying insects in an outside planted aviary.

### Genus *Mandingoa*

### GREEN-BACKED TWIN-SPOT *Mandingoa nitidula*

There are four subspecies, two of which, *M.n. schlegeli* (Schlegel's Twin-spot) and *M.n. chubbi* (Chubb's Twin-spot) differ sufficiently from the nominate subspecies, *M.n. nitidula* to be readily distinguished. *M.n. virginiae* is a little known subspecies, confined to the island of Fernando Po.

Green-backed twin-spots are active, vivacious birds which adjust well to captivity once established. Successful breedings have been achieved on the European continent, including the nominate subspecies *M.n. nitidula*, and *M.n. schlegli* and *chubbi*, but I can find no record of a breeding in the UK. Like all the twin-spots, breeding success is dependent on a constant supply of live food for the chicks. My birds have hatched chicks on one occasion; however, the nest was built on an exposed site and was washed out in a heavy rainstorm.

#### Description

114 mm (4½ in), sexually dimorphic.
COCK: Bill dull black; irides dark brown; lores, cheeks and chin red. Upperparts olive green, uppertail coverts and rump with a slight 'wash' of golden yellow. Wings dusky edged with olive green; tail black edged with olive green. Throat, sides of neck, upper breast and undertail coverts olive green; lower breast and abdomen black, densely spotted with white; legs and feet flesh colour or light brown.
HEN: Paler in colour than the cock, with lores, area around eyes and chin pale orange.

N.B. The cock of the subspecies *M.n. chubbi* differs from the nominate subspecies by having the throat to breast area tinged with golden olive, sometimes orange-red. *M.n. schlegeli* has a larger bill than that of the nominate race which is red with an area of purplish black at the base and upper mandible.

The throat and chest of the nominate cock bird is orange-red and these areas in the hen are golden olive.

Distribution and Habitat

From Sierra Leone to Zaire and Angola, southern Ethiopia and the Sudan, Kenya, Tanzania, Zambia and Mozambique to eastern Cape Province. The subspecies *M.n. virginiae* is confined to the island of Fernando Po. The main habitat of Green-backed twin-spots is forest and forest edges, thickets, long grass and clearings. Areas of cultivation are often visited by small flocks, where they feed on rice and other crops.

**Genus *Hypargos***

PETERS' TWIN-SPOT *Hypargos niveoguttatus*

OTHER NAMES: Red-throated Twin-spot, Peters's Spotted Fire-finch, Peters's Ruddy Waxbill. Five subspecies are recognised.

Although never commonly imported, Peters' Twin-spot was for some years the most readily available species of the group. Recently the situation has changed and Schlegel's Twin-spot (*M.n. schlegeli*), the West African race of the Green-backed Twin-spot, has been more frequently imported. Peters' Twin-spot has been bred on the European continent, as well as in the USA, the UK and South Africa. As with other twin-spots, successful breeding reports indicate a constant supply of live food in addition to a varied 'waxbill' diet to be essential.

Description

114–127 mm (4½–5 in), sexually dimorphic.

COCK: Bill black, light blue at the base of the lower mandible; irides dark brown; orbital ring light blue; top of the head to nape greyish brown; mantle to upper rump and wings a warm orange-brown with a slightly irregular wash of red; tail black and washed with crimson; uppertail coverts crimson; face, chin, throat and breast deep red; lower breast to uppertail coverts and flanks black with white spots; legs and feet grey.

HEN: Head greyish brown, face grey, the chin and throat deep buff; upper breast a paler red than the cock's; rest of underparts grey with white spots.

## Distribution and Habitat

From eastern Kenya, south to Zimbabwe and Mozambique. Inhabits dense cover along the edge of forest, thick bush in areas of high grass, and undergrowth on the banks of rivers and streams. Small parties will gather to feed in clearings, paths and along road sides.

## Breeding

PERIOD: Variable throughout its range, in the eastern regions mainly January to May and in the south March to June. Captive birds in outside aviaries have bred or attempted to breed from March to September on the European continent and in the UK. Two broods have been reared in captivity and the species is probably double brooded in the wild.
NEST: Domes with an entrance hole at the side, constructed of grass and lined with feathers (fibres and rootlets also recorded). The usual site is low down in a bush, sometimes on the ground. In captivity some nests have been built with the entrance in the form of a short 'tunnel'. Nest baskets and boxes have been used but the majority of nests have been free standing in low bushes or vines, on the ground in grass, in flower pots complete with soil and growing grass, and in clumps of cut branches. The material used has included grasses, leaves, animal hairs and feathers. Both sexes collect material and take part in building, but from the information available, the hen plays the major role. Most reports indicate the same nest is used for the second broods, often with material added.
EGGS: White. Clutch size usually 3 (3–6 recorded in captivity).
INCUBATION: Carried out by both sexes, the hen sitting at night and the cock during the day at irregular intervals. Incubation period 12 days.
CHICKS: Black in colour, with a few tufts of greyish down, the gape being bright chrome yellow (Harrison and Dormer). Fed by both parents and they leave the nest at approximately 21 days. At this stage their plumage is dark brown with a slight wash of red on the back and wings. The throat is light brown and the yellowish-white nodules at the corners of the gape are retained for some days.

## Behaviour

Harrison and Dormer record that the stem display is performed on the ground, the cock 'dancing' around the hen with a feather held in the bill-tip. The upward movement of the head and bobbing movement of the body is more exaggerated than similar movements in the displays of waxbills belonging to the genera *Uraeginthus*, *Estrilda* and *Lagonosticta*. In the case of the twin-spots, the head is thrown up with each upward bob of the body. Apparently this species indulges in a 'communal' display in the wild, a number of pairs collecting in an area of thick undergrowth and the cocks hopping from twig to twig and displaying to each other while the hens sit motionless and take no part in the activity.

The question of how well this species and other twin-spots interact with other birds in a mixed collection appears to be somewhat confused. The majority of breeding reports indicate they are fairly tolerant of other waxbill species and even conspecifics, although some aviculturists have recorded they are aggressive when breeding, and attack any smaller birds approaching the nest site. I have not found twin-spots aggressive, but my experience is limited to one unsuccessful breeding attempt with the Green-backed species.

## **Genus *Cryptospiza* (Crimson-wings)**

The Crimson-wings are a genus of four montane African waxbills, two of which, the Red-faced (*C. reichenovii*) and the Ethiopian (*C. salvadorii*), have been occasionally imported since the 1960s. The Dusky Crimson-wing (*C. jacksoni*) and Shelley's Crimson-wing (*C. shelleyi*), have rarely been available in the UK. The Red-faced and Ethiopian are similar in shape and general appearance, rather plump-looking little birds, with rounded wings and tails. In 1968, I looked after two pairs of recently imported Ethiopian Crimson-wings for a fellow aviculturist. They were housed in a small outside aviary, with an enclosed shelter heated to approximately 8–10°C (45–50°F) and electric light providing a twelve-hour photoperiod during the winter. These birds were with me for a year and did not seem too difficult to establish; they ate small canary seed, millets and picked-over mixed canary mixture. Mealworms were eaten avidly, seeding grasses and insectivorous soft-food mixture were also taken. They seemed to take most of the variety of live food collected from nettle beds and bushes in the summer. The Red-faced and Ethiopian have been bred in the UK; all four species have bred in captivity on the European continent.

RED-FACED CRIMSON-WING *Cryptospiza reichenovii* **Plate 24**
OTHER NAMES: Reichenow's Forest Finch. Three subspecies are recognised.

This Crimson-wing has been available more frequently in recent years and they were imported into the UK during 1989–90. Like all the Crimson-wings, it inhabits mountain forests, sometimes at high elevations. As with *C. salvadorii*, I have found this species easy to establish and they come through winters in the UK well, if provided with moderate heat and electric light to give them a 12-hour day. Paris (1970) wintered them in an outside aviary without heat. I think this is risky should a prolonged spell of sub-zero temperatures occur, especially if an extended day is not provided by electric light.

### Description

115 mm (4.5 in), sexually dimorphic.
COCK: Bill black; irides dark brown; plumage mostly olive, with a patch around the eye; lores, mantle, back, rump, wing coverts and flanks crimson-red; primaries, primary coverts and tail black; legs and feet brown or dark brown.
HEN: Patch around the eye and lores buff, not red; in general the plumage appears to be slightly paler.

### Distribution and Habitat

Howard and Moore (1980) list the distribution of the subspecies as follows: *C.r. reichenovii* — Cameroun to Uganda, North Angola; *C.r. australis* — southern Uganda, Tanzania, Malawi, Zimbabwe, Mozambique; *C.r. homogenes* — eastern Zimbabwe. The habitat is usually near the edge of mountain forests, with undergrowth, and along mountain streams, near paths and clearings up to elevations of 2000 m (7000 ft). Also on old cultivation and millet fields below the forest line, as low as 200 m (670 ft) in some areas of their distribution.

## Breeding

PERIOD: I can find no references to a breeding period for wild birds, Goodwin (1982) records varied breeding dates for *C. salvadorii*, dependent on the area of its distribution; these range from June–July to March–April. It is therefore very likely that the same variation occurs with *C. reichenovii*, with its more isolated populations. In captivity, breeding has commenced in April–May, in outside aviaries.
NEST: A domed structure, made of leaves or grass, some lined with the feathery heads of grass, usually 5–6 m (15–20 ft) above ground in tree ferns, or the saplings of forest pawpaw (Goodwin 1982). In captivity, nests have been built in boxes and baskets; materials used have included coconut fibres, grass, feathers and moss. The nest is built mainly by the cock and may be completed in two days.
EGGS: Usual estrildine eggs, white and unmarked. Clutch size 3–4.
INCUBATION: Both sexes incubate; period probably 12–13 days. They are tolerant of nest inspection in captivity.
CHICKS: The young fledge at 21 days and are fed, mainly by the cock, for another 10–12 days. It would appear that live food, as well as seeds, are fed to the young in captivity and in the wild. However, Paris (1970) recorded a pair in an outside aviary which reared a brood on seed, greenfly and chickweed.

## Behaviour

The courtship display is performed with, or sometimes without, a grass stem; both cock and hen give the display. In the wild the birds feed on or near the ground in clearings, cultivation and grass patches, never far from cover. If disturbed they fly into cover, keeping low at all times (Wöstendien 1965).

### ETHIOPIAN CRIMSON-WING *Cryptospiza salvadorii*

OTHER NAMES: Salvadori's Crimson-wing, Crimson-backed Forest Finch. Three subspecies are recognised.

The breeding, general habits and feeding behaviour of this Crimson-wing are similar to those of *C. reichenovii.* Captive breeding reports indicate that live food (or adequate substitutes such as insectivorous soft food) have always been available during successful breedings.

### Description

115 mm (4.5 in), sexes similar.
COCK: Bill black; irides dark brown; head, nape, upper back and underparts greyish olive; back, rump, flanks and wing coverts crimson-red; legs and feet brown on dark brown.
HEN: The crimson-red areas are slightly paler.

NB This species lacks the red eye patch (cock) and buff patch (hen) of *C. reichenovii.*

### Distribution and Habitat

The mountains of central Ethiopia, south-eastern Sudan, northern Kenya and Uganda, west and south to Kivu and northern Tanzania. Found at all elevations up to 2500 m (8500 ft); feeds on or near the ground in openings in the forest and flies to low cover if disturbed. I have found that both this species and *C. reichenovii* have the same behaviour in an aviary and low cover should be provided.

## Fire-finches, Blue Waxbills and Grenadiers, Typical Waxbills, Avadavats

There are four genera of waxbills which include all the species frequently and regularly imported and a few that are seldom available. Most of these are well known and popular, and regularly bred (some have been bred in captivity to such a degree that colour mutations have occurred). In Australia a few have been established to the extent that Australian breeders have, from necessity, become independent of imported birds for the maintenance of aviary stocks. As their care and breeding in captivity have many common factors, already covered, a detailed account for each species is superfluous.

### Genus *Lagonosticta* (Fire-finches)

This genus consists of eight species of small African waxbills, ranging in size from 90 to 115 mm (3½ to 4½ in). The two species of lavender waxbills (or finches), *Estrilda caerulescens* and *E. perreini*, were formerly included in this genus. The smallest and most commonly imported fire-finch is the Red-billed (*L. senegala*). Other species occasionally, or rarely, imported are the Dark Fire-finch (*L. rubricata*) and Jameson's (*L. rhodopareia*).

RED-BILLED FIRE-FINCH *Lagonosticta senegala* **Plate 14**
OTHER NAMES: Senegal Fire-finch, Common Fire-finch.

This is a delightful and attractive little bird which is 'tame' and confiding in many areas of its natural habitat. Often seen in villages and in the outskirts of towns, it will sometimes nest under eaves or inside buildings such as outhouses.

They are wintered outside with adequate shelter by many aviculturists, and were released to breed as liberty birds at Keston (in spacious grounds in a rural area), where a small flock used to roost at night in a carpenter's shed. The releasing of other species has been successful from time to time, the owner then having a small flock of 'homing' waxbills. There are two aspects to this which must be considered: firstly, if you live in an urban area, as I do, your 'flock' won't survive for long; secondly, legislation in the UK makes it an offence to deliberately release *any* foreign species of bird or animal without a licence (see Appendix).

On the question of wintering these birds without heat, you always hear about the successes, but never about the losses which must surely occur. I bring the birds in about November, and provide very moderate heat in hard weather. They are not delicate birds once established, but exposing them for long periods to temperatures below freezing, combined with 15–16 hour nights, is taking an unnecessary risk with their lives.

This Fire-finch is occasionally imported, and is a free breeding species in captivity, having the great advantage of being visually sexable. In the wild these birds are hosts to the parasitical Indigo bird (*Vidua chalybeata*), rearing the young Indigo bird with their own nestlings.

Description

90–100 mm (3½–4 in), sexually dimorphic.
COCK: Bill pale red, centre of upper and lower mandible blackish, light area around base; irides reddish brown or brown; yellowish or whitish yellow ring around eye; head,

rump and uppertail coverts red; back and wings light brown to dark brown; tail feathers brownish black, edged red; underparts red, pale on the lower abdomen; sides of the breast marked with a few fine white dots; undertail coverts brownish grey; legs and feet flesh colour.
HEN: Upperparts greyish to buffy brown, paler below; lores and uppertail coverts red.

## Distribution and Habitat

Wide distribution from south of the Sahara, south to the Cape and from the west to the east coast. A bird of savanna, scrub and thornbush, also cultivated areas and the vicinity of human habitation.

## Breeding

PERIOD: Varies throughout its vast distribution, but is usual from the end of the rainy season. In outside aviaries from April (sometimes March) until as late as September/October. The birds are best removed inside if they commence a nesting as late as this. Two or three broods are reared.
NEST: The usual estrildine domed nest with a side entrance. Made of dried grasses, stems or rootlets, lined with feathers. The site, in some areas of its distribution, is frequently in dwellings, especially the grass walls and roofs of African huts. Natural sites include low down in bushes or thorny growth. Favoured receptacles for captive nests include wicker 'waxbill' nest baskets. A crude, 'open' flat wooden box, with lathes nailed across, stuffed with dried grasses and hung up about 1.2 m (4 ft) under cover, is favoured by fire-finches and other waxbill species (also by mice if present). Aviary nests are made of grasses (or any similar material provided), lined with feathers. 'Natural' free-standing nests in a planted aviary are often difficult to spot. The nest is built by both sexes largely by the cock.
EGGS: White. Clutch size 3–5, rarely 6.
INCUBATION: Carried out by both sexes, apparently without any particular pattern. I have seen cock or hen in the nest at any time during the day; it would appear the hen sits at night, although I have seen the cock enter nests late in the evening.

Incubation period 12 days.
CHICKS: The chicks have the usual variable mouth markings of the estrildines. They are fed by both parents, and you can hear begging calls from about five or six days after hatching. They leave the nest at 18–20 days, becoming independent at 28–32 days. The plumage of the immature birds is greyish brown, similar to the hen's. There is a slight wash of red on the uppertail coverts and they lack the white breast spots.

Small live food for the young nestlings can be partly provided in a planted aviary by a fruit-fly culture and a forked over heap of dead semi-decomposed weeds and grasses. White worms and *small* maggots, mealworms, plus seeding grasses and rearing food, and ant pupae, if available, will be needed in much larger quantities in inside accommodation.

## Behaviour

The stem display given by these birds is similar to that given by other waxbills. When displaying from a perch, the feet do not leave the twig. They become 'territorial' when breeding, chasing other birds away from their nest site, but, unless kept with closely related birds or with birds with red plumage, the chasing is not persistent.

## Genus *Uraeginthus* (Blue Waxbills and Grenadiers)

This is a genus of five African species. The three blue waxbills are fairly frequently imported into the UK, the two grenadiers only occasionally. Like all waxbills (and seed-eating birds) they suffer from people's erroneous belief that they can be maintained in the long term on a hard seed diet. When purchased from an importer, the concept of completed quarantine leads to another false belief, that they are established and can be immediately exposed to the uncertainties of a spring or summer in the UK. European aviculturists seem to have a more sensible view and most avicultural literature from the European continent supports a varied diet and careful gradual adjustment to a new environment. Current information indicates that the importation of these birds could be reduced or cease in the near future.

## Blue Waxbills (Cordon-bleus)

This trio of beautiful birds differs from the typical waxbills of the genus *Estrilda* by not clinging to the stems of growing grasses to feed on the seeds. They are, like many species in the family, predominantly ground feeders, taking termites and green seeds picked up from the ground or from prostrate plants. They successfully hawk for flying insects and, like many seed-eating birds, the young are largely fed on these for the first few days after hatching. Even in the months when seeding grasses and weeds are available for collection, I doubt if one could supply anything like the variety available to the wild birds. However, the benefits obtained from collecting these and achieving an adequate diet are important, especially when the birds are breeding. Like other waxbills, all three species have a stem display.

In captivity the favoured nesting site is a wicker nesting basket with a side entrance, also selected by many other species of 'foreign finches'. My birds also build free-standing 'natural' nests in clumps of gorse. A basket fixed in a gorse clump seems to be their idea of a perfect site. Although some aviculturists winter these birds outside, without heat or extended lighting, cordon-bleus always look rather miserable during wet, cold spells, and I bring them inside by November — earlier if the weather deteriorates.

RED-CHEEKED CORDON-BLEU *Uraeginthus bengalus* **Plate 13**

OTHER NAMES: Formerly known, in avicultural language, as Cordon-bleu, before the Blue-headed Waxbill was commonly imported. Five subspecies are recognised.

This species has long been known in aviculture and the first UK breeding was in 1906. They have been regularly imported for many years and are generally considered to be the most difficult to establish of the blue waxbills.

### Description

115–130 mm (4½–5 in), sexually dimorphic.

COCK: Bill pink or mauvish pink, slight ashy marking at tip, the edge of lower mandible blackish; irides brown to reddish brown; narrow whitish margin around the eye; lores, sides of

head, throat, breast, sides of body and lower rump blue; dark red patch on side of face; tail blue; rest of plumage earth brown; legs and feet light horn colour.
HEN: Paler than cock and lacks the red patch on the side of the face.

## Distribution and Habitat

From Senegal through the semi-arid belt to Ethiopia and south through East Africa to Katanga and Zambia. Inhabits semi-arid thorn scrub, savanna woodland, fallow fields and the edges of villages. Often breed in the vicinity of wasps' nests; the assumption is that this affords protection against nest predators.

BLUE-BREASTED WAXBILL *Uraeginthus angolensis*
OTHER NAMES: Cordon-bleu, Angola Cordon-bleu. This species and *U. bengalus* have been treated as forms of a single species. Four subspecies are recognised.

The Blue-breasted Waxbill was considered easier to establish and freer breeding that *U. bengalus*, until the Blue-headed (*U. cyanocephala*) was imported. Currently most aviculturists think that *U. cyanocephala* is more prolific than its congenerics. There have been few importations of *U. angolensis* in recent years.

## Description

115–130 mm (4½–5 in), sexually dimorphic.
COCK: Bill steely grey, mauvish near the base and upper mandible; irides reddish brown; upperparts, except for a blue rump and tail, light greyish brown; face, breast and flanks light blue; centre of the lower breast and abdomen light pinkish buff; legs and feet horn colour.
HEN: Paler and with less extensive blue; there is subspecies variation.

## Distribution and Habitat

From Angola to Tanzania, Zambia, south to the Transvaal. Frequents low herbage, bush and cultivated areas.

BLUE-HEADED WAXBILL *Uraeginthus cyanocephala* **Plate 16**
OTHER NAMES: Blue-headed Cordon-bleu, Blue-capped Cordon-bleu.

A few Blue-headed waxbills were imported into Europe in about 1929/30. The first captive breeding was by Decoux (1931). They were not seen again, at least in the UK, until 1957/58, when a few small shipments arrived and were bred by Goodwin in 1962. From then onwards they have been frequently imported, sometimes in large numbers and for some time were more frequently available than *U. angolensis*. Since the early 1960s they have been bred regularly and are considered to be the most willing breeders of the blue waxbills.

### Description

115–130 mm (4½–5 in), sexually dimorphic.
COCK: Bill pinkish to crimson red; irides reddish brown; entire head blue; rest of upperparts brown; tail blue; upper breast and flanks blue; legs and feet light horn colour.
HEN: The blue areas are paler than those of the cock; lacks the blue head of cock, but sometimes has a little blue on forehead.

### Distribution and Habitat

Ethiopia to Tanzania. More restricted to arid scrub and semi-desert than the previous two species. Like *U. bengalus* will often breed in the vicinity of wasps' nests.

## Grenadiers

The two grenadiers are considered a superspecies, formerly placed in their own genus *Granatina*. It is now generally agreed that they are sufficiently like the blue waxbills to be regarded as congeneric. They are more strictly confined to thorn country than the blue waxbills, with the exception of *U. cyanocephala*, and are found in the more arid areas of Somalia and the Kalahari (Hall and Moreau). They are probably the most exotic looking of all the waxbills and are rather larger than the cordon-bleus. Both species (*U. ianthinogaster* and *U.*

*granatina*) are parasitised by *Vidua* whydahs, the Purple Grenadier by Fischer's (Straw-tailed) Whydah (*V. fischeri*) and the Violet-eared by the Queen (Shaft-tailed) Whydah (*V. regia*). The grenadiers are rather delicate when first imported, and are generally considered to be among the most difficult of the waxbills to establish in captivity. Termites and the seeds of grasses and other plants are the diet of both species in the wild. They are said to be more insectivorous than the blue waxbills and, like their congenerics, are ground feeders, picking up fallen seeds. They both build the usual domed estrildine nest, with an entrance at the side, and the sexes share incubation and feeding of the young. They have been imported fairly frequently, but the shipments are erratic and usually small. I have not bred either species, but the few I have kept thrived on the varied diet described for the waxbills *per se*. They took insectivorous soft food when mixed with small mealworms and maggots, later eating it without these attractions.

PURPLE GRENADIER *Uraeginthus ianthinogaster*
OTHER NAMES: Purple-bellied Waxbill. There are three subspecies.

This species was imported into Europe in 1928 but it was not until well after World War 2 that they were available in any numbers. The first captive breeding was at Keston (UK) in 1957. They were bred in Germany in 1964 and have been bred fairly frequently during the last ten years in Europe and the UK.

## Description

130–140 mm (5–5½ in), sexually dimorphic.
COCK: Bill red or reddish horn; irides reddish brown; orbital ring red with a patch of blue above and below the eye; head, neck and back chestnut brown, darker on the wings; tail black; rump blue; chin and throat russet brown; rest of underparts purple violet, unevenly marked; dark chestnut legs; feet blackish.
HEN: Whitish around eyes; upperparts brown, paler below; breast speckled with whitish and buff spots; rump blue; tail blackish.

## Distribution and Habitat

Somalia, Kenya and Uganda. Inhabits thorn scrub and open bush country.

## Breeding

PERIOD: Kenya, breeding begins March/April. No information for outside aviaries, dates not recorded (two records for inside accommodation), apparently double-brooded in captivity.
NEST: A loosely woven sphere of fine grasses, lined with feathers. Usually sited in low bushes. In captivity a nest box has been used, as have clumps of twigs in an aviary shelter. These nests are of grasses, lined with feathers. Both sexes build.
EGGS: White and glossy. Clutch size 3–5.
INCUBATION: Shared by both sexes, the cock during the day. Incubation period c 13 days.
CHICKS: The nestlings are fed by both parents. They leave the nest at 20–21 days and become independent some 14 days later. On leaving the nest they are earthy brown, darker on the wings and paler below, with short dusky blackish tails and dull blue rumps. They retain, for some time, the small blue nodules at the sides of the gape. The parents are tolerant of the young after they become independent. Their behaviour if a second brood hatches is not recorded. Rearing food has consisted of millet sprays, seeding grasses, ant pupae, mealworms, maggots and egg food, added to the basic seed diet and bread and milk. Small house crickets, buffalo worms, and collected 'wild' live food should also be available.

## Behaviour

From the limited information available they can be aggressive in a mixed collection when breeding, and the few I have kept have been self assertive. With their live food requirements and possible aggressive behaviour, a breeding pair should be housed on their own. They are secretive birds, especially when nesting but are not nervous and become quite 'tame' in aviaries.

VIOLET-EARED WAXBILL *Uraeginthus granatina* **Plate 17**
OTHER NAMES: Common Grenadier, Grenadier Waxbill. Three subspecies are recognised.

The importation and captive breeding results of the bird have had a similar pattern to those of *U. ianthinogaster*, although it was apparently known in Europe as early as 1874. The first captive breeding was in Zurich in 1927 and there have been several since. The first breeding in the UK was in 1936. Like *U. ianthinogaster* they need a varied diet, are insectivorous when breeding, and must be established with care.

Description

130–140 mm (5–5½ in), sexually dimorphic.
COCK: Bill red; irides reddish; orbital ring red; forehead and head blue, continuing in a violet stripe above the eye; rest of upperparts rich brown; rump and uppertail coverts blues; tail black; underparts brown; undertail coverts blue; legs and feet greyish.
HEN: The hen is much paler, especially on the lower abdomen.

Distribution and Habitat

Angola, Mozambique, south to Natal and northern Cape Province. Inhabits arid thornbush country.

**Genus *Estrilda* (Typical Waxbills)**

This genus of 14 to 16 species (depending on which checklist you follow) includes some six or seven species which, with *Lagonosticta* and *Uraeginthus*, constitute a large percentage of the frequently imported African waxbills. The *Estrilda* species differ from other waxbills by feeding when perched and clinging on growing grasses. They are agile and acrobatic, constantly moving their tails with a wagging motion, more frequently and deliberately than other waxbills. However, this agile and lively behaviour is carried out on *growing* plants. Goodwin remarks that *Estrilda* seen clinging to clumps of seeding grasses, hung up in their aviaries by well-meaning owners, are not 'switching their tails from side to side in pleasurable excitement', they are doing it to try and keep their balance.

The plumage of the sexes is alike in the majority of species in this genus and they are difficult to sex visually. As with all my birds, I ring new stock, bred or purchased, with coloured identification rings and this can help with the identification of true pairs. Their nests are specialised and elaborate, and they use their feet to hold down food, which reminds me of the feeding behaviour of the titmouse family. Some of the species, namely the commonly imported Red-eared waxbills (*E. astrild* and *E. troglodytes*), adjust well to captivity and are long lived. They are considered to be hardy enough to be wintered outside without heat or artificial light by some aviculturists, provided that they have access to adequate shelter. In a mild winter in the UK I suppose this is reasonable, but in many areas of Europe and the USA these thin-feathered birds, weighing perhaps 8–10 grams or less, need at least enough heat to prevent their drinking water freezing and an 'extended' day. Even in the comparative warmth of southern England I never leave these birds out later than November, whatever the weather. The *Estrilda* are a fairly homogeneous group which differ little in behaviour and breeding biology. Much is made of their 'seed diet' in the wild, but they also take lots of insects.

In planted aviaries many breedings occur without the owners knowing about them until the young leave the nests. In such cases it is hardly surprising that the young are sometimes reared successfully with little live food provided by the owner, if the competition from other birds for 'natural' live food is limited. As for all waxbills, I provide fruit-fly cultures, white worms, small mealworms, also ant pupae and collected live food whenever possible. With the addition of seeding grasses and soft food, if they will take it, the young can be reared successfully. On a few occasions my birds have reared young with limited live food, but without it or an adequate substitute breeding failures are frequent. Captive birds, like many other waxbills, favour the domed wicker nest basket, with side entrance, as their nesting receptacle. Nest boxes are also used, and free-standing nests are made in bushes and clumps of cut branches. These nests, like those in the wild, are often substantial and include a cock's nest (predator deception nest).

## RED-EARED WAXBILL *Estrilda troglodytes* **Plate 22**

OTHER NAMES: Grey Waxbill, Black-rumped Waxbill, Pink-cheeked Waxbill.

These delightful little birds have been imported in large numbers for many years. Because they were so cheap, few people bothered to breed them, so they were kept in mixed collections for their vivacity and attractive appearance. Usually they travel well, and their plumage remains immaculate unless they are very stressed. Visual sexing is difficult. To obtain true pairs, six birds can be obtained and observed in a cage during their period of isolation and adjustment to a new environment. They are willing breeders and, if housed with unrelated species which do not bully them, will rear two or three broods in a season.

### Description

90 mm (3½ in), sexes alike.
Bill red; irides reddish brown; upper plumage greyish brown, finely barred with dusky brown, with a crimson stripe extending through the eye; underparts light grey; centre of the lower breast and abdomen pink, sometimes extending as a paler pink to the vent; feet and legs light brown.

N.B. The pink on the underparts of a hen is paler and less extensive and the eye-stripe is paler and smaller. This method of sexing suffers from individual variation and I find the vigorous stem display and 'bolder' look and behaviour of the cock a surer guide.

### Distribution and Habitat

Senegal to Ethiopia, in areas of high grass, marshy areas and drier hills, never far from water.

## ST HELENA WAXBILL *Estrilda astrild*

OTHER NAMES: Common Waxbill, or sometimes in ornithological literature just Waxbill. There are 18 subspecies.

This species is one of the larger species in the genus, it is probably the most vivacious in a lively group of birds. A healthy pair are never still in an aviary. The cock gives stem displays, bouncing on a perch, full of excitement, then breaks off to join the hen in catching flying insects or clinging to plant growth, with jerking tails. They are probably the most free-breeding of the genus and are the easiest to establish. If free-standing 'natural' nests are built in an aviary, a cock's nest is often built on top. My birds have sometimes built two or three nests together with a cock's nest. In the wild the cock's nest is lined with feathers while the real nest is unlined, although in my aviaries the reverse has sometimes occurred; the real nest being lined with feathers.

They are more self assertive than most other species in the genus, but unless housed with congenerics, the chasing and bickering is seldom serious enough to disrupt breeding activity. In a compatible group or, better still, on their own in a small aviary, they will rear two or three broods in a season.

Some aviculturists have found that these birds desert easily if their nests are inspected, but I have found them to be tolerant, providing inspection is carried out without causing disruption; the accessibility of the site being the crucial factor. In the wild this species and at least three other *Estrilda* act as hosts to the parasitical Pin-tailed Whydah (*Vidua macroura*). The future availability of *E. astrild* and its congenerics is uncertain, so no opportunity for breeding should be lost.

## Description

115 mm (4½ in), sexes similar.

Bill red; irides brown; crimson stripe through eye; upperparts fawn grey, marked with fine wavy darker lines, with pinkish wash on rump and uppertail coverts; tail dark greyish-brown; chin and throat whitish; rest of underparts grey brown, finely barred with dull whitish and dusky brown; centre of breast and belly red; lower belly and undertail coverts black; legs and feet brown. Hen generally paler; areas of red and black on the underparts less extensive.

## Distribution and Habitat

Wide distribution south of Sahara. Introduced successfully on a number of islands and also in Portugal. Habitat in many areas is grassland, usually close to water, also found in cultivated areas.

## ROSY-RUMPED WAXBILL *Estrilda rhodopyga* **Plate 23**

OTHER NAMES: Crimson-rumped Waxbill, Ruddy Waxbill, Sundevall's Waxbill. There are two subspecies.

This species is also a willing breeder in captivity. Its only disadvantage is the difficulty in selecting a true pair. Importations are not as frequent as those of *E. troglodytes* and *E. astrild*, but on many occasions in recent years they have been more often available than *E. astrild*. They are very similar to *E. troglodytes* in behaviour, vivacious but lacking the more robust self assertiveness of *E. astrild* in a mixed collection. They will often use the 'waxbill' type wicker baskets, or half-open boxes, for their nests and will sometimes build a 'natural' nest low down in a bush or grass clump. The nests are often difficult to find in a planted aviary of any size.

### Description

115 mm (4½ in), sexes alike.
Bill very dark steel colour or black; irides brown; red stripe through eye; upperparts fawn brown with fine wavy markings of darker brown; rump and uppertail coverts crimson; wings brown, the secondaries edged with crimson; chin and throat whitish; underparts greyish buff, marked with fine darker wavy lines on the sides. The hen has crimson areas slightly paler; eye-stripe is sometimes narrower and less extensive. The differences are marginal and visual sexing difficult.

### Distribution and Habitat

The Sudan, Ethiopia and Somalia, Uganda, Tanzania and Malawi. Inhabits grasslands, open country and scattered clumps of bush and old cultivation.

## ORANGE-CHEEKED WAXBILL *Estrilda melpoda* **Plate 21**

There are two subspecies.

This is another commonly imported, attractive little bird which, as with so many formerly very cheap waxbill species, few people bothered to breed. It is still occasionally imported and, in common with many other species, serious attempts to breed them are now more frequent. They are difficult to sex, but I find them easier than many other species in the family which are not sexually dimorphic. In the wild the nests are quite substantial structures and free-standing nests in aviaries are usually large. Only on one occasion have my birds built a small nest. This was in a privet bush about 50 cm (19 in) high, between two vertically growing shoots, a domed structure about 62 mm (2½ in) across and 100 mm (4 in) high. These birds are quite prolific if you have a compatible true pair and will rear two or three broods.

### Description

100 mm (4 in), sexes alike.
Bill red; irides brown; top of head and nape grey; sides of head bright orange; rest of upperparts fawn brown; lower rump and uppertail coverts crimson; tail greyish black; throat whitish; rest of underparts pale grey, fading to whitish at centre of lower abdomen. The hen is generally slightly paler; orange area on sides of head sometimes smaller. Individual variation can be misleading.

### Distribution and Habitat

West Africa from Senegal to the Congo, northern Angola and Lake Chad. Successfully introduced in Puerto Rico. Inhabits grass savannas, grasses bordering river banks, old cultivation and sometimes gardens.

## FAWN-BREASTED WAXBILL *Estrilda paludicola*

This species resembles *E. melpoda*, but lacks the orange on the sides of the head. It is more difficult to establish than *E. melpoda* and is delicate when newly imported. A few small shipments arrive on occasion and they were imported in 1980. The only pair I have ever owned built a nest and laid eggs, but they got no further. They were successfully bred in the UK in 1959.

## LAVENDER FINCH *Estrilda caerulescens*

OTHER NAMES: Lavender Waxbill, Bluish Waxbill, formerly known as *Lagonosticta caerulescens*.

This species, with *E. perreini* and *E. thomensis*, forms a superspecies, the lavender waxbills. The main plumage colour of all three is a beautiful blue-grey. The Lavender Finch has been known in aviculture for many years and is frequently and regularly imported. The Black-tailed Lavender Finch (*E. perreini*) is occasionally imported and resembles *E. caerulescens* apart from a black chin, tail and undertail coverts. The São Thomé Waxbill (*E. thomensis*) is a little known species from Angola and São Thomé island. These species were formerly placed with the fire-finches in *Lagonosticta*.

The Lavender Finch is a lively, attractive bird which is a good breeder if a true pair can be chosen, as the sexes are alike. They are insectivorous and rather delicate birds which are difficult to establish. As with many other species which allo-preen, if kept in the sterile environment of an isolation cage for long periods, feather plucking will occur. The normal preening behaviour becomes stereotyped and large areas of plumage are plucked bare. This can be overcome by limiting the number of birds in a cage and giving them millet sprays, seeding grasses, turves of grass, soil, white-worm culture and leaf mould in which they can hunt for seeds or insects, thus preventing the inactivity which is the cause of the problem. Even when established, these birds should not be wintered outside in colder weather without moderate heat and extended day-length provided with electric lighting. They are not aggressive birds, but when breeding are best housed with unrelated species. The usual waxbill wicker basket is favoured for nesting, sometimes a nest box, also bushes and clumps of gorse or similar cover. Small live food is essential rearing food for the first crucial days after hatching, and my birds have successfully bred on fruit-flies, ant pupae, white worm and small maggots, as well as soft food, seeding grasses and the usual hard seeds.

## Description

115 mm (4½ in), sexes alike.

Bill black, reddish at base; irides brown; lores black, with a small black spot behind the eye. The general colour is bluish grey, with the rump, uppertail and lowertail coverts and tail crimson. There are often a few white dots on the flanks; legs and feet blackish. The hen is slightly smaller and paler in colour.

### Distribution and Habitat

Senegal to the Central African Republic. Inhabits the arid parts of the savanna, the edges of thickets, open areas where the grass is short and grass verges of roads.

## BLACK-CHEEKED WAXBILL *Estrilda erythronotos*

There are three subspecies.

This is one of the less frequently imported species although occasionally shipments are numerous for a season and it has been available in 1989–90. These waxbills are attractive, but not colourful birds, active and lively in an aviary and more arboreal than most *Estrilda* species. The species is considered to be a link between the *E. astrild* group and the lavender waxbills. They are difficult to establish but have been bred on several occasions. The ideal accommodation is a planted aviary with a shelter and artificial lighting and heat available as required. They are a more insectivorous species than some other waxbills and live food is essential for successful breeding.

### Description

115 mm (4½ in), sexually dimorphic.
Bill blackish, or dark steel grey; irides reddish brown; head grey; forehead blackish; upper body ash grey, with fine barring of dusky grey; secondaries and wing coverts barred black and white; rump and uppertail coverts crimson; tail black. Underparts grey, with vinous wash on throat and breast; middle abdomen black; flanks red; vent and undertail coverts black; legs and feet black. The hen has paler red on the flanks and vent and undertail coverts are greyish or brownish grey.

### Distribution and Habitat

From southern Kenya south to Angola and the Cape Province. Inhabits areas of scrub country, also heavier bush growth and trees.

**Genus *Amandava* (Avadavats)**

This genus consists of three species: the African Golden-breasted Waxbill (*A. subflava*), the Asiatic Red Avadavat (*A. amandava*) and the Asiatic Green Avadavat (*A. formosa*). The Golden-breasted Waxbill and the Red Avadavat have been common imports for many years and are free-breeding species in captivity, especially the Red. They are long lived and reasonably hardy once established. The Green Avadavat is less frequently imported and is seldom available, it is also more difficult to establish and often does not travel as well as the other species. Avadavats build the typical domed estrildine nest and lay 4–6 white eggs. Both sexes share building, incubation and the rearing of the chicks.

RED AVADAVAT *Amandava amandava* **Plates 17 and 18**
OTHER NAMES: Red Munia, Bombay Avadavat, Tiger Finch. There are three subspecies, *A.a. punicea* is noticeably smaller than the nominate, the red of the plumage is brighter and the white spotting is heavier. This subspecies is called the Strawberry Finch, Chinese or Cochin Avadavat.

This species is often the first 'exotic' foreign bird to be kept after perhaps an apprenticeship with Zebra Finches or Bengalese. Formerly it was imported into Europe and the UK in vast numbers, especially from the mid-1950s until the late 1960s. During the period small flocks of escaped birds, often in the company of Asiatic munias and African waxbills, could be seen flying about in the sewerage farm and marshy areas outside the perimeter of Heathrow Airport. Although many escaped in the warm weather and obviously lived well on the insects and grass seeds, there was apparently not a single case of these birds or other species surviving a winter. I keep the birds outside from April to November mainly because they often do not start breeding until July/August.

They are free breeders (they have bred in cages) providing they are supplied with enough small live food to rear the chicks. I have bred them with only seeding grasses, fruit-flies and small maggots apart from the basic diet, but this was in a planted aviary so they must have obtained a good deal of their own live food. They are very suitable subjects for establishment as a breeding species in captivity and have been bred for many generations by a few aviculturists. The Red Avadavat was the first really foreign bird I ever bred (in 1949). They are one of the most rewarding birds to keep, the cock having a beautiful nuptial plumage and a pleasant little song. For many years, they were probably the frequent and numerous Asiatic species to be imported. This position has changed in recent years, and they are now seldom available.

## Description

90–100 mm (3½–4 in), sexually dimorphic.
This species is the only estrildine which has a nuptial plumage, the cock bird in eclipse plumage resembles the hen.
COCK: Bill red; irides orange-red; head bright red, except for blackish lores; back and wings brown, with a few small white spots; wing coverts and inner secondaries tipped with white; rump red; uppertail coverts marked with a few white dots; tail blackish, with outer feathers edged white; underparts red, with white spots on the breast and flanks; legs and feet brownish.
HEN: Sides of head, breast and body brownish grey; throat whitish; breast and abdomen greyish buff or yellowish, with few white spots on the wings; lower rump red. The eclipsed cock is more yellowish on the abdomen, which often has blackish markings; a few red feathers are sometimes retained on the head and underparts, also the white spots on the flanks.

This species often becomes melanistic in captivity, some birds becoming almost black except for the red bill. Usually this is due to being kept inside without benefit of sun and rain and on a poor diet of only hard seed. This melanism is not permanent and a cock bird I purchased from a dealer which was almost black, moulted into the normal red after a season in an outside aviary.

## Distribution and Habitat

Wide distribution including the Indian subcontinent, South-east Asia, Burma, China and has been introduced in many areas, including Singapore, Mauritius, Reunion, Fiji and other places. Inhabits dry grasslands, grassy jungle, the reeds and tall grasses of river banks, bush, paddy fields and gardens.

## Breeding

PERIOD: On the Indian subcontinent the breeding season varies with the region and nests may be found at any month of the year, the majority during the rains and early winter. In outside aviaries breeding can commence in April but in my experience imported, established, and even aviary-bred birds often commence nesting as late as September and October and young have left the nest in late November. They are apparently sometimes double-brooded in the wild and two, sometimes three broods have been reared in aviaries.

NEST: A large domed structure, with a side entrance, made of various types of grasses and lined with finer grasses and sometimes feathers. The site is well concealed, low in the bases of thick bushes or reed and grass clumps, seldom higher than 91 cm (3ft) and sometimes practically on the ground (Whistler). Small pieces of burnt wood and charcoal have been found in nests, a behaviour shared with some Australian grass finch species. It has been suggested this controls humidity. In my aviaries I have found small pieces of dried peat and earth in nests and once some tiny stones. Aviary nests with few exceptions are also low in bushes or on the ground in clumps of grass. The favoured receptacle is the waxbill-type nest basket with a side opening. Unlike many estrildines and birds in other families, Red Avadavats seldom nest in the gorse clumps I provide, even if stuck into or laid on the ground. The nest is built by both sexes but the cock seems to play the major role, often bringing material to the nest after the hen is incubating eggs.

EGGS: White. Clutch size 4–5, sometimes 6.

INCUBATION: By both sexes, difficult to be sure of any pattern of sharing. I have observed either sex on the nest during the day at various times. The usual incubation period is 12 days; in my aviaries there have been several 14-day periods recorded, especially later in the year.

CHICKS: The nestlings have a very dark skin with sparse brownish or greyish brown down, the mouth markings are small blackish spots, with whitish nodules at the corner of the gape. Begging calls can be heard a few days after hatching, they are fed by both parents and leave the nest at c20 days. The plumage is light brown, the wings darker brown with two buffy bars, the tail dark brown. Bill very dark horn, almost black; legs and feet a pale flesh colour. The chicks become independent some 12 days after leaving the nest and are fed by the cock if the hen starts another clutch. The cock does not harass them even after the second brood are hatched, but once the young cocks show red feathers they must be separated. Parent Avadavats have been known to feed Golden-breasted Waxbill chicks, when both species are housed together.

### Behaviour

Lively and vivacious, the cock has a bowing display, lowering his head to the left and right sometimes holding a grass stem. They are not very aggressive, but will chase other birds away from their nest site. Red Avadavats should not be housed with other species who have red plumage, such as the Fire-finch (*Lagonosticta senegala*). Out of colour cocks will sing but I have not known them to breed until at least half the nuptial plumage is showing.

## GREEN AVADAVAT *Amandava formosa* **Plate 19**

OTHER NAMES: Green Munia.

This beautiful, predominantly green plumaged waxbill has a limited distribution compared to the Red Avadavat and has never been a common import. The first captive breeding was probably in 1899 and they have been bred on numerous occasions since, but to my knowledge they have not been bred for many generations like *A. amandava*. They have a similar behaviour and breeding biology to the Red Avadavat, but information is limited and they have not been as extensively studied. The cock has a bowing display but a stem is not used. It is generally accepted they are very insectivorous when breeding but given reasonable seclusion and live food they can be as free breeding as *A. amandava*. Green Avadavats can be wintered with moderate heat when established. Newly acquired birds must be established with care and are best released into outside accommodation in late May or June for their first season. Their breeding and care in captivity is the same as for *A. amandava*. There is some evidence that the young of the first brood will help to rear the next if left in the aviary. They were available in 1989–90.

Description

100 mm (4 in), sexes similar.
Bill red; irides brown; sides of head and uppertail coverts yellowish green, rest of upperparts olive green. Paler below, yellow on the breast and abdomen fading to whitish lower abdomen; flanks marked with horizontal white lines on an olive-green background; legs and feet brownish. The hen is generally paler and the flank markings are often ill-defined.

Distribution and Habitat

Central India. Inhabits grassy areas, scrub and cultivation.

GOLDEN-BREASTED WAXBILL *Amandava subflava* **Plate 20**
OTHER NAMES: Orange-breasted Waxbill, Zebra Waxbill. Two subspecies are recognised: *A.s. clarki* has a more southerly distribution and is larger. It is offered on dealers' lists as the Giant Golden-breasted (or Clarke's) Waxbill.

This waxbill is a small bird which, like similar-sized estrildines, must be confined with aviary wire of 12 × 12 mm (½ × ½ in) mesh (minimum) to prevent escapes. These birds have been commonly imported for many years and like its Asiatic relative, the Red Avadavat, they adjust well to captivity and are prolific breeders in an aviary or indoor flight. It has been suggested by some aviculturists that they can be wintered outside without heat or artificial lighting. However, although not delicate birds when established, they are best housed inside in the hard weather and short nights from November onwards unless the aviary has a shelter attached with electricity. In a temperature of about 8°C (45°F) and extended lighting they will winter well. They need small live food for breeding and this, combined with seeding grasses, small soaked and germinated seeds and soft food, is needed for success.

Golden-breasted waxbills have been bred for many generations by a few aviculturists and, like the Red Avadavat, are an excellent species for establishment in captivity, being easy to sex visually, attractive and still frequently imported. For nesting they favour the usual wicker type basket with a side entrance. My birds choose clumps of gorse nailed low down under cover and they prefer a basket fixed in a clump to any other site. They can be housed with other unrelated waxbills and silverbills and in an aviary of reasonable size with cover, two pairs will successfully breed. However, I think the best results are obtained with one pair to each aviary housed with other species.

### Description

90 mm (3½ in), sexually dimorphic.
COCK: Bill red, culmen black, blackish at base; irides reddish brown; red stripe above eye; lores black. Upperparts greenish grey; lower rump and uppertail coverts red; underparts orange-yellow or orange; sides of breast and flanks barred with dark grey; undertail coverts yellow-orange; legs and feet flesh coloured.
HEN: The hen is duller in colour and lacks the red stripe above the eye.

### Distribution and Habitat

Much of Africa south of the Sahara, except the extreme south. Inhabits grasslands, reedbeds and other vegetation near water, also areas of cultivation.

## Grass Finches and Parrot Finches

These birds are probably the most colourful group of seed-eating passerines, especially the Gouldian Finch, which impresses anyone who sees it, especially for the first time. Some species have been established in captivity and the Zebra Finch is domesticated. With a few exceptions, the sexes are alike or the differences are minor and the visual sexing of some species is difficult.

In some cases the stem display of the waxbills has been replaced by ritualized beak wiping, bowing and body shaking. They are typical estrildines in many ways, building domed nests, laying white eggs and the nestlings having the variable gape markings characteristic of the family. The grass finches come from Australia and their export from that country has been banned since the 1st January 1960. Parrot finches have a distribution from Burma to northern Australia; some species, however, are confined to a limited range of island groups or to one island. Several species have been established in captivity and are free breeding.

The group has undergone a good deal of systematic change over the years and some grass finch species such as the Gouldian Finch (*Chloebia gouldiae*), which is currently placed between the parrot finches *Erythrura* and the *Lonchura* mannikins, has been considered a 'link' species. There has probably been more avicultural literature devoted to these birds, especially the grass finches, than to any other passerines and they probably arouse the most controversy. The Gouldian in particular has been the subject of much debate owing to the variability of breeding results obtained from the different captive environments and diets provided.

Parrot finches and grass finches with the exception of the Zebra Finch, are not suitable for the beginner. They have always been more expensive than most other African and Asiatic estrildines even before the ban on the export of native birds by the Australian Government. Captive breedings on the European continent, in the USA, the UK and other areas have ensured that most of the grass finches and several parrot finch species are available.

## Accommodation and Breeding

For the grass finches, especially the Gouldian, most aviculturists currently seem to favour indoor cages or flights, but I think an outdoor aviary with heat and light available is the ideal. If cages are used a *minimum* size of 120 × 41 × 41 cm (4 × 1¼ × 1¼ ft) enables the birds to exercise and keep fit. Both grass finches and parrot finches will use wicker nest baskets with a side entrance, half-open nest boxes of various shapes, domed wire baskets and short funnels with grass in them. With the exception of the Gouldian (*Chloebia gouldiae*), which in the wild breeds in a hole in a tree or termite mound, the other species will also build free-standing domed nests in bushes and other vegetation in a planted aviary, or in clumps of cut branches and twigs; the Gouldian rarely builds a free-standing nest in the wild or captivity. In all species both sexes build the nest, and in most cases the cock collects and carries the material to the site while the hen sits in the nest and builds. Incubation and feeding is also carried out by both parents; the usual clutch size is 4–6 but some species will lay up to 9.

For pairs which prove to be poor parents, many breeders use the domesticated Bengalese Finch (*Lonchura striata*) as foster parents, but this, like so many aspects of Australian Finch breeding has engendered a good deal of controversy. The Gouldian Finch is the main species to be reared by the use of Bengalese, but other grass finches have also been reared by this method. Some aviculturists maintain this is the reason for infertility sometimes occurring in some strains of Gouldian Finches. They also point out the evils of imprinting, that is Gouldians reared by Bengalese 'think' they are Bengalese, and when of breeding age, fail to respond to the reproductive behaviour of other Gouldians. Others say this is not a problem and there is no evidence to suggest such imprinting occurs. Gouldians and other species have been bred under the colony system, and in spite of bickering the results have been quite good; however, if a 'strain' is being established, there is no control over pairing.

## Food and Care

The grass finches in the wild live on grass seeds and flying termites. The Star Finch (*Neochmia ruficauda*) and the Gouldian, (*Chloebia gouldiae*) are among the most insectivorous and take other flying insects besides. The Gouldian becomes almost completely insectivorous when breeding and has been observed at cobwebs waiting for spiders and taking beetles from the ground. The large bills of some of the parrot finch species indicate a specialised feeding behaviour; some are forest birds and fruits, such as figs, appear to be an important part of their diet in the wild.

The captive diet for the group includes a basic seed mixture of millet and canary seed, and ripe and half-ripe grass seed are taken by both grass and parrot finches. High protein food in the form of live food such as mealworms and ant pupae is required during breeding, and for fitness in the long term; I have found some species will also take small house crickets and white worms. Green food both collected and cultivated is taken by most birds, and the diet can be varied still further by giving soft food for rearing, insectivorous mixtures and egg food. The Zebra Finch has reared young on little else but the basic seed and green food, but soft food, soaked and germinated seed, and millet sprays give better results. On the question of live food, individuals vary as well as species; I have kept Heck's Grass Finches which would seldom take live food of any kind whilst others would eat mealworms ad lib. Like so many diverse groups of seed-eating birds, grass and parrot finches have a need for minerals which can be supplied by crushed cuttle-fish bone, mineralised grit, oyster-shell and egg-shells baked in an oven and crushed. Most Gouldian Finch breeders also give charcoal granules.

There seem to be three different schools of thought regarding the question of ambient temperature for these birds. Before I list these I will make two points: The first is that no birds do well in cold, dark, damp and draughty accommodation; the second concerns that frequently heard remark, applied to so many foreign birds, about the temperature falling below freezing in their natural habitat — that is true for many species, but it does not stay below freezing for several weeks as it will in a hard UK winter, or longer in parts of Europe and North America, nor is it combined with a 16-hour night. That said, the three opinions are as follows:

1 Gouldians should always be kept in a temperature of above 21°C (70°F) with a humidity of 70%. Other species should have a minimum temperature of about 16°C (60°F) with the exception of the Zebra Finch.

2 All species should be kept at the above temperatures when *breeding*, but wintering them in such temperatures is unnecessary.

3 Established birds, especially those bred in the UK, Europe and USA, are said to breed and remain fit at temperatures far below those quoted above and with adequate shelter are able to overwinter without heat in regions with mild climates. As far as my own experiences are concerned, I last kept Gouldian Finches in 1956, my initial stock having been imported from Australia. After the birds had been carefully established I bred them in an outside aviary between May and September and wintered them in the house in box cages, with

extended lighting at night. I have kept Heck's Grass Finches, Star Finches and Diamond Firetails under the same conditions, and the first two I now winter in an outside bird room in a temperature of 10°C (50°F) with extended lighting until 20.00 hours. Where new stock is concerned, those bred on the European continent and obtained after a quarantine period I treat with extra care, especially as they are kept at high temperatures for prolonged periods under conditions that create stress. During the winter I keep the sexes separate and, unlike some other foreign birds, do not release them in outside aviaries until the end of May.

### Genus *Emblema*

DIAMOND FIRETAIL *Emblema guttata* **Plate 27**

OTHER NAMES: Diamond Sparrow, Diamond Finch, Spot-sided Finch. Formerly known as *Zonaeginthus guttata.*

This is a beautiful bird which has received the most inappropriate common name. It is certainly nothing like a sparrow or taxonomically related. The ornithological Diamond Firetail Finch is at least descriptive, giving an indication of the bird's beauty. The species was formerly placed in *Zonaeginthus* with two other firetail species and the Painted Finch. These are now removed to *Emblema*, a former monotypic genus comprising the Painted Finch (*E. picta*).

Diamond Firetails have a reputation for obesity due to sluggish behaviour in captivity. Certainly the birds imported to the UK from Australia prior to the ban looked more elegant and shapely than the captive-bred birds now available. This species was first imported into Germany in 1870, but apparently had been available in France before then. They are now bred in captivity in many parts of the world and are frequently available. The temperament of the Diamond Firetail is a matter of some disagreement, opinions vary from 'can be aggressive in mixed company' to 'peaceable'. Cage breeding is a viable method, but in the summer months a small aviary or indoor flight for a single pair will give good results. Most aviculturists consider a temperature of 16°C (60°F) a minimum for wintering this species. One of the most important factors for breeding is compatibility of a pair, a true pair (as with many birds) may not agree or breed.

### Description

115–130 mm (4½–5 in), sexes alike.
Bill red, darker at base; irides reddish brown, with a red ring around eye; head and nape grey; lores black; sides of head whitish; mantle and wings brown; rump and uppertail coverts bright red; tail black; underparts white, with a black band crossing the breast; sides of breast and flanks black, the feathers having a large white subterminal spot; legs and feet brownish grey.

The hens have paler, occasionally brownish lores, and are sometimes noticeably smaller. The orbital eye ring is paler.

### Distribution and Habitat

Western, central and southern central Australia. Inhabits open forest, mallee and grasslands, can be found in gardens and parks. The species is decreasing in numbers owing to destruction of habitat.

## Genus *Poephila*

This genus contains many of the Australian finches which are well known and free breeding in captivity. These species are bred in the UK and captive-bred stock is imported from the European continent and Asia.

STAR FINCH *Poephila ruficauda* **Plate 28**
OTHER NAMES: Red-faced Finch, Red-tailed Finch, Ruficauda, Rufous-tailed Finch. Also *Neochmia ruficauda*. Two subspecies are recognised.

This species was formerly placed in its own genus, *Bathilda*, and is currently listed by some taxonomists in *Neochmia* with the rarely available Crimson Finch (*N. phaeton*). However, I have included it in *Poephila* as aviculturists will look for it in that genus.

The Star Finch is well established and is a free-breeding species in captivity. When imported into the UK from Australia it soon adjusted to life in cages and aviaries and was easier to establish than some of its congenerics. They are very popular birds and a suitable species for newcomers to Australian finches after keeping zebra finches for a time.

They build nests in the usual baskets and half-open nest boxes, and in aviaries, free-standing nests are built in bushes and cut branches. Most pairs will rear broods without live food if supplements of soft food, seeding grasses and soaked and germinated seed are provided. I winter them at a temperature of 10°C (50°F) with extended lighting.

## Description

100–115 mm (4–4½ in), sexually dimorphic.

COCK: Bill red; irides light brown; oribital ring red; forehead to centre of crown, sides of head, lores and throat red, dotted with white spots, more heavily on the ear coverts and throat; upperparts greyish green; uppertail coverts dull red; tail dull reddish, the centre webs brighter red; underparts whitish; base of throat, upper breast and sides of body greenish grey, with white dots; undertail coverts white; legs and feet light flesh colour or very pale brown.

HEN: The plumage is somewhat duller and the red on the face is paler and less extensive, also appears slightly smaller than the cock. A yellow-headed colour mutation has occurred in Australia and is apparently a dilute form, also an albino mutation.

## Distribution and Habitat

North-western Australia to northern and central Queensland. Frequents the grasses and rushes of swamps, rivers and creeks. In the dry season they assemble in huge flocks near areas of surface water including irrigated rice fields.

## LONG-TAILED GRASS FINCH *Poephila acuticauda* **Plate 30**

OTHER NAMES: Long-tailed Finch and, in Australia, Black-hearted Finch or Blackheart. The subspecies *P.a. hecki* is known as Heck's Grass Finch and is distinguished by having a red instead of a yellow bill.

This is another species which is well established in captivity and is readily available. They are not delicate birds but should be wintered with moderate heat and extended lighting and the sexes separated until the breeding season. Some aviculturists suggest they can be wintered without heat but the long, cold, often wet nights are, in my opinion, too much for them, especially for birds obtained from importers. They need the same careful initial care as those caught in the wild and imported from Australia before the ban. Long-tailed Grass Finches are bred in cages and aviaries and although they have been reared without live food, my birds take more live food than other Australian finches I have kept, even when not breeding. They can be aggressive in a mixed collection.

### Description

150–165 mm (6–6½ in), including long central tail-feather spines. Sexes alike.
Bill yellow; irides reddish brown; top and sides of head and neck bluish grey; chin, throat and area of crop black, forming a bib; upper body and wings brown, with white edging on outer primaries; lower rump and uppertail coverts white; tail black with central feathers extending to fine 'spines' or 'bristles'; underparts pale brownish wine colour; legs and feet flesh colour.

The hen has the black bib slightly smaller and appears a smaller bird.

N.B. The tail-feather spines of most current stock available seem to be much shorter than those of the once imported Australian birds. A fawn colour mutation has been bred.

### Distribution and Habitat

Northern and north-western Australia. Inhabits savanna and tree growth near water courses.

## PARSON FINCH *Poephila cincta*

OTHER NAMES: Black-throated Finch. Three subspecies are recognised.

This species resembles the Long-tailed Grass Finch and its care and breeding in captivity is the same. I have not bred this species, but apparently they do not take a lot of live food, and they are considered aggressive in mixed collections. This and *P. acuticauda* are sibling species and their behaviour is almost identical. Both species have a habit of bobbing their heads up and down in varied situations. Immelmann considers this to be the last remnant of a stem display like that of the African waxbills. Like the Masked Finch and the Long-tailed (*P.*

*personata* and *P. acuticauda*), they drink water by sucking. The curious behaviour of placing bits of charcoal in their nests is also shared, but it is found more frequently in the nests of *P. personata*. The Parson Finch is established in captivity and is a free-breeding species in cage and aviary.

### Description

100 mm (4 in), sexes alike.
This species closely resembles its sibling *P. acuticauda*, but its bill is black and the central tail-feather spines are much shorter. The hen Parson has a smaller black bib than the cock.

### Distribution and Habitat

Queensland and the northern part of New South Wales. Inhabits open timbered country with a few high eucalypts and ground cover of grass and scrub.

## ZEBRA FINCH *Poephila guttata* **Plate 29**

OTHER NAMES: Chestnut-eared Finch, Spotted-sided Finch. Formerly placed in its own genus, *Taeniopygia*. Two subspecies are recognised, *P. g. castanotis* is the bird of the Australian mainland.
The Zebra Finch is the commonest of the Australian finches in the wild and captivity. Like other *Poephila* species they drink by sucking, a method which is considered to be an adaption to life in dry, open country enabling them to drink large amounts of water quickly. This means they spend less time at water holes where they are particularly vulnerable to predation. The Zebra Finch is bred in large numbers in many countries and numerous colour varieties have been established. They are vivacious and self-assertive birds which will breed in cages or aviaries and it is one of the most prolific species bred in captivity. For breeding they are best kept in pairs although they are successfully bred in colonies. If this method is used the nest boxes provided must exceed the number of pairs and they should be fixed at the same height, otherwise there will be constant bickering over nest sites. They have been used as foster parents for other seed-eating species, but they are not as good as the Bengalese Finch. The

Zebra Finch is a hardy bird which can be wintered outside in a dry, draught-proof, well-lit shelter, although in a hard winter I think a temperature of about 7°C (40°F) should be provided.

### Description

100–115 mm (4–4½ in), sexually dimorphic.
COCK: Bill coral red; irides reddish brown; crown and nape grey; back and wings greyish brown; tail brown; rump white; uppertail coverts black, with white tips on individual feathers; lores and front of cheeks white, with a black bar edged with white at the base of lower mandible; chestnut brown patch at the side of head; chin to breast finely barred with black and white; flanks chestnut, spotted white; abdomen and undertail coverts white; legs and feet flesh coloured.
HEN: Has no chestnut brown at side of head or flank and no chest markings; throat and upper breast grey without markings; bill paler.

### Distribution and Habitat

*P. g. castanotis* ranges over most of Australia except north-eastern Queensland. *P. g. guttata* inhabits the Lesser Sunda Islands. Found in many varied habitats, grasslands, open savanna, woodlands and any area where artificial water sources, such as bores and tanks have enabled them to extend their range. Also gardens, orchards, parks and areas of cultivation.

## Genus *Aidemosyne*

CHERRY FINCH *Aidemosyne modesta* **Plate 31**
OTHER NAMES: Plum-capped Finch, Plum-headed Finch, Modest Finch, Modest Grassfinch, Plain-coloured Finch.

The Cherry Finch is a monotypic form which has been the subject of dispute with regard to its affinities, some taxonomists listing it with the typical grassfinches. Others have proposed it is more closely allied to the *Lonchura*; Keast (1958) listed it in that genus. In aviculture, the Cherry Finch once had the reputation for being a difficult and delicate species, but that is no longer the case. They have the great advantage of the sexes being visually distinct and they are not aggressive to other species. In my experience, they are more likely to be a victim rather than an aggressor, so I have always kept them in an aviary with a pair of small doves, such as the Masked and Waxbills, e.g. Cordon-bleu and Red-eared. Cherry Finches are very steady birds, which soon settle in new surroundings, and I winter established birds in an outside bird room heated to 16°C (60°F) and given the all-important extended day-length, with electric lighting provided for approximately 14 hours.

## Description

100 mm (4 in), sexually dimorphic.
COCK: Bill black, greyish at base of lower mandible; forehead, crown and chin dark purplish red; hind crown, nape and upperparts dull brown, darker on the wings, with wing and tail coverts edged with white; lores black; sides of face, throat and underparts to tail coverts dull white, with brown barring mainly on the breast and flanks; legs and feet brownish flesh colour, sometimes greyish brown.
HEN: Similar to the cock, but purplish red on chin is absent, or much reduced; the hen is generally slightly paler.

## Distribution and Habitat

The temperate areas of Queensland and New South Wales. Inhabits riparian areas with rank grass and reeds, also open flats with bushes and along the dense growth of watercourses. Locally in cultivated grain fields and gardens; they often visit human habitations, taking crumbs from gardens and verandahs.

## Breeding

PERIOD: In the wild the breeding season is from September to January and at other times when the conditions are suitable. In captivity, breeding in outside aviaries is dependent on when the owner decides the weather, season and other factors are promising. It appears that the majority of birds in the UK are still bred in cages, with environmental control, so the breeding season under this regime is irrelevant.

NEST: Wild birds build a domed nest with a side entrance, but no entrance tube; the material used is green grass stems. Grasses growing nearby are incorporated into the walls of the nest and some nests are lined with feathers. The site is usually less than 1 m (3 ft 3 in) above ground, in a bush shrub, grass clump or other vegetation (Immelmann 1977). Captive birds will build in half open boxes or domed 'waxbill' baskets, but almost any type of box or basket can be used. In an aviary they will also build 'natural' nests in cut branches hung in the aviary and growing plants. Materials used are dry and green grass stems, coconut fibres and feathers.
EGGS: Usual estrildid white eggs. Clutch size 3–7.
INCUBATION: Both sexes incubate by day. The incubation period is 12 days.
CHICKS: The young fledge at 22 days and sometimes return to the nest to roost at night. They are independent of their parents within 14 days of fledging. The immature birds are a lighter brown on the upperparts than the adults, without white markings, except for a few spots on the wings. They lack the purplish red on the head and the underparts are pale buffish brown, with an obscure pattern of spots rather than the barred markings of the adults. The chicks have often been reared on hard and soaked seed, green food, millet sprays etc, without any live food or substitutes such as egg food or insectivorous soft food. However, I have experienced no difficulty in getting my birds to take soft food or live food.

## Behaviour

In an aviary with other birds, they will chase intruders from their nesting site, but this is not persistent, especially in an aviary with adequate cover. They should not be housed with weavers, African mannikins, serins and other potentially aggressive species. The courtship display consists of the cock approaching the hen, with a grass stem held in his bill and the feathers of his bib, cheeks and belly erected; he then bobs slowly up and down without his feet leaving the perch. The stem is then dropped, the cock sings and bill wipes on the perch. This is followed by copulation if the hen solicits. Goodwin (1982) remarks that some males apparently never hold nesting material and the 'form' of the display varies.

## Genus *Chloebia*

### GOULDIAN FINCH *Chloebia gouldiae*

OTHER NAMES: Rainbow Finch, Painted Finch.

The Gouldian Finch has been the subject of much systematic debate (as well as the diet and environment for successful breeding). It has been placed in the genera *Erythrura* (parrot finches) and *Poephila* but is currently placed in its own genus, in a position following *Erythrura*. I have not kept or bred Gouldian Finches since the 1950s and then they were wild birds imported from Australia. They were established in large box cages inside the house with heat and artificial lighting until about 22.00 hours. For breeding they were released in an outside planted aviary which had a shelter with glazed windows and approximately a third of the flight enclosed with old glazed window frames on the roof and sides. Half-open nesting boxes were hung in this area. The birds were not put out until the end of May and only when the weather appeared to be settled. Three pairs bred well but nesting did not commence until early July, sometimes later. Their diet was dry, soaked and germinated seeds, including millets, canary, maw, rape, niger, seeding grasses and green food, wild and cultivated. Collected and purchased live food was provided every day when they were breeding and canary rearing food was given daily. Unless they had chicks in the nest, they were returned to the house for the winter at about the end of September. The birds did well under this regime but there is no doubt the Gouldian is happiest at a high temperature with cold, damp conditions the worst possible. Today in bird rooms with sophisticated heating, humidity and lighting controls and using cage breeding methods, stock is bred to show standards and colour mutations have been obtained, although I must confess that it is difficult to envisage how the colours of this beautiful bird can be changed for the better. My objective was easier to achieve; I just wanted to breed healthy Gouldian Finches.

#### Description

130 mm (5 in), sexes alike.
There are three colour morphs in the wild: the Black-headed,

Red-headed and Yellow-headed. The black-headed form is the most common.
Bill pale pinkish white, with red tip; irides brown; top of head, cheeks and throat black, edged with a narrow light blue stripe; upperparts from upper neck to rump and wings grass green; rump and uppertail coverts greenish blue to blue; tail blackish; breast purplish lilac; rest of underparts yellow, becoming paler, almost white at undertail coverts; legs and feet flesh coloured.

The hen is paler on the breast and underparts. The Red-headed and Yellow-headed morphs have the black areas of the head and red or yellow cheeks.

Distribution and Habitat

Tropical northern Australia. Never found far from water, frequents open grassy plains with groups of tall trees, the edges of mangroves and thickets.

**Genus *Erythrura* (Parrot Finches)**

Several species of parrot finch are established in captivity, and it was generally considered that they are aviary birds and too active, fast flying and nervous to be successfully bred in cages. However, many aviculturists have used cages and Walther Langberg of Copenhagen has been very successful with this method. The Pin-tailed Parrot Finch (*E. prasina*) is without doubt the least known and most difficult species, although once imported in vast numbers.

PIN-TAILED PARROT FINCH *Erythrura prasina*
OTHER NAMES: Pin-tailed Nonpareil; this name is the one most often used in aviculture and importer's lists, which can lead to confusion with the New World Nonpareil (Painted) Bunting (*Passerina ciris*). There are two subspecies.
For many years this bird, which has a wide distribution, was imported into Europe and the UK in large numbers, yet breeding results have been limited. Other species of *Erythrura* with a restricted distribution and often seldom imported by comparison, have been established as breeding species in captivity. I think there are a number of reasons for this: firstly they were too freely available and cheap to buy until the last

few years (imports are now much smaller in number); secondly they had a reputation for being delicate, difficult to establish and 'wean' from the diet of paddy rice on which shipments are fed; thirdly many 'hens' turn out to be immature cocks. (These birds also moult twice a year; for example, of my birds a hen moulted in March and September and the cock in January and July the year after importation.)

I have only known of a few successful breedings in the UK, although they have been bred on the European continent fairly frequently. After trying for six years I managed to get a pair in which both sexes had moulted and were in breeding condition at the same time. The nesting was in an outside planted aviary and, as so often happens, two young left the nest in the morning and that night there was a violent thunderstorm with torrential rain and I found them dead next day. If established with care they are long lived and adjust well to captivity, although they never seem happy in a cage. I have had no trouble changing their diet from paddy rice, mixing it with a canary mixture containing seeds such as rape, linseed, hemp and niger. A supply of paddy rice is continued in a separate dish, although I have found most birds will take little once they are accustomed to a varied diet. Seeding grasses, soaked and germinated seed, millet sprays and green food such as chickweed and cut apples (from which they will remove the seeds) are all taken. Live food is also taken, and they always show interest in the variety of collected live food, but little interest in live food such as white worm; mealworms are always taken. Once established they winter well with moderate heat at 8°C (45°F) and artificial light.

## Description

140 mm (5½ in), sexually dimorphic.
COCK: Bill heavy, upper mandible black, lower dark blackish grey; irides brown; forehead, sides of head and throat blue; lores black; crown to lower back and wings green; uppertail coverts scarlet; tail feathers blackish with scarlet outer edges, central tail feather scarlet and elongated, ending in a fine point; underparts yellowish buff; abdomen scarlet; legs and feet flesh coloured.
HEN: Similar to cock but the blue on the forehead and throat

is absent or the area is small; no red on abdomen; elongated tail feathers are shorter.

### Distribution and Habitat

From Burma through Thailand and Malaysia to Indonesia. Frequents undergrowth or jungle edges, bamboo thickets and rice fields, where it feeds in vast flocks.

### Breeding

PERIOD: In the wild the bird is said to breed in the rainy season. Aviary nestings have begun 'in the spring', my birds began nesting in late May; 2–3 broods have been reared (on the European continent).
NEST: In the wild the typical estrildine domed nest with an entrance hole at the side is built in low bushes and trees, sometimes as high as 18.6 m (60 ft). The nest is made of dry leaves and fibres on an underlay consisting of grasses and small roots (Robiller). Aviary nests are usually made of dried grasses lined with finer grasses; straw, sisal, coconut fibres and moss have also been used. They seem to prefer to nest as high up in the aviary as possible and my birds built in nest boxes, except for the nearly successful breeding, which was in half of a damaged lobster pot, hung up near the roof of the aviary, about 2.4 m (8 ft) high. All the nests built by my birds were of grasses and other stems lined with a few finer grasses.
EGGS: White. Clutch size 3–5, rarely 6.
INCUBATION: Carried out by both sexes, the cock and hen will sit in turn during the day and it appears the hen sits at night. Incubation period 13–14 days.
CHICKS: The nestlings are flesh coloured and naked; the chicks are closely brooded for the first seven to eight days and are fed by both parents. They leave the nest at about 22–24 days and become independent some 14 days later. They can be left with the parents until the next brood hatches, or until the young cocks start to show red feathers, at which time the cock parent might harass them. The plumage of the young birds is mainly pale grey on the upperparts, faintly tinged with green on the back, the primaries are blackish grey with a slight greenish tinge on the outer edges. The tail is short, grey in colour, underparts brownish grey, turning yellowish on the flanks,

undertail coverts whitish; the bill is blackish, dark greyish on the lower mandible; legs and feet flesh colour.

Behaviour

Like other *Erythrura* species, Pin-tailed Parrot Finches are active and fast flying birds and rather nervous in a cage until they are well established. In an aviary my birds were secretive at first, hiding in privet bushes when the aviary was approached. Housed with *Lonchura* mannikins in a planted aviary, they were not aggressive, but dominant at the feeding sites. Only one pair of this species should be kept in an enclosure, but with unrelated species (other than waxbills) no problems should arise. Birds such as the larger weavers, which may well bully them, are not suitable companions.

The sexes frequently bill-fence at the beginning of pair-bonding, then later the cock will approach the hen on a perch, sidling up to her with his tail twisted towards her. When close he will arch his neck and stretch it over her head; afterwards he will mandibulate, rapidly opening and closing his beak and making an audible noise. The species has a stem display, the stem being held crossways in the bill, and the head bobbed in the manner of the Long-tailed Grass Finch (*Peophila acuticauda*). The cock will also make 'abbreviated' bows to the left and right (the head is only slightly lowered).

BLUE-FACED PARROT FINCH *Erythrura trichroa*

OTHER NAMES: None valid, those sometimes used are also listed for other species of *Erythrura*.

The Blue-faced Parrot Finch is well established in captivity and bred frequently in cages and aviaries in many European countries, the UK, USA and South Africa. This consolidation has escalated during the last 10 years; certainly this species, in common with other *Erythrura*, was once regarded as too nervous for cages and only suitable for aviaries. However, if space is available, I think all non-domesticated species are best kept in aviaries. Even in small outside aviaries you have at least a partial chance of reproducing some 'natural' conditions. There is a better opportunity to observe the birds and record their behaviour. Evans and Fidler (1990) record that *E. trichroa* are such excellent parents that they have been used as foster parents for more 'difficult' species.

I winter established birds with heat and the usual 14-hour extended day, provided by electric light. Apart from hard and soaked seed, they are given green food, millet sprays and insectivorous mixture and live food. The birds will take mealworms, wax-moth larvae and small house crickets, but have shown no interest in buffalo worms or white worms. As found with Pin-tailed Parrot Finches, they will take cut apples, if firmly fixed; they remove and eat the seeds first.

### Description

115 mm (4.5 in), sexually dimorphic.
COCK: Bill black; irides dark brown; forehead and sides of face blue; upperparts dark green; upper tail coverts and rump red; throat and underparts a lighter green; legs and feet are brownish.
HEN: Blue on the face is paler and less extensive and general plumage duller, but these differences can be masked by subspecific variation.

### Distribution and Habitat

*E. trichroa* has a wide geographic range, extending from north to south from the Caroline Islands to the north-east tip of Australia and from west to east from the Celebes to Vanuatu (Evans and Fidler 1990). Found at varying elevations in different parts of its range. Inhabits forest, where there are clearings, forest edge, secondary growth, grassland, cultivated areas, plantations. Also, for feeding purposes, playing fields, pastures and airfields.

## Mannikins and Munias

This group of birds has a distribution from Africa, India, south and east to Australasia. Their breeding biology and behaviour is typically estrildine, building domed nests with an entrance hole at the side and laying white unmarked eggs. The nestlings have distinctive mouth markings of horse-shoe shape, dark lines or dark blotches. Unlike many waxbills, the parrot finches, and to a lesser extent the grass finches, sexual dimorphism in this group is rare, the African *Amadina* species — the Cut-throat and Red-headed finches — being well-known exceptions.

Mannikins and munias are attractive, but lack the bright colours of many waxbills, grass finches and parrot finches. They travel well, even in a crowded transit cage most species seem to retain their immaculate plumage. For many years they were imported into Europe in vast numbers and are still available. Although some species are domesticated (the Bengalese Finch and the white mutation of the Java Sparrow), and others can be considered established as a captive breeding species (the silverbills), breeding results for many species are infrequent considering the numbers imported. This is due to their comparative cheapness, lack of bright colours and the fact that in most cases visual sexing is difficult, if not impossible. They are certainly not among the world's main songsters — the 'song' of many species is inaudible at any distance.

Their care and breeding in captivity differs little from the other estrildine groups except that in general they are more tolerant of environmental change. They adjust readily to captivity and are relatively easy to acclimatise. Many aviculturists winter *established* birds in adequate shelters without heat. I personally think that from November onwards, in the UK, they should have at least enough heat to prevent their water from freezing and an extended day length provided by artificial lighting. If these conditions are met, the birds seem to come through the winter fitter and attain breeding conditions sooner. In colder parts of the world heat and lighting is essential.

The diet of this group is basically the same as that of other estrildines, although more species rear their young in captivity without live food or with very little. The problem of sexing can be overcome by releasing six or more birds in the same aviary as they are with a few exceptions sociable birds, and serious aggressive behaviour is rare. However, colony breeding has a disadvantage, as there is evidence that in some species (such as the Java Sparrow) only the dominant pair will breed. Most species will use the large size 'foreign finch' wicker nesting basket with side entrance, or a half-open nesting box. Java sparrows will use budgerigar nesting boxes or the half-open type. Some species are bred in cages but apart from those that are domesticated or established, aviaries are preferable. Mannikins and munias have been a rather neglected group in aviculture, for although most species lack bright colours, with a few exceptions they make good companions for many other birds which are not territorial.

## Genus *Lonchura*

### AFRICAN SILVERBILL *Lonchura malabarica cantans* **Plate 32**

OTHER NAMES: In common with the Indian Silverbill (*L. malabarica malabarica*), they are often called White-throated munias. The 'African' and 'Indian' silverbills are now considered subspecies, the nominate Asiatic *L.m. malabarica* with the two African subspecies *L.m. cantans* and *L.m. orientalis* constituting a single species. They were formerly placed in the now defunct genus *Euodice*. I have retained them as two separate forms, for aviculturists will look for them with this status and they can be readily distinguished.

Both subspecies are long known in aviculture and have been imported regularly for many years. Currently the African Silverbill is readily available; the Indian, in common with other species whose distribution includes the Indian subcontinent, is not so frequently imported. Both subspecies are quietly coloured little birds, free breeding and adjusting well to captivity. Like other *Lonchura* species visual sexing is difficult, although one can listen for the song of the cock and watch for the stem display. They have been used as foster parents for other more 'difficult' species, but the results have not been as successful as those from using the Bengalese Finch. In the wild their choice of nesting sites are varied both in the Ethiopian and Asiatic regions. They are confiding birds and are often found in gardens and villages, sometimes nesting in walls and thatched roofs. More natural sites are thorn bushes, scrub jungle and long grass. They will also use the old nests of other birds. The domed nest is large compared to the bird's size. The usual clutch size is 5–8, but often more than one hen will lay in the same nest and as many as 25 eggs have been found in one nest.

In captivity silverbills will breed in cages and aviaries. I have found them suitable companions for other birds, including waxbills, and they are suitable birds for beginners in aviculture. Their only vice is they will often try to take over the occupied nest of another pair of birds and this can result in disruption. They will rear young without live food, but small live food is taken if provided, by most pairs.

Description

100–115 mm (4–4½ in), sexes alike.
Bill bluish grey; irides reddish brown; upperparts pale sandy brown, faintly barred and darkest on the wings; uppertail coverts and tail blackish; throat whitish, rest of underparts very pale light brown; legs and feet flesh colour.

Distribution

Northern tropical Africa, Senegal, Tanzania, south-western Arabia.

INDIAN SILVERBILL *Lonchura malabarica malabarica*

Description

100–115 mm (4–4½ in), sexes alike.
Bill lead grey, lighter on lower mandible; irides brown. Forehead to rump light brown; rump and lower tail coverts white, with black edges to outer feathers; sides of head and underparts fawn; legs and feet flesh colour.

Distribution

From Muscat and south-eastern Iran through the Indian subcontinent and Sri Lanka.

GREY-HEADED SILVERBILL *Lonchura griseicapilla*
OTHER NAMES: Pearl-headed Silverbill. This species was formerly placed in its own genus Odontospiza (*O. caniceps*).

The avicultural history of this species is similar to that of the Blue-headed Waxbill (*Uraeginthus cyanocephala*). Both were first imported into the UK in small numbers in the 1930s and were not available again until the late 1950s or early 1960s. The first successful captive breeding for *L. griseicapilla* was in 1963. They have been frequently imported since then and have been available in 1989–90. Breedings have been fairly frequent since 1963, although they are not as easy to breed as the Common Silverbill; they appear to be more insectivorous and the best breeding results are obtained when live food and rearing food supplements are provided. They do not adjust to environmental change as readily as many other *Lonchura* species and should be established with care. I winter established birds with a minimum temperature of 10°C (50°F) and with artificial lighting until 20.00 hours.

### Description

100–115 mm (4–4½ in), sexes alike.
Bill, upper mandible dark grey, lower lighter grey; irides blackish; head grey; sides of face and throat speckled with white; upperparts brown; rump and uppertail coverts white; wings brown, with the primaries and secondaries black; tail black; underparts vinous brown, growing paler on the lower abdomen; legs and feet dark horn colour.

N.B. As first noted by Landberg, the chest plumage of cock birds is noticeably darker.

### Distribution and Habitat

Southern Ethiopia to Tanzania. In arid thornbush country.

### Breeding

PERIOD: Nesting commences in May/June in Kenya. In outside aviaries in the UK nest building starts in May/June. Two or three broods are reared.

NEST: In the wild a rather untidy domed nest made of grasses and lined with feathers, with side entrance hole, is built in a tree. In captivity I have found they will use domed wicker baskets and half-open boxes. They also share the Common Silverbill's behaviour of taking over the old and occupied nests of other birds, but (so far) they have not tried to evict the rightful owners of an occupied nest. My birds have used dried and sometimes green grass stems for the nest, with feathers the favourite choice for lining. The nest is built by both sexes,

although the cock seems to gather most of the material.
EGGS: White and unmarked. Clutch size 4–6.
INCUBATION: Carried out by both sexes; it would appear the hen sits at night, but both birds spend a good deal of time in the nest and the share of incubation by the sexes is difficult to ascertain. Period 13–14 days.
CHICKS: The nestlings are pink-skinned with little down; the gape flanges are bluish white and unlike many estrildine species have no papillae at the gape commissures. They are fed by both parents and leave the nest at 20–22 days and are fed for a further 14–16 days. The immature plumage is a duller version of the adult's, and on leaving the nests the chicks lack the white markings on the sides of the face and throat.

### Behaviour

The cock has a stem display similar to that of the waxbills, but the stem is held crossways in the bill in munia fashion. Feathers are also frequently used in this display, for which the feather is held in the bill by the quill end (much as waxbills hold the stiff end of a grass stem). Bill fencing and the tail-twist postures are among the frequently seen behaviour common to estrildines. Landberg remarks that he saw a cock bird carrying beakfuls of sand to a nest containing young. I have frequently observed the adults carrying pieces of dried earth to the nest after the chicks have hatched. These birds are not aggressive and they have bred in the company of *Uraeginthus* and *Estrilda* waxbills without conflict.

## African Mannikins

The three species included here are occasionally imported and although typical of the *Lonchura* species in behaviour and breeding biology, most authors have found them to be more aggressive in mixed company than the silverbills or Asiatic munias. The only species I have bred, the Bronze-winged Mannikin (*Lonchura cucullata*) proved to be self-assertive and prone to 'explore' the nests of other birds (with a view to a roosting or nesting site). This often causes disruption, but overt aggression is rare. When a small 'flock' of six Bronze-wings are released into an aviary, it is always amusing to 'find' their chosen site; often within an hour, six little heads will peer out of a basket or nest box as you approach. However, if lots of nesting receptacles and sites are provided, the conflict is minimal. A small aviary containing the mannikins and a species they will not worry, such as a pair of doves or sparrows such as the Golden Sparrow (*Passer luteus*), may be the wisest policy. African mannikins were formerly placed in the now defunct genus *Spermestes*. Due to the similarity of their common name they are sometimes confused with the rarely imported and brightly coloured manakins (Pipridae) which are 'soft-billed' birds of American tropical and subtropical forests.

BRONZE-WINGED MANNIKIN *Lonchura cucullata*

OTHER NAMES: Bronze Mannikin. Two subspecies are recognised.

The Bronze-winged Mannikin is the most frequently imported of the African *Lonchura* species. Because of this, their lack of bright colours, and problems of sexing, breeding results are infrequent considering the numbers imported — factors shared with most of the mannikin-munia group. This species should not be kept with waxbills or any birds which cannot resist the mannikins' self-assertive behaviour. For breeding they will utilise practically any sort of basket or box. A small flock will sort themselves out into pairs, and the use of coloured rings can help to identify true pairs which can then be isolated. Once established they are prolific breeders and three to four broods can be reared in a season. They have been bred without live food, but my birds take maggots and small mealworms when breeding, even in a planted aviary.

Description

90 mm (3½ in), sexes alike.

Bill, upper mandible dark horn, lower pale bluish grey; irides brown; head and neck black with a greenish sheen; nape mantle and wings greyish; uppertail coverts barred greyish and black; tail black; small patches on the wing scapulars and the sides of breast blackish, with a green tinge; underparts white; flanks greyish brown, with indistinct white stripes; legs and feet blackish.

Distribution and Habitat

From the west coast of Africa to the Sudan and from Ethiopia south to Angola and the Cape Province. Inhabits savanna and forest clearings, gardens, cultivated and waste land near towns and villages.

BLACK AND WHITE MANNIKIN *Lonchura bicolor* **Plate 33**

There are six subspecies, one of which, the Rufous-backed Mannikin (*L.b. nigriceps*) is quite distinct in plumage and has been considered a species. This subspecies is also called the Red-backed Mannikin and has the mantle, wing coverts and inner secondaries chestnut brown, sometimes with an indistinct blackish wash.

The Black and White Mannikin has a reputation for aggressive behaviour in mixed company and, unlike the Bronze-winged Mannikin, is rather nervous and does not settle well in a cage. Opinions on the Rufous-backed subspecies are varied; some consider it aggressive and others have found it compatible in a mixed collection, breeding without serious conflict and steady in a cage. I have kept them in mixed company in aviaries and cages and found *L.b. nigriceps* to be far less aggressive then the Bronze-winged. However, I have not bred them, and breeding pairs are often a different proposition. From the information available, the best results are obtained when seeding grasses, live food and other supplements are provided.

Description

90 mm (3½ in), sexes alike.
Bill lead grey, lighter on the lower mandible; irides brown; head and neck black, with a greenish sheen; back and wings black, with indistinct white marks on inner primaries; rump, lower tail coverts and tail black; underparts white; flanks black, with a few white markings; legs and feet blackish.

Distribution and Habitat

Fernando Pó and Africa south of the Sahara to Angola and Natal, Zanzibar, Pemba and Mafia. Inhabits open country, forest clearings and cultivation seldom in the vicinity of habitation.

## MAGPIE MANNIKIN *Lonchura fringilloides*

This species is easily distinguished from other mannikins by its larger size and longer, rather heavy bill. They have been bred fairly frequently on the European continent in outside and indoor aviaries, and have been bred in cages. Once established they are fairly hardy birds. The one pair I have kept will 'see off' other birds with a jab of their powerful bills, and the reputation the species has for aggressive behaviour when breeding appears to be justified. Except for one record (which took place in a planted outside aviary), live food and supplements have been provided for breeding pairs.

### Description

115 mm (4½ in), sexes alike.
Head, neck, rump, uppertail coverts and tail black; mantle brown, with black centres to feathers; wings dusky; underparts white, with a black mark on the sides of breast and ill-defined black and rusty-brown markings on the flanks; legs and feet greyish.

### Distribution and Habitat

Senegal to Somalia, south to Natal. Found in open grassy country and areas of cultivation.

## Asiatic Munias

There are four Asiatic *Lonchura* species which have, in the past, been imported into the UK in large numbers and are still frequently available in small numbers. They adjust readily to captivity, but are rather nervous in a cage and are best kept in aviaries. Once established they are hardy and long lived and when breeding are not aggressive. The sexes are alike and often when breedings occur in a mixed collection the first knowledge of the event is when the young birds leave the nest. In the wild they feed by clinging to growing grasses, crops, and take seeds and insects from the ground. Their claws are naturally rather long and in the wild are kept under control by the wear involved in clinging to growing grasses and crops. In captivity the claws must be regularly checked and clipped when required, otherwise they can become caught on cage fronts and in aviary mesh. This happens with other munia and mannikin species, but the Asiatic *Lonchura* species seem especially prone to overgrown claws. These munias will nest in half-open nest boxes, baskets and clumps of cut branches, and free-standing domed nests are built in bushes and other growing plants. They need a varied diet for rearing young, including seeding grasses, and soaked and germinated seed. Live food will be taken and although young have been reared without it, the breedings in question have often been in an outside planted aviary where natural live food must have been available. The White-backed Munia (*L. striata*) apparently feeds its young entirely on live food in the wild, yet will seldom take live food in captivity.

WHITE-BACKED MUNIA *Lonchura striata*

OTHER NAMES: Striated Munia, White-rumped Munia, Sharp-tailed Munia. There are six subspecies varying slightly in colour and overall length.

This munia is the wild ancestor of the domesticated Bengalese Munia or 'Finch' as they are called. Like many other related species they cause considerable damage to crops in many areas of their distribution. They are not colourful birds but have a longer tail than other *Lonchura* species which tapers to a point and this gives them an elegant appearance. The domesticated Bengalese variety is thought to have originated in China and was brought to Japan in about 1700. A number of colour mutations have evolved. Because of its use as a very successful foster parent for Australian grass finches and other estrildines, the Bengalese Finch is one of the best known passerines in aviculture. The wild birds have frequently been bred in aviaries but do not adjust well to life in a cage.

## Description

115 mm (4½ in), sexes alike.

Bill, upper mandible blackish, lower dark grey; irides brown; forehead, lores, sides of head and neck dark brown or blackish brown; back and wings greyish brown; rump white; tail black; underparts white except for flanks and undertail coverts which are brownish grey; legs and feet bluish grey.

### Distribution and Habitat

The Indian subcontinent, Sri Lanka, South-east Asia, southern China, Taiwan, Banka Island, the Andamans and Nicobars.

## SPICE FINCH *Lonchura punctulata*

OTHER NAMES: Nutmeg Munia, Spice Bird. Eleven subspecies are recognised.

This is another species which has a wide Asian distribution. They adjust well to life in aviaries. I have kept them with waxbills and other small estrildines and found them retiring and peaceable. If six birds are housed together to establish true pairs, there is no serious conflict. They will nest in baskets and half-open nest boxes, and free-standing nests are built in cut branches and bushes. Once a pair built their nest in the top of a mound of dead leaves and grasses placed in the aviary as a source of live food, and it was discovered only when I began to turn the mound over after leaving it for a couple of weeks. Luckily the sitting bird flew out just as I began to move the mound with a fork. These birds seem to take live food more readily than other munias, even when not breeding. The Spice Finch is prolific, and would make an excellent subject for establishment in aviculture.

### Description

115 mm (4½ in), sexes alike.
Bill bluish-grey; irides brown; head, back, wings and tail brown, slightly reddish brown on the head; rump, uppertail coverts and central tail feathers yellowish brown or light brown; breast and flanks white, covered with brown to black scaly markings; lower abdomen and undertail coverts white; legs and feet bluish grey.

The Philippine subspecies, *L.p. cabanisi*, which used to be available fairly frequently, is much paler and a noticeably smaller bird.

Distribution and Habitat

Indian subcontinent, Sri Lanka, South-east Asia, southern China, Taiwan and Hainan, through Greater and Lesser Sundas to the Celebes and Philippines. Established in Australia from aviary escapes.

CHESTNUT MUNIA *Lonchura malacca* **Plate 34**
OTHER NAMES: Tri-coloured or Three coloured Nun. In current systematic lists, it will be found as the Chestnut Mannikin or Munia, or Black-headed Munia. This last common name was used for the subspecies *L.m. atricapilla* which was formerly considered a species. There are ten subspecies recognised.

This munia is an attractive bird which shares with other *Lonchura* species the immaculate plumage which makes them look so elegant. They are less inclined to use nesting receptacles than other munias, and a free-standing nest will be built if suitable cover is provided such as bamboo or, if possible, reeds. They will take live food readily when breeding, but have reared young with little provided.

Description

115 mm (4½ in), sexes alike.
Bill light grey; irides brown; head and neck black; upperparts chestnut; reddish brown on rump and uppertail coverts; underparts white, except for the lower abdomen, vent and undertail coverts which are black; legs and feet dark grey.

The subspecies *L.m. atricapilla* is chestnut brown on the entire underparts.

Distribution and Habitat

India and Sri Lanka, South-east Asia, Sumatra, Taiwan, the Philippines, Celebes and Java. Inhabits grasslands, reedbeds, paddy fields and other cultivation.

WHITE-HEADED MUNIA *Lonchura maja*
OTHER NAMES: Maja Munia, Pale-headed Munia or Mannikin; white or pale-headed forms have been included with *L. maja* as subspecies but are now regarded as good species.

The White-headed Munia in captivity is very similar to the Tri-coloured. It prefers to build a free-standing nest where suitable cover is provided and has reared young with little or no live food, if a varied diet, including seeding grasses, germinated seed and green food is available.

### Description

115 mm (4½ in), sexes alike.
Bill bluish-grey; irides dark brown; head, throat and nape white; upperparts chestnut; wings brown; primaries blackish brown; rump and uppertail coverts lighter; lower breast, abdomen, thighs and undertail coverts black; flanks dark chestnut; legs and feet brownish grey.

There is some indication that the hens have duller white on the head, throat and nape and the white area is less extensive.

### Distribution and Habitat

Malaysia, Sumatra, Simeulue, Nias, Java and Bali. Frequents grasslands and cultivation, especially rice fields.

## CHESTNUT AND WHITE MUNIA *Lonchura quinticolor*

**Plate 35**

OTHER NAMES: Five-coloured Mannikin, Five-coloured Munia, Chestnut and White Mannikin.

This Munia is another of the *Lonchura* species which were seldom imported, but have been available fairly frequently in recent years. They have been bred on the European continent and in the UK on several occasions; the first UK breeding was in 1981 (Green 1986). Like most *Lonchura* species they adjust well to captivity and thrive on a good seed diet, with green food and seeding grasses in season.

### Description

115 mm (4.5 in), sexes alike.
Bill bluish grey; irides dark brown; forehead crown, nape and face dark chestnut; throat dark brown; mantle, back and wing coverts a lighter chestnut brown; tail and upper tail coverts light reddish brown; under tail coverts black; rest of underparts below the throat are white; legs and feet grey.

### Distribution and Habitat

The Timor and Lesser Sunda Islands. No information on habitat preference.

### Breeding

PERIOD: Captive birds in outside aviaries have bred from the Spring to the Autumn; two broods (possibly three) have been reared in a season.
NEST: Elliptical in shape and made of dried grasses. Built in various sites: a nest box, ball of wire and a clump of seeding grasses. This site was 1.2 m (4 ft) from the ground (Green 1986).
EGGS: Usual white eggs. Clutch size 5–6 (few records as yet).
INCUBATION: The usual estrild pattern: the sexes sharing incubation by day, the hen sitting at night. Period 14 days.
CHICKS: The chicks are brooded by their parents for 10 days and leave the nest at 21 days. At this stage they are a dull buffish grey, with some dull white on the abdomen. Chicks have been reared on soaked seed, small maggots, egg food and green food.

### Behaviour

Green (1986) remarks that these mannikins have not been observed to clump (perching or sitting in contact) or allopreen. His birds always kept a few inches distance from each other, except when the cock displays.

## JAVA SPARROW *Lonchura oryzivora* **Plate 36**

OTHER NAMES: Rice Bird, Paddy Finch, Rice Munia. Synonym *Padda oryzivora*.

The Java Sparrow is probably the most colourful species in the munia-mannikin group. The plumage always has a subtle 'sheen' which is only lacking in a *very* sick bird. A domesticated white mutation has long been established and a cinnamon (fawn) mutation was first bred in Australia and has been bred in Europe recently. The wild 'grey' bird is, to my mind, the most attractive and until about 10–12 years ago was considered difficult to breed. There is little doubt that this was because they were housed in pairs and needed contact with conspecifics. Better results have been obtained with a colony system, although there is some evidence that only the dominant pair will breed under these conditions. I have found a single pair will sometimes fail to breed or only make half-hearted attempts, but if conspecifics are in visual and auditory contact they will breed. This method has the advantage of stimulating breeding without housing more than one pair together.

In the wild they will nest under the eaves of buildings, in holes in buildings or trees and will build domed free-standing nests in bushes and trees. The white mutation will breed in cages, as will the wild grey although this is best kept in aviaries. Suitable nesting receptacles are budgerigar-type boxes or half-open boxes. The usual budgie box is a little on the small side, as Javas usually like to use a lot of material such as dried grasses and other plant stems. Young are often reared without live food providing a varied diet, including germinated soaked seed, green food, soft food and a variety of minerals are provided. I always supply live food even though my birds are housed in outside aviaries, and they take a good deal when breeding. The white mutation will rear young on hard, soaked and germinated seed with green food. Java Sparrows should not be kept with waxbills, but can share an aviary with the most self-assertive birds which seldom, if ever, nest in boxes. The smaller *Euplectes* weavers such as the Napoleon (*E. afer*) make suitable companions.

Description

130–140 mm (5–5½ in), sexes alike.
Bill large, pinkish red, lighter at the edges and the tip; irides reddish brown; orbital ring reddish; entire head black with a large white cheek patch; upperparts bluish grey; rump, uppertail coverts, tail and primaries black; underparts bluish grey, shading to pale pinkish grey on the lower abdomen; undertail coverts and thighs white; legs and feet flesh coloured.

N.B. The cock in breeding condition has the base of the upper mandible swollen, often becoming a deeper red in this area.

## Distribution and Habitat

The original distribution is thought to have been Java and Bali. It has been introduced, or become established, from captive escapes in many regions. These include Sumatra, Borneo, Lombok, the Malay peninsula, southern China, Taiwan and the Philippines. In the Ethiopian region it is established on Pemba, Zanzibar, the East African coast and St Helena.

## TIMOR SPARROW *Lonchura fuscata*

OTHER NAMES: Brown Rice Bird, Brown Mannikin, Timor Finch. Synonym *Padda fuscata*.

This close relative of the Java Sparrow was bred for the first time in the UK in 1960 (Martin 1961). Martin first saw the species in the collection of G. H. Gurney; this was in 1928, which was probably the year of their first importation. They have been bred in Germany to the fourth generation, and have also been bred in the UK since the first occasion. The reports indicate that *P. fuscata* could be as prolific as the Java Sparrow; one pair reared 19 young in three consecutive broods. In captivity, they will breed when kept in flocks, the pairs breeding in synchrony.

The Timor Sparrow has been imported into Europe and the UK quite often in recent years and they were available in 1989–90. The information on their feeding, general habits and voice, has been obtained from captive studies (Goodwin 1982). There is apparently little information on their displays or social behaviour, thus presenting yet another opportunity for the aviculturist. Breeding in captivity seems to present few problems (except that the sexes are alike). They have nested in Budgie nest boxes using hay, moss, bits of paper, feather and coconut fibres. They have, on at least one occasion, reared young without live food, using hard seed, seeding grasses and chickweed. Adults in captivity have been observed to eat mealworms and possibly insectivorous soft food.

## Description

130 mm (5.0 in), sexes alike.
Bill pale blue-grey; irides dark brown; orbital eye rim bluish

grey; upperparts chocolate brown shading to black on the head; cheeks white; breast chocolate brown, separated from white underparts by a narrow black band; legs and feet are grey.

Distribution and Habitat

Timor and Samau Island. There is apparently no information on their habitat.

**Genus** ***Amadina***

The two munias in this African genus, the Cut-throat Finch (*A. fasciata*) and the Red-headed Finch (*A. erythrocephela*), are distinguished by being sexually dimorphic and together form a superspecies. Both species are often in the vicinity of human habitation and will nest under the eaves and in holes in buildings. They will also use the nests of weavers and other birds.

CUT-THROAT FINCH *Amadina fasciata* **Plate 25**
OTHER NAMES: Ribbon finch. There are three subspecies; *A.f. alexanderi* is a slightly larger bird with darker and more defined barring. In dealers' lists they are called Alexander's or East African Cut-throats.

The Cut-throat is a hardy and free-breeding bird once adjusted to a new environment and could easily be established as a captive-breeding species. They are lively, active and are still frequently imported. This species has many avicultural virtues, its only disadvantage is its aggression when breeding. They should only be housed with birds such as weavers which are self-assertive and have different nesting habits. Plenty of baskets and half-open nesting boxes should be provided because in the wild and captivity this bird will take over the nests of others, giving the rightful owners a hard time. I have bred them in mixed company without trouble, but I always put up plenty of cut gorse branches and provided a minimum of four nesting receptacles for each pair of birds. They will rear young on a varied diet without live food, but I have found them very insectivorous, even when not breeding. The Cut-throat has been bred in cages quite frequently, although better results are obtained in aviaries.

Description

115–130 mm (4½–5 in), sexually dimorphic.
COCK: Bill pale horn colour; irides brown; upperparts greyish fawn, barred and speckled with black; rump and uppertail coverts pale brown; wings greyish to yellowish brown; tail black, outer feathers tipped with white; a red band crosses throat to sides of head; underparts pale fawn or pinkish fawn, with a chestnut patch on abdomen; flanks have ill-defined black barring; legs and feet flesh colour.
HEN: Lacks the red throat band, plumage paler and the chestnut patch on underparts is absent or vestigial.

Distribution and Habitat

The semi-arid country from Senegal to the Sudan, and south through East Africa to the Orange Free State. Found on the fringes of deserts, steppes, agricultural land, villages and small towns.

RED-HEADED FINCH *Amadina erythrocephala* **Plate 26**
OTHER NAMES: Paradise Sparrow, Aberdeen Finch. There are two subspecies.

This species is not frequently imported but some shipments arrive every season and they were available quite often in 1989–90. Boosey did not think much of this bird's colouring and would not have approved of the name Paradise Sparrow. In his opinion they were a rather rare and dull Cut-throat. However, I find them attractive and if given enough nesting sites they will not try to steal those of other birds. Even when breeding I have had no trouble from them at all in a planted aviary, shared with the more benign *Lonchura* species such as spice finches and even waxbills. Red-headed finches are not so free breeding as the Cut-throats and are slightly more difficult to establish; they should not be wintered outside without moderate heat at about 8°C (45°F).

However, when settled in (which is often not until their second year after importation) they can be good breeders and will equal the two or three broods of the Cut-throat. They also favour nest boxes as a site, using dried grass and feathers to build a nest which is rather crude. Both sexes spend a lot of time in the nest box whatever the stage of reproduction and it is difficult to ascertain their share or pattern of incubation. Like the Cut-throat they will take live food readily at any time and become very 'insectivorous' when breeding, but in my experience they have been bred without live food.

## Description

130 mm (5 in), sexually dimorphic.
COCK: Bill pale horn colour; irides brown; crown, sides of head and throat dull red; lores whitish; upperparts greyish brown, with the tips of feathers of wing coverts and secondaries dotted with white; breast has scaly black and white markings; flanks irregularly barred with black; undertail coverts greyish brown, with a white dot outlined in black on each feather; tail dark brown with the same markings; legs and feet flesh colour.
HEN: Plumage greyish brown without any red; throat whitish; underparts duller and markings ill-defined compared to cock.

## Distribution and Habitat

South Africa north to Angola and Zimbabwe. Inhabits dry, open country and thorn veld; also found in the vicinity of human habitation and will nest under the eaves of houses or other cavities.

# 8
# Ploceidae — Whydahs, Weavers and Sparrows

This family of seed-eating birds is divided by most authors into three subfamilies:

1 Subfamily Viduinae: parasitical whydahs and indigo birds.
2 Subfamily Passerinae: sparrows, sparrow-weavers and petronias.
3 Subfamily Ploceinae: weavers and non-parasitical whydahs.

Some authors list a fourth subfamily, the Bubalornithinae, containing the buffalo weavers, but as these birds are seldom imported and really only suitable for a very large aviary, they are omitted here.

## Subfamily Viduinae: Parasitical Whydahs and Indigo Birds

This group of parasitic African birds are sexually dimorphic in the breeding season; the nuptial plumage of the whydahs is exotic, with long tail feathers, and that of the indigo birds (or combassous) black or steely-blue. Outside of the breeding season, the mature *Vidua* cocks, like the ploceid weavers, have the same dull sparrow-like plumage as the hens and immature cocks.

The indigo birds are an especially problematic group for the taxonomist, one question being whether the different forms are separate species or a single polytypic species. They were formerly placed in their own genus *Hypochera* but are now included with the parasitic whydahs in the genus *Vidua*, although there is considerable evidence from captive breeding that at least one indigo 'species' will build their own nest and rear young. The Viduinae on the whole resemble the estrildines because of their small size, bill shape, and the nestlings' palate markings with conspicuous gape nodules. They also lay white unmarked eggs like the estrildines, although such reproductive similarities are considered evolutionary adaptations owing to the fact that the Viduinae birds lay their eggs in estrildine nests to be reared by estrildine species.

Most *Vidua* species are brood parasitic on a single species of estrildine host whose range correlates with that of the *Vidua* species — for example, Fischer's Whydah (*Vidua fischeri*) and its host the Purple Grenadier (*Uraeginthus ianthinogaster*). The Pin-tailed Whydah (*V. macroura*) is one of the few to use several *Estrilda* species as hosts. It is possible, therefore, that the *Vidua* species group is evolving either a multi-host opportunistic pattern or a host-specific parasitical behaviour. In the latter case, the *Vidua* cock mimics the song of the specific host species and the palate markings of the whydah nestlings are the same as the host species. In captivity, breedings have occurred where the *Vidua* chicks have been reared by an 'abnormal' host.

## Accommodation and Breeding

The *Vidua* species are active, lively birds which need space; cages for isolation, reception or winter housing should be large and perches arranged to prevent their tails becoming worn and frayed. Breeding is difficult and seldom successful; two or three pairs of the host species should be accommodated in an aviary with a cock whydah in nuptial plumage and two or three hens. If the host species is the Melba Finch (*Pytilia melba*), for example, more than one Melba pair would lead to conflict and make successful breeding doubtful, unless the aviary was a large one. The hen whydahs are stimulated into breeding condition by the reproductive activity of the host species. The cock whydah mimics the song of the host species and evidence suggests that he also locates the host's nest for the hen to lay two or three eggs. The *Vidua* chicks are reared along with the host's young (unlike cuckoo chicks which eject the host's young from the nest). Young whydahs are successful as parasites because they mimic accurately the palate markings, growth rate and other characteristics of the host nestlings.

## Food and Care

The *Vidua* species are mainly ground feeders and scratch away loose soil with a rapid backward movement of both feet for seeds; they also take insects. In captivity they will thrive on mixed millets — dry, soaked and germinated — also seeds such as small canary, niger and maw. They will feed on seeding grasses, green food and pupae, mealworms and soft food. Seeds mixed with leaf mould or the peat substrate from a white-worm culture and thrown on the aviary floor will keep them scratching away for a long time. Once established they are not delicate birds but I treat them as waxbills, that is wintering with heat at 8–10°C (45–50°F) and artificial lighting from November until about March in an average UK winter. Cocks imported during the period of attaining nuptial plumage seem particularly vulnerable to stress and must be treated with extra care.

**Genus *Vidua*   (Indigo Birds [Combassous] and Whydahs)**

SENEGAL INDIGO BIRD   *Vidua chalybeata* **Plate 37**
OTHER NAMES: Village Indigo Bird, Senegal Combassou. There are six subspecies recognised.

This form is the most frequently imported of the four species currently considered 'good species' by some taxonomists. These birds were previously placed in the defunct genus *Hypochera*, now merged with *Vidua*. The indigo birds are brood-parasitic on the fire-finches (*Lagonosticta* spp.) and the host of the Senegal Indigo Bird is the Red-billed Fire-finch (*L. senegala*). However, the relationships are complex and in any one area each form of indigo bird parasitises one *Lagonosticta* species. These correlated distribution patterns between host and parasite could change the whole concept of what constitutes a species in the genus *Vidua*. Like its host species, the Senegal Indigo Bird has a strong association with human habitation and areas of cultivation. The cocks have a display flight shared with other *Vidua* species which consists of a hovering flight over the head of the perched hen. Among the few successful captive breedings recorded, there have been cases of Senegal Indigo Birds rearing their own young.

Description

100–115 mm (4–4½ in), sexually dimorphic (nuptial plumage).

COCK: (Breeding plumage) — Bill pinkish-white; irides brown; entire plumage blue-black; primaries blackish; legs and feet variable in colour, light brownish to orange.
HEN: Crown of the head has a pale central streak bordered with dark brown; upperparts buff white.

The cock in eclipse plumage resembles the hen, but the crown streaks are darker.

### Distribution and Habitat

Widely distributed through much of Africa south of the Sahara, to Botswana. Inhabits dry savanna, edges of woodland, cultivation, farms and villages.

### PIN-TAILED WHYDAH *Vidua macroura* **Plate 39**

This whydah has been the most frequently imported of the *Vidua* species (and cheap to buy), especially when the cocks are 'O.O.C.' (out of colour). A dealer's cage of apparently rather drab sparrow-like birds makes it difficult for the uninitiated buyer to envisage the glory to come. They are long lived and hardy when established; a cock bird bought by a lady as a 'pet', lived for 17 years and died in full nuptial plumage. This bird was allowed out of its cage to fly around the room and was fed lots of extras, such as green food in variety, millet sprays and seeding grasses.

The Pin-tailed Whydah is still frequently imported but obtaining hens can be difficult; as with other Ploceidae which have a male eclipse plumage, many hens turn out to be cocks. This whydah is the only *Vidua* species to parasitise more than one host species, the primary host group being waxbills of the genus *Estrilda*.

Pin-tailed whydahs have been bred in captivity on a few occasions, probably the first in the UK was in 1909 when it took place in a large planted aviary. I have tried to breed these birds, but found one difficulty is getting the host species to breed when the cock whydah is in nuptial plumage. The answer to this problem is probably to have a breeding group of proven pairs of St Helena or Red-eared waxbills (*E. astrild* and *E. troglodytes*) housed with a cock and two or three Pin-tailed whydah hens, with some 'spare' cocks kept in isolation, so that if the breeding cock goes out of colour you have a second chance. In my experience, males in captivity are seldom in or out of colour at the same time, even if they have been imported some years before. The cock birds can be disruptive in an aviary with their display flights and sometimes aggressive behaviour (which does not help the breeding of waxbills). However, I have found this species displays far less overt aggression than the Paradise Whydah (*V. paradisaea*).

## Description

280 mm (11 in), including tail of 180–200 mm (7–8 in), sexually dimorphic (nuptial plumage).
COCK: (Breeding plumage) — Bill red; irides brown; crown, lores and feathers of nape, back and scapulars black; sides of head, a bar in nape and underparts white; chin and sides of upper breast show a black patch; wings black with a broad white transverse stripe; rump white, uppertail coverts black; tail black, the four middle tail feathers long and ribbon like; legs and feet reddish-brown.
HEN: Black stripes on pale brown upperparts; two black stripes over crown. Middle of crown, rump and uppertail coverts reddish brown.

The cock in eclipse plumage resembles the hen but streaking is darker. The bills of both sexes fade to a pinkish red or pale red.

## Distribution and Habitat

Much of Africa south of Sahara, with the exception of dense forest and deserts. Frequents karoo, savannas, grass clearing in forests, cultivation and vicinity of villages.

### PARADISE WHYDAH *Vidua paradisaea*

OTHER NAMES: Paradise Widow Bird.

Next to the Pin-tailed Whydah, this species is often available and, like *V. macroura*, until quite recently large shipments were imported. This is the well-known Paradise Whydah of aviculture, with long central tail feathers which narrow to a point. A second species, the Broad-tailed Paradise Whydah (*V. orientalis*), has five or six subspecies (depending on which checklist is followed) which vary in plumage pattern and tail feather shape. All may be distinguished from *V. paradisaea* because of the tapering of its central tail feathers, although the difference is slight in the case of *V. o. togoensis*. Both these species were formerly placed in the now defunct genus *Steganura*, and parasitise the *Pytilia* species (see *Pytilia*, under Estrildidae). The Melba Finch (*P. melba*) is host to *V. paradisaea*.

Like other *Vidua* species, this bird has seldom been bred in captivity and those few successes usually occurred by accident rather than design, with the exception of some ornithological studies in aviaries. The Paradise Whydah has the same hovering display flight as other *Vidua* species and this can be disruptive to host species in the same aviary. *V. paradisaea* is the most aggressive of the genus in my experience. During an unsuccessful attempt to breed them using the Red-winged Pytilia (*P. phoenicoptera*), as host, a cock in nuptial plumage killed a young pytilia with a couple of blows of its bill, before I could do anything about it. They have been bred in captivity with 'abnormal' host species. Fire-finches were the hosts on one occasion. They were bred in South Africa in a very large well planted aviary with 'normal' Melba Finch hosts.

## Description

400 mm (16 in), including tail of 280 mm (11 in), sexually dimorphic (nuptial plumage).

COCK: (Breeding plumage) — Bill black; irides dark brown; head, chin, throat down to upper breast, back, upper and undertail coverts, thighs, wing coverts and tail black; two central feathers of tail graduate to a point; vent area white; flights dark brown with brown edges. Nape bar, sides of neck and underparts yellow ochre; upper breast golden brown towards abdomen, paler near vent; legs and feet dark horn colour.

HEN: Black crown with a buff longitudinal stripe; side of head and eye-stripe sand colour; behind irides black stripe to ear coverts; upperparts yellowish brown, with black stripe in middle; underparts white and slightly rust coloured towards throat.

The cock in eclipse plumage resembles the hen, but the plumage appears darker and the tail appears slightly longer; the bill of the cock changes to a horn colour.

Distribution and Habitat

East and South Africa from the Sudan to Angola and Natal. Inhabits tree- and brush-covered savannas, also areas of thorn bush.

FISCHER'S WHYDAH *Vidua fischeri* **Plate 38**
OTHER NAMES: Straw-tailed Whydah

Another beautiful and elegant *Vidua*, which has never been frequently imported into the UK, but was available in 1980/81. It was first imported into Europe in 1911. The natural host for this species is the Purple Grenadier (*Uraeginthus ianthinogaster*).

Description

280 mm (11 in), including tail of 180–200 mm (7–8 in), sexually dimorphic (nuptial plumage).
COCK: (Breeding plumage) — Bill red; irides brown; crown buff; rump and uppertail coverts dull brown with darker stripes; remaining upperparts, head, neck, scapulars and back all black; underparts straw yellow to rust-coloured-yellow; wings and tail black and blackish brown, with the four middle tail feathers straw yellow; legs and feet orange.
HEN: Upperparts buff brown, with brown markings; underparts buff yellow.
Cock in eclipse resembles hen.

Distribution and Habitat

Somalia to Uganda and northern Tanzania. Frequents dry thornbush and desert scrub.

QUEEN WHYDAH *Vidua regia*
OTHER NAMES: Shaft-tailed Whydah.

The Queen Whydah is imported into the UK most seasons, but shipments are usually small or a few arrive in a mixed waxbill shipment. They were available in 1989–90. They have been bred on several occasions, the normal host being the Violet-eared Waxbill (*Uraeginthus granatina*), although they were bred in the UK using the Red-cheeked Cordon-bleu (*U.*

*bengalus*) as the host species. In South Africa they were bred in a large planted aviary and the young were reared by Violet-eared waxbills. I had a pair of these whydahs and attempted to breed then using the St Helena Waxbill (*Estrilda astrild*) as host species. The hen whydah was seen flying out of a nest box the waxbills were using, but unfortunately none of the eggs hatched. When I put what had been gathered from ants' nests — pupae and ants, including winged ants — out for the waxbills, the whydahs immediately flew down to them, eating pupae and ants, winged or without wings.

### Description

300 mm (12 in), including tail of about 200 mm (8 in), sexually dimorphic (nuptial plumage).
COCK: Bill coral red; irides brown; upperparts black; nape, sides of head and underparts dark honey; wings black and blackish brown with narrow brown edges; undertail coverts and thighs black; underwing coverts white; tail blackish brown, with white mottling on inner edges of tips; four extended tail feathers like stiff black wires with the end quarter webbed and shaped like a paddle; legs and feet coral red.
HEN: Upperparts brown, with dark brown markings; head and neck yellowish brown; underparts yellowish brown, merging to white towards middle of abdomen.

The cock in eclipse plumage is like the hen, but the dark brown markings on the head are darker and the underparts browner.

### Distribution and Habitat

Southern Angola to Cape Province. In dry thorn country.

## STEEL-BLUE WHYDAH *Vidua hypocherina*

OTHER NAMES: Long-tailed Combassou.

This Whydah has been imported in small numbers for many years, usually among a number of mixed waxbill species. They have not been bred in the UK as far as I can ascertain; this is probably due to their parasitic and polygamous breeding habits as many 'hens' turn out to be cocks in eclipse plumage.

In the wild, this whydah was once thought to be a brood parasite on the Rosy-rumped Waxbill (*Estrilda rhodopyga*). It is now thought that the host species are the Black-cheeked Waxbill (*E. erythronotos*) and the closely related *E. charmosyna*.

Description

305 mm (12 in), including tail of about 200 mm (8 in), sexually dimorphic (nuptial plumage).
COCK: (Breeding plumage) — Bill dull white to greyish white; entire plumage glossy bluish or purplish black, including the four long slender central tail feathers, which widen towards their ends; legs and feet brownish grey.
HEN: Buffy brown with upperparts streaked with black and brown; underparts buffish fading to whitish on the lower abdomen and under tail coverts.

The cock in eclipse plumage resembles the hen, but the streaking on the upperparts is darker.

Distribution and Habitat

Ethiopia and Somalia to Tanzania. Dry bush country.

## Subfamily Passerinae: Sparrows, Sparrow-weavers and Petronias

Sparrows have never been popular birds in aviculture and if importers can find a justification for avoiding the name, they will — an opportunity which can occur with species of sparrow-weavers and petronias. Because of their lack of popular interest, importers receiving shipments 'in error' will rapidly take steps to prevent another 'error' occurring. But in the last few years there have been signs of growing avicultural interest in sparrows with the realization that some species are attractive, a few colourful and that all are interesting birds. Some aviculturists have been sparrow enthusiasts for a long time, myself included.

The sparrows are among the world's successful passerines; most species are opportunistic and gregarious breeders to some extent, whether nesting in colonies or in the vicinity of other pairs. The House Sparrow (*Passer domesticus*) and other congenerics will build crude, domed, weaver-type 'ancestral' nests if holes and cavities in buildings are not available. The 'typical' sparrow (genus *Passer*) is sexually dimorphic to some degree, the Ethiopian region *Sporopipes* and *Pseudonigrita* being examples of somewhat aberrant genera with the sexes alike. Unlike the Estrildidae the sparrows and other members of the Ploceidae family are not 'contact' birds, and, with a few exceptions such as the *Sporopipes* species, body contact and mutual preening are largely unknown or perfunctory.

## Accommodation and Breeding

With a few exceptions the Passerinae are not happy in cages; if cages are used for winter accommodation and the reception of new stock, they should be large and of the enclosed box type. In planted aviaries, unlike the weavers (Ploceinae), they are not destructive to growing plants. Most of the species are fairly large — 140–178 mm (5½–7 in) — and although their aggression is usually intraspecific, they should not be housed with waxbills and similar birds. They are inclined to monopolise feeding sites and being by nature self-assertive, birds of their size can be very disruptive for less robust species. Many sparrows in the wild use holes in trees, rocks and buildings for their nests and most will also build free-standing nests in bushes and trees. Some species of the sparrow-weaver group build specialised nests in thornbush and trees. The Social Weaver (*Philetairus socius*) makes a huge community nest, the occupants (of both sexes) keeping the nest roof in constant repair throughout the year.

Both sexes take part in nest building and the incubation and care of the young, but the extent and share of these duties vary among different genera. In captivity nesting sites are provided by half-open and budgerigar nest boxes, bushes and clumps of cut branches, especially spiky gorse. Dried grasses and feathers are the preferred nesting materials but most *Passer* and *Petronia* species will use practically anything including paper, straw and rags. I always provide plenty of feathers as wild *P. domesticus* and captive *Petronia* species will pull out the feathers of doves (or any bird they can catch) to line their nests.

## Food and Care

Although seed-eating birds, sparrows feed their young largely on insects for the first few days of life. Species in the genus *Passer* are less insectivorous than others like the *Petronia* species. A basic diet in captivity is mixed millets with about 30% canary seed. This is supplemented with green food both cultivated and collected and soft food, which most birds will 'learn' to take. Mealworms should be offered twice a week, and mineralised grit, cuttle fish bone, oystershell and sand should always be available. When breeding, live food should be given in generous amounts, and for non-breeding adult sparrow-weavers and petronias, live food or soft food substitutes appear to be essential in the long term.

### Genus *Passer*

Most *Passer* species are hardy once established and can winter outside with adequate shelter. Some of the African sparrow-weavers are difficult to establish and even after a season in captivity should not be wintered without moderate heat.

SUDAN GOLDEN SPARROW *Passer luteus*
OTHER NAMES: Yellow Sparrow, Golden Song Sparrow. Some authors place this species and the Arabian Golden Sparrow (*P. euchlorus*) in their own genus *Auripasser*.

This African species is the most frequently imported sparrow, and they are still among the cheapest birds to buy. In spite of their colourful appearance, few people bother to try and breed them. They are active, rather nervous birds and the dealers' name of 'Song' sparrow is most inappropriate. Like so many imported species in which the cocks' plumage is colourful, hens make up a small percentage of shipments and many turn out to be immature cocks. They have been bred fairly frequently, often by accident.

The best results are achieved with a colony system and Herbert Murray was very successful using clumps of gorse in which the colony bred. I have only bred Sudan Golden Sparrows once, the single pair built in a gorse clump about 1.8 m (6 ft) high in an aviary. The nest was a rather untidy, domed structure of grasses and weed stems with an entrance hole at the side and lined with feathers. Owing to its situation it was almost impossible to examine the nest, and until two young birds left the nest I did not check it. The birds took lots of live food both collected and commercial. They were not aggressive to the other birds in the aviary, which were Asiatic munias. Although this pair were housed on their own they were in visual and auditory contact with other Golden Sparrows in another aviary. It would appear that with this species and other colony breeders, this can be enough to stimulate a single pair.

### Description

130 mm (5 in), sexually dimorphic.
COCK: Bill horn colour, turning black in the breeding season; irides brown; head and underparts bright yellow; mantle and edges of inner primaries chestnut brown; rump yellowish; tail blackish brown with pale edges; legs and feet dark flesh colour.
HEN: Paler brown head, mantle and rump; underparts greyish white.

### Distribution and Habitat

Northern Nigeria, Chad, the Sudan and northern Ethiopia. Inhabits open steppe country with trees and scrub, and moves into areas of cultivation and villages out of breeding season in large flocks.

ARABIAN GOLDEN SPARROW *Passer euchlorus*
OTHER NAMES: This bird is sometimes considered a subspecies of *P. luteus*.

*P. euchlorus* is distinguished from *P. luteus* by having the mantle and wings yellow instead of chestnut. It is rarely imported but probably has turned up in mixed shipments without being identified. They have been bred in captivity.

## Genus *Sorella*

CHESTNUT SPARROW *Sorella eminibey*
OTHER NAMES: This monotypic genus has been merged into *Passer* by some authors.

This is a very interesting little African sparrow, but I can find no record of them being bred in captivity. They are imported occasionally and were available in 1989. I have kept them over a period of ten years, and all but one of the 'hens' proved to be immature cocks.

There has been some doubt as to whether chestnut sparrows build their own nests, or take over the old nests of weavers and line them with fine grasses and feathers. I can confirm that they are industrious builders; the only pair built nests in wicker baskets and later made an ambitious structure in a large gorse clump. This was shaped like a sack with a narrow tube-like entrance.

The hen would often give a wing-quivering posture to the cock as if soliciting food. Later four cock birds housed together were observed giving this display to each other when flying away. The rapid wing beat was continued and their flight was slower than normal flight, as if the extra wing beats gave a hovering effect. When gathering nest material (both the true pair and the four bachelors) they always collected the stems and feathers by the bill tip — stems were never held crossways in the bill. They are cheerful and constant singers and a series of typical sparrow-like chirps have other more melodious notes in between, some resembling the notes of serins. The true pair later went to nest in a basket; chicks did hatch but by then it was late November in an outside aviary and they died after about three days. The hen did not live through the winter and I have not been able to obtain hens since. Chestnut sparrows are not aggressive birds and any bickering and squabbles are intraspecific — however, I would not house them with waxbills.

## Description

115 mm (4½ in), sexually dimorphic.
COCK: Bill horn colour, slate-black in breeding season; irides blackish brown; plumage mainly chestnut brown, darker on head and neck; primaries and tail blackish brown; wing coverts chestnut brown; legs and feet reddish brown.
HEN: Crown ash-grey; upperparts dull brown with black stripes; rump and uppertail coverts reddish brown; underparts white.

Distribution and Habitat

The Sudan to northern Tanzania. Usual habitat is on islets of trees and scrub among papyrus swamps. In some areas they are found in gardens and among houses.

**Genus *Petronia***

*Petronia* species are more slender and elegant-looking birds than the larger members of the genus *Passer*. Their conical bills are longer and pointed, an indication that they are more insectivorous in feeding habits, which has proved to be true when they breed in captivity. Of the five species, three are imported occasionally and I have bred two of these for a number of years. They are hole nesters and can fill an 'ecological niche' in an aviary without displaying the aggression which some hole nesters such as titmice (Paridae) demonstrate.

YELLOW-THROATED SPARROW *Petronia xanthocollis*

OTHER NAMES: Yellow-throated Rock Sparrow, Yellow-spotted Petronia. Some checklists record the species as *P. xanthosterna*.

This species is a lively, active bird, which, although rather nervous until established, adjusts well to life in an aviary. They are willing breeders, but like the other *Petronia* species, will seldom breed the first season following importation, and sometimes not for a period of three or four years. Once started, they are consistent and will breed regularly; aviary-bred birds will breed the season following their hatching.

Description

150 mm (6 in), sexually dimorphic.

COCK: Bill dark horn, showing seasonal change (paler); irides dark brown; upperparts ashy brown; wings brown with two bars, the upper white, the lower pale buffish and a chestnut patch on the lesser wing coverts; chin greyish white, with a pronounced yellow patch on the throat; underparts greyish becoming white on the abdomen; legs and feet light brown.

HEN: Bill greyish brown; the yellow throat patch is very faint and the chestnut wing patches are replaced by a very pale ruddy brown.

## Distribution and Habitat

From Iraq, Iran and Afghanistan almost throughout the Indian subcontinent. Essentially a bird of the trees in both cultivated and barren land but avoids heavy forest. They will nest in gardens and readily use nest boxes where provided.

## Breeding

PERIOD: Whistler records a breeding season from April to July on the Indian subcontinent and they are double brooded. In outside aviaries nesting begins in April or May, ending with a second brood in July. It is interesting to note that this species and *P. dentata* (which has a distribution in the Ethiopian region) are apparently affected by the declining photoperiod in the UK from the summer solstice onwards — even if a single brood is reared or nesting is commenced later they will not breed into the late summer or autumn. Estrildidae species with a similar distribution will breed well into November, or even later if they are left in the aviaries.

NEST: These birds are hole nesters both in the wild and in captivity. A budgerigar nesting box is the favoured receptacle, or a larger box of the same type. This is filled with an untidy nest of grasses, paper and any other material provided, and the cup of the nest is always lined with feathers. The cock will gather material but the hen does most of the building. The same nest will be used for the next brood.

EGGS: Ground colour greenish white, marked with brown and ashy brown. Clutch size 3–4.

INCUBATION: The hen plays the major role in incubation, but the cock will cover the eggs while she is feeding or bathing and occasionally for longer periods. Incubation usually commences with the third egg laid; the period is 13–15 days.

CHICKS: The nestlings have a very dark purplish skin with dark grey down, the mouth is dark red and the gape flanges are white. They are fed largely on live food; in my aviaries the parents will fly down and wait for me to empty a bag of collected live food onto the aviary floor. The chicks' begging calls can be heard from about the seventh day after hatching. They leave the nest at 14 days and are fed by the cock for a further 12–14 days. The hen will start a second clutch within two days of the first brood leaving the nest. The immature plumage is like that of the hen; the small yellow throat spot is absent and the chicks are paler overall, showing very faint buff-coloured bars on the wings. When the second brood hatches, the first should be removed otherwise the cock will harass them.

Behaviour

In display, the cock approaches the hen with the head and bill lifted exposing the yellow throat patch, and the wings lifted and moved to show the chestnut patches. *P. dentata* has a similar display but the posture is more upright and since this species lacks the wing patches, the wings are not moved. They are not aggressive birds except towards other petronias and related species. They can be safely housed with the more robust *Lonchura* munias and the smaller *Euplectes* weavers (those without yellow plumage) or other species which are not hole-nesters.

**Genus *Sporopipes***

This African genus consists of two small 'sparrow-weavers' which have two widely separated distributions: the Scaly-crowned Weaver (*S. squamifrons*) and the Speckle-fronted Weaver (*S. frontalis*). Their systematic position has been the subject of a good deal of debate, as some aspects of their behaviour and breeding biology have similarities with the estrildines. These include contact behaviour (sitting on a perch in bodily contact with another bird), mutual preening and social behaviour. However, these are outweighed by physiological and other similarities with the Ploceidae, especially the Passerinae.

Both *Sporopipes* species are fairly frequently imported into the UK and were available in 1989–90. They have been bred occasionally but successful breeding results are seldom reported.

The sexes are alike, and in the wild and captivity they become insectivorous when breeding — factors which make breeding difficult. They are also said to become very aggressive when breeding and this must come as a surprise to those who equate only large birds with aggression, especially as the Scaly-crowned has an 'innocent' pink-billed 'waxbill' appearance. I have not bred either species and have found them self-assertive but not aggressive. When breeding, however, a different situation could occur.

*Sporopipes* species are more difficult to establish than other Passerinae, especially *S. squamifrons*, and they should be wintered with heat at about 10°C (50°F). In the wild both species build free-standing, untidy, domed nests with a side entrance; both sexes build and feed the young although in *S. squamifrons* it is thought only the hen incubates. In aviaries, nest boxes and the old nests of other birds have been used. Unlike most Passerinae, they become steady and are not nervous in a cage once established.

SCALY-CROWNED WEAVER *Sporopipes squamifrons*
OTHER NAMES: Scaly Weaver, Scaly-fronted Weaver. Two subspecies are recognised.

Description

100 mm (4 in), sexes alike.
Bill pink; irides brown; white ring around eye; top of head black, with white scale markings; lores and chin black; throat white with black stripe on sides; rest of head, ear coverts and upperparts ash grey; wing coverts, inner primaries and tail black, with white edges; rest of wing dark grey; underparts whitish grey; legs and feet greyish brown.

Distribution and Habitat

From Angola through Namibia and Botswana to Zimbabwe and South Africa. Inhabits dry thorny bush country, also areas of cultivation, parks, villages and towns.

SPECKLE-FRONTED WEAVER *Sporopipes frontalis*
OTHER NAMES: Has been called Red-fronted Finch, also Scaly-fronted Weaver. There are three subspecies.

Description

115 mm (4½ in), sexes alike.
Bill horn coloured; irides brown; forehead, top of head and

beard-stripe black, flecked with white; back of head and neck tawny brown; mantle and rump ashy brown; wings and tail grey, edged yellowish white; sides of head and breast greyish; rest of underparts white; legs and feet horn coloured.

### Distribution and Habitat

Senegal to the Sudan and south to Tanzania. Frequents arid thornbush, also areas of cultivation and villages.

## Subfamily Ploceinae: Weavers, Bishops and Whydahs

This subfamily consists of about 90 species whose main distribution is confined to Africa south of the Sahara and off-shore islands. The exceptions are five species whose distribution includes the Indian subcontinent and other Asian regions. There are a number of generalisations one can make about this subfamily; with few exceptions the cocks have a brightly coloured nuptial plumage in which reds and yellows are predominant and when in eclipse they resemble the more dully coloured hens; many species feed on insects as well as seeds which are rarely taken from the ground, and generally speaking, like the sparrows, those with the more slender bills are the most insectivorous.

Many species build elaborate, beautifully woven nests which are often suspended from the branches of trees or built in reeds and grasses, often with an entrance tube hanging down from the nest. They are generally social nesters, the numbers and type of colony varying from a small 'loose' group nesting in the vicinity of other pairs to colonies of hundreds. The eggs of weavers are variable in colour and markings and in one species may be white, greenish, bluish or brown, unmarked or with spots and blotches of black and brown, or other colours and shades.

### Accommodation and Breeding

Once established most weavers are hardy and if a good dry enclosed shelter is provided they can be left outside in the average UK winter. It is most important that the shelter should have adequate windows, as birds will not fly from light into dark. Electric power should be connected to the shelter so that if really harsh weather sets in, the birds have instant heat and light if needed. If wintered in cages, the large box type is the best. I always move my weavers inside about November and provide enough heat to stop their water freezing, with extended lighting to shorten the long nights. Weavers will destroy bushes in a planted aviary, but this activity can be controlled by putting up clumps of gorse for nesting sites and providing lots of nesting material.

A few weaver species have been bred occasionally, but among the problems there is the usual one of obtaining hens and the fact that some weavers can be very aggressive. Also the commonly imported species were very cheap for many years and therefore the motivation to breed them was lacking. The usual method recommended is to have one cock to two or three hens in a fairly large aviary (if you can obtain the hens in the first place). However, successes have occurred with single pairs in aviaries of modest size. The nearest I have ever got to a success was with a pair of Zanzibar Red Bishops (*Euplectes nigroventris*); chicks were hatched but the parents deserted them at about five days as it was very late in the season (November).

## Food and Care

Weavers will thrive on a basic diet of mixed millets and canary seed with the essential minerals, grit and green food also provided; in addition, seeding grasses which form a part of their feral diet are always eaten. All the weavers I have kept (some 14 species) have taken almost any kind of live food at any time. Most species travel well but as they have to cope with a further one or two changes of environment after quarantine, imported stock should be established with care.

### Genus *Ploceus*

This genus, along with *Euplectes* and *Quelea*, contains all the species of commonly imported weavers. Like other large genera in the family there has been some rearrangement of species into genera and subgenera; currently it would appear the 'lumpers' have won and most taxonomic lists include some 57–60 species. The males in the main have bright yellow in some areas of their plumage combined with black or various shades of brown. A common factor with the nesting of many species in this genus and *Malimbus* is the employment of nest-protective devices. These vary from nesting near the sites of raptors' and wasps' nests at the extreme tips of twigs, over water, or having a long entrance tube hanging from the bottom of the nest.

The males are polygamous, or near polygamous in the majority of species. They nest in colonies which can consist of vast numbers of nests or, more rarely, solitary nests are built. The cocks begin the building but, having made a frame, the building method from then on varies with different species. He displays by hanging from the nest and, with wings flapping, produces the buzzing, wheezing notes which pass for a song in the Ploceinae. This display is to attract a hen who will complete the nest with the cock.

RUFOUS-NECKED WEAVER *Ploceus cucullatus*
OTHER NAMES: Village Weaver, V-marked Weaver, Black-headed Weaver. Formerly placed in the genus *Textor*. The name Black-headed Weaver can cause avicultural confusion with *P. melanocephalus*, a smaller bird. There are seven subspecies.

This large African weaver is still occasionally imported but the only breeding records for the UK were at the London Zoo in 1905 and again in 1913. They have been bred on the European continent on a few occasions. This species (and others) which nest in colonies with their noisy, displaying, colourful males, would make a wonderfully interesting exhibit in a large zoological aviary. I have seen a few small groups of weavers in zoos over the years but not breeding colonies.

These birds have a reputation for aggressive behaviour and most 'hens' turn out to be immature cocks. Some years ago I managed to obtain a true pair and released them in a planted aviary with a 'pair' of Pope Cardinals (*Paroaria dominicana*), which are able to take care of themselves. Besides some privet bushes the aviary had the usual gorse clumps hung up at various heights. The weavers built a nest woven into the wire netting (a common occurrence with weavers). The nest was well made but the Pope Cardinals became aggressive so I had to remove the weavers. Some avicultural authors condemn 'wire netting' nests as useless. However, providing the nests are 'finished' and not exposed, wire netting makes a more secure support than the ends of twigs or many other nest supports used in the wild. Canon Lowe had a pair of Half Masked Weavers (*Ploceus vitellinus*) breed successfully in a nest woven in the wire of an aviary roof. He described the nest as 'strong and efficient' and the young were reared on lots of mealworms.

Robbiller (1974) summarises breedings on the European continent as successful with a colony system. The cocks are aggressive towards smaller birds and large flights are necessary for accommodation. Live food is essential for the rearing of young.

### Description

150–180 mm (6–7 in), sexually dimorphic (nuptial plumage).
COCK: (Breeding plumage) — Bill black; irides bright orange red; head and throat to upper breast black; chestnut-brown bar to upper breast; upperparts and underparts yellow; flanks and breast tinged with chestnut; wing coverts black, yellow tipped; primaries blackish brown, with greenish-yellow edges; tail olive brown, tinged with green; legs and feet brown.
HEN: Olive-coloured upperparts, with dark brown longitudinal stripes; underparts yellow; sides of body tinged with brown; abdomen whitish.

The eclipsed cock has the head yellow and the upperparts ash grey with darker streaks; breast pale yellow; whitish on abdomen.

### Distribution and Habitat

From Senegal east to the Sudan and Ethiopia; south to Angola and eastern South Africa. Forest and savanna showing a preference for towns, villages and cultivated land.

## HALF-MASKED WEAVER *Ploceus vitellinus*

OTHER NAMES: Vitelline Masked Weaver. There are two subspecies.

This species, in common with some of its congenerics, has been frequently available for many years. A smaller bird than the preceding species, some aviculturists are of the opinion that they are less aggressive, but once in breeding plumage, the cocks are not to be trusted. They are best housed in an aviary on their own, or perhaps with a pair of doves or quail. The size of the aviary and the cover provided can, of course, affect their behaviour. Like most weavers, they are destructive to growing plants because of their constant nest-building activity. It is usually recommended that one cock to 2 or 3 hens is the ideal breeding group. However, I know of one successful breeding with a pair housed in a small aviary on their own. Live food seems to be essential for the rearing of the chicks.

Description

130 mm (5 in), sexually dimorphic (nuptial plumage).
COCK: (Breeding plumage) — Bill black; irides yellow; forehead chestnut; crown orange-chestnut; nape yellow; face, chin and cheeks black; mantle black; wings and tail olive-yellow marked with dark streakings; underparts yellow; legs and feet brown.
HEN: Brownish upperparts, with dark striations; underparts buffish with a slight wash of yellow on the throat and breast.

The eclipsed cock resembles the hen and lacks the black facial mask.

Distribution and Habitat

Senegal to Chad, western Sudan, northern Central African Republic. Generally a bird of the arid savanna; frequents open thorn scrub.

**Genus *Quelea***

*Quelea* is a small African genus of three species, two of which are commonly imported and well known in aviculture. They lack the brighter colours of some *Ploceus* and *Euplectes* species, but they are attractive and long lived, adjusting well to captivity.

RED-HEADED QUELEA *Quelea erythrops*
OTHER NAMES: Red-headed Dioch.

This small weaver is a most attractive bird which, although fairly frequently imported, has received little attention from aviculturists. One problem is the usual lack of hens in the shipments and, as they are comparatively cheap to buy, the motivation to breed them is lacking. They have been bred on the European continent but apparently not in the UK.

Its congeneric, the Red-billed Quelea (*Q. quelea*) is one of the few weavers which is monogamous, so it is reasonable to assume that the Red-headed has the same reproductive behaviour. I have only kept one pair of these birds and found them less aggressive and self-assertive than many other weaver species. A UK aviculturist who had a single pair which hatched chicks (but failed to rear them) found they were not aggressive in a mixed collection. The breeding failure he considered was due to insufficient live food as only maggots were provided. In the wild they are colony nesters in reedbeds, building a small spherical nest with a side entrance.

## Description

115 mm (4½ in), sexually dimorphic (nuptial plumage).
COCK: (Breeding plumage) — Bill black; irides dark brown; head and throat scarlet, throat with black base; upperparts striated brown; rump and uppertail coverts paler brown; underparts light brown; abdomen and undertail coverts often white; wings brownish black, edged yellow; tail brownish black, edged light brown; legs and feet flesh coloured.
HEN: Bill horn colour. Lacks red on head and throat.

The cock in eclipse plumage resembles the hen, may sometimes show a slight tinge of red on the forehead.

## Distribution and Habitat

Senegal to Ethiopia, south to Angola, Natal and Cape Province. Inhabits open country such as grassy woodland, and marshland.

### RED-BILLED QUELEA *Quelea quelea*

OTHER NAMES: Common Quelea, Red-billed Weaver, Black-faced Dioch. There are three subspecies.

This quelea is the most frequently imported of the Ploceinae.

They are attractive and, when established, are among the hardiest of the subfamily. In the wild, they breed in vast colonies but, unlike many *Ploceus* species, they are monogamous, retaining a pair bond within the colony. Captive breedings have occurred quite often. One record concerned a single pair breeding in a mixed collection. The aviary was small and there was no aggressive behaviour from the queleas. Another success (Coupe, 1964) occurred in a large aviary which housed other birds, including different species of weaver. An interesting aspect to this breeding was the feeding of the young queleas by other weaver species. In both these successful breedings, live food was supplied and in the first, the parents also collected aphids from growing plants and caught flying insects.

Wild queleas are a pest of plague proportions to crops, and the agricultural departments of the countries in which they occur are permanently engaged in total war against these birds. The methods employed in destroying breeding colonies, some of which have been estimated to number ten thousand nests, include chemical spraying from aircraft, explosives and flame-throwers.

## Description

115–130 mm (4½–5 in), sexually dimorphic (nuptial plumage).

COCK: (Breeding plumage) Bill red; irides brown; orbital ring red; bar across forehead, sides of head and throat black; crown, sides of neck and underparts buff, tinged with pink; abdomen and undertail coverts white; upperparts yellowish brown, with black bars; wings brown, with light edges; legs and feet flesh colour.

HEN: Brownish-grey head; underparts light buffish; whitish at throat and lower abdomen.

The eclipsed cock resembles the hen but is often more heavily streaked on the upperparts with a few black feathers retained on the throat.

## Distribution and Habitat

From West Africa south of the Sahara to the east and south to

South Africa, extending from the south into Angola. Inhabits semi-arid savannas and cultivated areas.

### Genus *Euplectes*

*Euplectes* is an African genus of 15 species which includes the weavers known as bishops and a group of whydahs which are not parasitical. All have a nuptial male plumage, the cocks resembling the hens out of the breeding season. The whydahs were formerly placed in their own genus *Coliuspasser*, some in their own monotypic genus. At present all are included in *Euplectes* as there is little doubt they are a homogenous group. The nuptial plumage of the bishops has either a red or yellow colour contrasting with black. The whydahs are similar but the black areas are usually more extensive and they have longer tails which can measure 406 mm (16 in). The genus includes a few species in the 'bishop' group which are still frequently imported. Only two species of whydah are occasionally available and some, such as Jackson's Whydah (*E. jacksoni*), have always been rare imports. As breeding prospects, the whydahs are only suitable for the more extensive aviaries; they are larger and generally more aggressive than the bishop members of the genus who are themselves not noted for a lack of self-assertive behaviour. For these reasons the whydahs are not included in the following notes on the *Euplectes* species.

The bishops (or weavers) in this genus are polygamous, the cocks holding territories which vary enormously in size depending on the species, and which they retain by displays and aggressive behaviour. The displays are patrol flights over the territory as well as boundary displays, the perched cock erecting its conspicuous plumage and holding a vertical posture with the bill raised or directed at a possible rival. This display is accompanied by the whizzing, rattling and buzzing notes which in *Euplectes* passes for a song. Having established a territory the cock builds the framework of several nests which are selected by a hen who lines them with finer material. The hen incubates and rears the young, with the cock's role consisting of guarding the occupied nests.

In aviaries a cock with two or three hens would be a suitable ratio although there have been records of single pairs breeding successfully. A planted aviary of a reasonable size would give the best chance of success. It would appear from observations in smaller aviaries that the limited space puts pressure on the hens because the cock constantly chases them back to the nest. Also, I have often had a hen complete a nest only to have the cock pull it to pieces and start another frame. The amount of cover provided in the aviary has a bearing on such aggression — plenty of cut branches and tough bushes such as privet should help to keep conflict at bay. I can find no record of a successful captive breeding without some live food being provided and the birds have always been housed in an outside aviary.

NAPOLEON WEAVER *Euplectes afer*

OTHER NAMES: Golden Bishop, Yellow-crowned Bishop. There are four subspecies.

This species is probably the most frequently imported of the genus; they are attractive birds which have been bred on a few occasions. Among the breeding methods, I have tried a cock with two hens which, although not successful, at least resulted in completed nests and eggs laid. Two pairs in the same aviary ended in constant bickering and chasing. They can be kept with unrelated birds of a robust nature (e.g. Java sparrows) or those whose breeding biology and behaviour is very different, such as a pair of doves. Like other *Euplectes* species, in the wild they are birds of the savanna, nesting and feeding largely in grasses and reedbeds. They become insectivorous when breeding and live food should be provided for the young to be reared.

Description

115–130 mm (4½–5 in), sexually dimorphic (nuptial plumage).

COCK: (Breeding plumage) — Bill black; irides yellowish brown; upperparts and undertail coverts golden yellow; nape feathers edged with black, with black bar running across; sides of head, throat, breast and abdomen black; a reddish-brown patch below the upper breast; wings and tail dark brown, with light brown edges; legs and feet flesh colour.

HEN: Bill yellowish horn; upperparts brown; underparts whitish; upper breast and sides of body tinged with brown.

The eclipsed cock resembles the hen, except for somewhat darker upperparts.

Distribution and Habitat

Africa south of the Sahara to South Africa. Inhabits well-watered grasslands and marshes.

ORANGE WEAVER *Euplectes orix franciscana* **Plate 40**
OTHER NAMES: Orange Bishop. This subspecies is treated as a species by some workers. Hall and Moreau separate this bird as a species and include *E. orix* and *E. nigroventris* as a superspecies. Including *E. o. franciscana*, there are four subspecies of *E. orix*.

The Orange Weaver is like *E. afer*, having been commonly imported into the UK and Europe for many years. I have seen them both kept together in fairly large aviaries, the red plumage of this species making a pleasing contrast with the yellow of *E. afer*. The Orange Weaver has also been bred occasionally in the UK, Europe, Australia, New Zealand and North America.

Description

130 mm (5 in), sexually dimorphic (nuptial plumage).
COCK: (Breeding plumage) — Bill black; irides brown; crown, sides of head and underparts black; rest of plumage orange red; back reddish brown; wings blackish brown, with light feather edging; legs and feet flesh coloured.
HEN: Bill yellowish horn-colour; upperparts light brown, with blackish-brown stripes; eye-stripe yellowish white; underparts white; upper breast and sides of body tinged with brown; legs and feet yellowish horn.

The eclipsed cock resembles the hen except for traces of retained black areas of the nuptial plumage.

Distribution and Habitat

From Senegal to Ethiopia, Somalia, Kenya, Tanzania south to South Africa and west to Angola. Inhabits karoo and savannas moving into areas of cultivation out of the breeding season, feeding on millet and other grain crops.

## Breeding

PERIOD: Variable throughout their vast range of distribution, November–April in the south and May–October in the north. Aviary birds in the UK and Europe often commence breeding late in the year, which can cause problems if the weather is cold and wet combined with the declining photoperiod from October/November onwards. In the wild some hens rear two broods in each season; second broods have been commenced in aviaries but apparently not reared.

NEST: The usual nest site is a bush, especially thorn bushes. Using grass stems the cock weaves the frame of the nest in a perpendicular ring, the outer weave enclosing the vertical stems of the bush or other vegetation. A hen in breeding condition will then complete a selected nest. In captivity this behaviour is retained, if anything approaching a natural habitat is provided. My birds will usually use the new vertical growth of privet bushes to build their nests. Other aviary sites have been among growing plants or the nest has been woven into the wire of the aviary. On the European continent half-open nest boxes and wire baskets have been used. As in the wild the materials used in aviaries are grass stems, and my birds have used wood-wool (commercial packing material) as lining. The nest often has a flimsy appearance but is surprisingly strong and durable; it is oval in shape with an entrance at the top of one side. A lining of finer material is added by the hen after incubation has commenced.

EGGS: Variable, but it would appear they do not show the variety of colour found in some Ploceinae species. They are immaculate and pale greenish blue or bluish grey. Clutch size usually 3, but anything from 2–7 has been recorded.

INCUBATION: Carried out by the hen alone. Period 13–14 days.

CHICKS: Fed by the hen. If a single breeding pair is housed in one aviary the cock can be removed after the chicks have hatched (as he can harass the hen by driving her to nest again). In a polygamous group the cock may be occupied by building a nest and mating another hen, so he will have an outlet for his reproductive drive. The young leave the nest at approximately 13–16 days and are fed by the hen for at least another 14 days. They should be removed if the cock is present as he may harass the young birds. The immature plumage is like that of the hen but paler, with the yellowish eye-stripe visible when the chicks leave the nest. Gleghorn records a successful breeding in a large planted aviary, the hen being provided with a wide variety of live food, from spiders to moths and 60 mealworms a day. This was in addition to an egg and biscuit mixture and a varied seed mixture.

### Behaviour

The cocks are self-assertive birds when in colour and if housed with other cocks or unrelated weaver species breeding is disrupted with constant bickering. Actual injury seldom occurs, but I had a cock kill a Napoleon Weaver very quickly on one occasion.

## GRENADIER WEAVER *Euplectes orix orix*

OTHER NAMES: Red Bishop, Grenadier Bishop, Crimson Grenadier.

This *E. orix* subspecies is a beautiful bird less frequently imported than *E. o. franciscana*. They have been bred, although records are few; the shipments are small and, as usual, 'hens' turn out to be immature cocks. Like other *Euplectes* species they require live food for successful breeding and can be aggressive in a mixed aviary. I have housed them with Java Sparrows, without conflict.

### Description

150 mm (6 in), sexually dimorphic (nuptial plumage).
COCK: (Breeding plumage) — Bill black; irides dark brown; forehead, crown, sides of head and throat black; rest of head, neck, upper and undertail coverts scarlet; remaining underparts black; thighs rust yellow, tinged with red; wings and tail blackish brown with light edges; legs and feet flesh coloured.
HEN: Bill horn coloured; upperparts pale brown, with dark brown stripes; eye-stripe rust-coloured yellow; underparts light brown, with brownish-black stripes.

The cock in eclipse is like the hen, but may retain faint indications of black from the nuptial plumage. The hen generally shows darker striping on the underparts.

RED-SHOULDERED WHYDAH *Euplectes axillaris* **Plate 41**
OTHER NAMES: Fan-tailed Whydah, there are 7 subspecies. This species was formerly listed as *Coliuspasser axillaris*.

This whydah has been imported in small numbers for many years, in common with the White-winged (*E. albonatus*), Yellow-shouldered (*E. macrocercus*), Red-collared (*E. ardens*) and, occasionally, others. The *Euplectes* whydahs, like all the Ploceidae, are best kept in aviaries; they are active birds, with an energetic courtship display. I can find no record of a breeding in the UK in spite of their former frequent availability. They have been bred on the European Continent and elsewhere; all the breedings have been in aviaries and live food has been provided. In the wild, they nest close to the ground in coarse grass, usually in swampy areas, the cock building a frame of living grass, which is lined by the hen. Incubation and rearing is by the hen alone, the species is polygamous.

## Description

180 mm (7 in), sexually dimorphic (nuptial plumage).
COCK: (Breeding plumage) — Bill bluish grey; irides dark brown; entire plumage velvety black, except for orange-red wing shoulder, wing coverts which are edged with brown, and brown underwing coverts; legs and feet blackish grey.
HEN: Upperparts brownish buff, streaked with black; below pale buff, whitish on belly, with darker streaks; wings have a blackish shoulder patch edged with red.

The cock in eclipse plumage resembles the hen, except for the wing patch and coverts and the streaking is more pronounced.

## Distribution and Habitat

Widespread in Africa south of the Sahara, where suitable habitats occur. Usually grasslands, but also in cultivation and cane fields in some areas of its distribution.

WHITE-WINGED WHYDAH *Euplectes albonotatus*
OTHER NAMES: White-winged Widow-bird, there are four subspecies. Formerly listed as *Coliuspasser albonotatus*.

This species, like *E. axillaris*, is still available and was imported in 1989–90. Its breeding behaviour and general habits are similar to many *Euplectes* species. They are polygamous and a planted aviary, with a heavy growth of rank grasses and other herbage, established before the birds are released into the aviary, will provide the best environment for breeding.

### Description

229 mm (9 in), sexually dimorphic (nuptial plumage).
COCK: (Breeding plumage) — Bill bluish grey; irides brown; entire plumage velvety black, except for a yellow shoulder patch (cinnamon in the subspecies *eques*) and a white patch at the base of the primaries; legs and feet, blackish grey.
HEN: Upper parts brownish buff with sparse dark streaking; slight yellow wash on face and throat; pale buff underparts; faint yellow shoulder patch.

The eclipsed cock resembles the hen, except for heavier dark streaking above.

### Distribution and Habitat

Widespread in grasslands, Africa, south of the Sahara. Usually rank grass and reedbeds, but also inhabits old cultivation and dry acacia savanna in some areas of its distribution.

# 9
# Phasianidae — Quail

Quail is the substantive name used for two distinct groups of birds in the Phasianidae family. The American quails of the subfamily Odontophorinae differ from the Old World members by having a stronger bill (the edges of which are sharp and more or less serrated), although there are other anatomical differences. The quails of the Old World are included in the subfamily Phasianinae and are smaller with rather weak bills and legs. This group includes the 'true' quails of the genus *Coturnix*, the genus *Excalfactoria* (included in *Coturnix* by some taxonomists), and the erroneously named Bush 'quails' (*Perdicula*) of the Indian subcontinent which are really small partridges.

Quail nests are rudimentary, usually consisting of a hollow or 'scrape' in herbage or soil under a grass tuft, bush, tree base, fallen log or similar site. Occasionally some New World species may nest off the ground on a tree stump or where fallen branches make a platform, and sometimes in the old nests of other birds. In most cases the nest hollow is lined with plant material from the immediate vicinity and in some Old World species there may be little or no lining. With the exception of little-known neotropical forms, quails lay large clutches of eggs — up to 20, and sometimes more, in certain New World species. The young are downy, precocial, and active within a short period after hatching. (But even although they can feed themselves, they are still tended and directed towards food by the parents.) The share of parental duties varies in the two subfamilies and genera.

Most species are sexually dimorphic, although in some the differences are negligible. Courtship feeding, the cock calling the hen on finding an insect or other live food is part of the nuptial behaviour in many species. He calls the hen with a special posture, the head often lowered and held to one side, then he gives a low call, holding the offering in the bill tip, to be taken by the hen. A lowered wing display, the cock circling the hen usually with the wing nearest to her lowered and with the secondaries and primaries splayed open, is found in the Old World *Coturnix* and *Excalfactoria* genera, as well as some other genera. Quails find much of their seed and insect food by scratching away loose substrate in the classic 'chicken scratch' fashion of the galliformes. They are also adept at catching insects on growing herbage.

Quails breed in pairs; the strength of the bonding varies with different species and is maintained by behaviour patterns such as the courtship feeding of the hen and the mutual preening in *Excalfactoria* species. The breeding season of some Ethiopian and Asiatic species is opportunistic following rainfall and plant growth. They are gregarious outside of the breeding season and some gather to a limited extent when breeding. The New World species include many which perch to roost and sometimes nest off the ground, while the Old World groups are completely terrestrial. Quails rely on running and concealment in herbage to escape from predators; they are assisted in this by plumage patterns which blend with the surrounding cover, and if pressed, they can explode into almost vertical flight.

## Accommodation and Breeding

There are three main factors to be considered for quail accommodation. Firstly, it should be dry, well protected from prevailing winds and heavy rain, and well drained, especially if it has a flight with a soil or gravel floor. (Wet, muddy floors and poor drainage will result in ill health and breeding failure.) Secondly, the rather nervous nature of quail must be taken into account; until established, they will fly up into the roof when startled and injure their heads. This is overcome to some extent by having aviaries with a height of 1.8–2.4 m (6–8 ft) and providing cover so the birds can hide; or special quail aviaries and cages with a false roof of polythene, hessian or other soft material nailed beneath the true roof can be used. Another method is to cut short the primary feathers of *one* wing which will prevent any explosive vertical flights, and by the time the feathers have regrown after a moult, the birds will be established in their new environment. Although practically all the quail available today have either been bred in the UK or are imported, captive-bred stock, even the domesticated Japanese Quail (*Coturnix japonica*) and the semi-domesticated Chinese Painted Quail (*Excalfactoria chinensis*) will suddenly panic if anything unusual and unexpected occurs. The third important aspect concerning quail accommodation is the control of rodents and predators (the methods for dealing with this problem are given in Chapter One).

The specialised quail aviary is the answer to many of these problems and has been recommended by several authors for some years. There are various designs, but basically they are an enclosed 'aviary' or house with a wire front containing feeding and access doors. A simple sloping roof can be made of polythene roof sheeting, with a false roof of hessian or thin polythene sheeting nailed underneath to prevent head injuries from panic flights. For one pair this house or aviary should be approximately 1.2 × 1.2 × 1.1 m high (4 × 4 × 3 ft) and raised some 60 cm (2 ft) off the ground on an enclosed base or legs. (This ensures the whole structure is kept dry and access for rodents made more difficult than in a conventional aviary.) The best floor covering in a converted or quail aviary is sharp sand and cover can be provided with such items as clumps of twigs tied into bunches and placed upright in two of the corners, thus creating a screen with an entrance at each end. In general, however, the larger quail species will not breed naturally in this type of accommodation, although the fertile eggs can be collected and artificially incubated (described below).

In a conventional aviary that is dry, well drained and protected, one pair of quail will live and breed well. They will co-exist amicably with the seed-eating passerines and also doves, except for the more terrestrial species. Problems can arise with some of the perching New World forms which may frighten the passerines and doves when they go up to roost.

If suitable ground cover in a sheltered area is provided, such as shrubs or clumps of twigs, quail will make a nest scrape lined with a few plants, grass stems, or other available material, although often the scrape is left unlined. Under these conditions they will usually rear their chicks without problems. Many 'natural' breeding failures are due to a spartan environment, no cover for nesting or concealment being provided. The larger New World species need an aviary with a minimum size of 3.8 × 2.4 × 1.8 m high (10 × 8 × 6 ft) for breeding, as they will seldom settle to breed naturally. The Old World *Coturnix* and *Excalfactoria* genera are sometimes kept in trios of one cock to two hens, but I have not found this method very successful. Two cocks of any quail species should never be kept together; even if housed in adjoining aviaries they will try to fight through the wire and their restless behaviour will prevent successful breeding.

## Artificial Incubation and Rearing

In addition to the failure of quail to incubate and rear their chicks due to the insecurity engendered by lack of cover and insufficient space, the natural egg-rolling behaviour of some quail species such as the Chinese Painted Quail (*Excalfactoria chinensis*) has become stereotyped in captivity — the hen lays eggs at random and rolls them around the aviary instead of laying in the next scrape. This species is well on the way to domestication and some strains have been artificially reared for many generations. When these birds were imported from the country of origin, in my experience the imported stock and their naturally reared offspring seldom failed to roll the eggs to the scrape and incubate and rear their chicks. Apart from egg-rolling behaviour, there are other indications that certain quail are losing the instinct to incubate their eggs — the long domesticated Japanese Quail (*Coturnix japonica*), for example, will seldom breed naturally. However, with the incubators, time switches and other equipment now available, hatching and rearing rates for artificial methods are superior to natural breeding methods. In my opinion, however, the latter are the most desirable, as one of the greatest pleasures in aviculture is to watch a hen quail with her brood of tiny chicks.

Artificial incubation is not always a complete success story, and failure is often due to events before the incubation is commenced. On many occasions dirty, slightly cracked and misshapen eggs are incubated and the owner is surprised when the hatching rate is poor. Eggs to be incubated should also be as fresh as possible, for after ten days the hatching rate is often reduced to a very low percentage. Storage until incubation should be in a temperature range of 10–15°C (50–59°F) and the eggs should be turned daily. In static-air incubators a temperature of 38.9–39.4°C (102–103°F) is recommended with a relative humidity of 55%, raised to 70% for the last nine days of incubation. The eggs should be turned by hand at least twice daily if the incubator is 'manual' — that is, without an automatic egg-turning mechanism.

When the chicks hatch, they are transferred to a brooder box, with ventilation holes around the top and dark (infra-red) radiator bulbs suspended over the box, or fixed in the rear panels, to provide heat. The temperature can be adjusted by moving a glass cover over the box top in the case of the fixed lamps or by lowering and raising the suspended lamps. If the number of chicks to be reared is small, a commercial or custom-made hospital cage will make an excellent brooder as it provides an even ambient temperature coupled with efficient control (see Chapter 3). For large numbers, a custom made brooder with a thermostatic temperature control is optimal.

The incubation period for most New World species is 22–23 days and for the Old World *Coturnix* and *Excalfactoria* species 16–18 days. The chicks should be kept at a temperature of 35°C (95°F) at first, which is slowly reduced by 2–3°C (3.6–5.4°F) per week until they are fully feathered. As with the chicks of domestic fowl, observation will indicate if a temperature is satisfactory: if too hot they will spread out away from the heat source, if cold they will huddle in groups. Chick starter crumbs will provide a high protein diet and should be scattered on the floor of the brooder at first until they become used to a feeder or dish. With small groups it is sometimes necessary to use live food to get them feeding. After a few days, chopped green food and millets are added to the diet, although the millet is not essential. Small grit and mineral sources (i.e. crushed oyster shell) should be made available when the chicks show signs of feathering. Water must be provided; the fountain type of inverted water container over a small rimmed dish will prevent the chicks drowning in and fouling the water.

Unlike passerine and dove species, quail from the Ethiopian and Asiatic regions, although opportunistic breeders to some extent, seldom breed in outside aviaries in Europe and the UK in the later months of declining photoperiod. Ivey and Howes found that the egg laying rate of *Coturnix japonica* in *inside* accommodation is optimal with a 14-hour day length, and inhibiting this period reduces the laying rate. In my outside aviaries quail of any species will rarely breed successfully after September.

### Food and Care

The nutrition of quail kept in mixed species aviaries was for many years dismissed by the comment, 'they pick up seed dropped by the other birds'. It was, therefore, hardly surprising that many aviculturists had poor breeding results from their birds. Chick or turkey starter crumbs provide a high protein source for quail and with the essential addition of green food, minerals and grit, will constitute an adequate diet for successful reproduction. I always supplement this with mixed millets and maw seed for smaller species such as the Chinese Painted Quail (*Excalfactoria chinensis*) and the chicks of any species. Young quail should be separated from their parents as soon as the cocks begin to show sexually dimorphic plumage, usually at six to eight weeks.

In many areas of Europe and the USA quail should be wintered in dry sheltered accommodation at a minimum temperature of 10°C (50°F). The worst possible conditions are prolonged periods of rain combined with low temperatures — a common feature of UK winters. Although some aviculturists winter these birds without heat, this is only possible if the accommodation is dry and completely sheltered; I am personally in favour of providing moderate heat in all types of outside accommodation. Quail will dust-bathe at every opportunity, and a large shallow tray filled with clean sand should be provided. It is most important to give drinking water in containers in which newly hatched chicks cannot drown; the dish type of container should have flat stones placed in them to prevent this happening.

## Subfamily Odontophorinae

This subfamily includes the quail of North America which are well known in aviculture and captive-bred in the USA and many other countries. They are attractive, elegant birds with a distinctive head crest; their tarsi carry no spurs.

**Genus** ***Lophortyx***

This is a genus of three species of crested quails which are placed in the genus *Callipela* by some authors. Two are frequently available in the UK: Gambel's Quail (*L. gambelii*) and the California Quail (*L. californica*).

CALIFORNIA QUAIL *Lophortyx californica*
OTHER NAMES: Valley Quail, Crested Quail. There are six subspecies.

This elegant and attractive species has been successfully bred in captivity for many years and soon adjusts to aviaries if kept in well-sheltered accommodation. With adequate nesting cover and space they will rear their own young. I have found they will thrive in a well-drained and sheltered aviary measuring 4.3 × 2.4 × 2.4 m high (14 × 8 × 8 ft) with adequate ground cover and perching facilities. They are popular game birds in the United States and have been successfully introduced into New Zealand and Chile.

Description

255 mm (10 in), sexually dimorphic.
COCK: Bill grey to dark grey; irides brown; forward-bending crest of black spatulate feathers; brow yellowish white with narrow black eyebrow stripes; upper part of head black, shading to reddish brown on nape; throat, chin and cheeks black; throat outlined with brown and black; neck and mantle grey with black and white markings; upper flanks olive brown, abdomen brown with black and dark brown markings; legs and feet greyish brown.
HEN: Shorter crest; head blackish brown. Lacks the brown on abdomen.

Distribution and Habitat

The United States from Oregon to Baja California. Introduced in other western states. A bird of arid country, living in valleys and the lower slopes of mountains, wherever suitable vegetation occurs, usually open bush and areas of cultivation.

## Breeding

PERIOD: In the wild the breeding season commences in January in the south and up to May in the north of their distribution. Breeding in outside aviaries in the UK will begin from the end of March to the beginning of April. They are double brooded in the wild and two broods are reared in captivity by the parents.
NEST: Feral nests are a scrape in cover, lined with nearby vegetation. Sometimes found off the ground in the old nest of another bird in a bush or tree, or where branches and creepers make a suitable site, or a tree stump (Harrison). Aviary nests are the usual scrape in cover, or an open-fronted box with peat and sand on the floor. They will sometimes use a wire basket lined with hay and fixed in a bush or small tree. (The chicks drop from these raised nests without harm.)
EGGS: Ground colour pale creamy-buff, creamy white or yellowish, with fine speckles, spots and blotches of a brown, dull brown and buffish colour. Clutch size usually 12–17, sometimes up to 28 (two hens?).
INCUBATION: Usually carried out by the hen with the cock nearby, who may incubate if the hen dies (Harrison). Period 21–23 days.
CHICKS: The chicks are precocial and downy; sides of head and forehead yellowish buff; crown and nape rufous-brown with darker edges, tapering to a point on the forehead and bordered by a creamy-buff stripe. The back is dark brown with three broad longitudinal yellowish-buff stripes; underparts buffish white. The chicks are active soon after hatching and are tended by both parents who will call them when food is found, the parents' bill pointing at the position of the food. The cock will tend the chicks when the hen commences a second clutch. A suitable rearing food is chick crumbs, or other small-grain commercial preparations which can be ground smaller when the chicks are young. Chopped green food and small live food such as maggots and mealworms

should also be offered, and seeds such as millets and maw can be mixed with the basic commercial food or fed separately.

Behaviour

Courtship feeding is a nuptial behaviour of the California Quail and some other galliform birds. In many species the cock on finding an insect or other choice morsel calls the hen while holding the tit-bit in his bill, and a particular posture, often with the head lowered or tilted to one side, is adopted. The hen then runs to the cock and takes the food from his bill tip. This behaviour is often followed by copulation which would seem to suggest that its functions are to reduce the hen's fear of the cock and increase the likelihood of a successful mating, as well as to maintain the pair bond. In many species a similar posture and call are given when the cock calls the chicks for food. The courtship feeding of the California Quail is less ritualised than that of some other species and often consists of the cock mock-pecking at food on the ground rather than holding it in his bill for the hen. The cock also gives a bowing display to the hen during which the distinctive crest becomes more conspicuous as the head is moved.

These quail are not agressive except towards conspecifics and other terrestrial birds which, if housed together, may squabble over food and nest sites. It must also be remembered that quails will frighten doves and small passerines such as waxbills when they fly up to a perch for roosting.

GAMBEL'S QUAIL *Lophortyx gambelii* **Plate 42**
OTHER NAMES: Desert Quail. Five subspecies are recognised.

This is another attractive quail, closely related to the Californian, which it resembles in appearance. Gambel's Quail was rarely imported into the UK and Europe for many years, but currently captive-bred stock (imported and UK bred) is frequently available. These birds, which are not as nervous as the Californian species, often roost on the ground and are more suitable for housing with passerines and doves. The usual nest site in the wild is a scrape at the base of a bush or tuft of grass, and lined with plant material; occasionally they will nest off the ground on a tree stump. Gambel's Quails are birds of arid country and deserts and although those that are available are bred in captivity, they are often hatched in incubation and reared in brooders. New stock should therefore be established with care and outside accommodation must be sheltered and protected from rain and low temperatures.

Description

240 mm (9½ in), sexually dimorphic.
COCK: Bill greyish; irides reddish brown; tall, forward-bending crest of black, fan-like plumage; forehead, sides of head and throat black, edged with white. Crown and nape reddish brown; upperparts olive brown, abdomen black and breast brownish yellow; flanks reddish brown with buff stripes; legs and feet greyish brown.
HEN: Smaller crest; grey head. No black on the abdomen.

Distribution and Habitat

Colorado to south-western United States and Mexico. In arid desert scrub.

**Genus** ***Colinus***

This genus consists of four or in some checklists three species of Bobwhite Quail. Their distribution includes the USA, Central and South America. Some authors include the White-faced Bobwhite (*C. leucopogon*) with the Crested Bobwhite (*C. cristatus*). The species commonly available in European aviculture is the Common or Virginian Bobwhite, *C. virginianus*.

BOBWHITE QUAIL *Colinus virginianus*
OTHER NAMES: Virginian Bobwhite, Virginian Colin, Common Bobwhite. Eighteen subspecies are recognised.

The Bobwhite receives its common English name from its whistling call, interpreted as 'bob-whoit' or 'poor-bob-whoit'. They are delightful birds and one of the smaller members of the subfamily; rather 'rounder' in appearance and lacking the distinctive head crest of the *Lophortyx* quails.

Bobwhites are free breeding in captivity. The strong pair bond is maintained by courtship feeding and various displays, including the male lateral and bowing displays, and mutual preening. Both sexes take part in building the nest which is domed when enough vegetation is present, often with a tunnel entrance. The cock takes over the care of a brood when the hen commences a second clutch. If the hen dies after laying a clutch, cocks have been known to incubate and care for the chicks. They are far less disruptive towards the other birds in a mixed collection, as they usually roost on the ground and use perches less frequently than the *Lophortyx* species.

Description

230 mm (9 in), sexually dimorphic.
COCK: Bill grey or greyish horn; irides brown; white throat, white eyebrow stripe extending to neck; black band across eyes and bordering white throat; back, upper breast and wings rust brown with yellow and brownish-yellow spots; breast brownish-yellow and white with narrow black stripes; slight crest; legs and feet brownish flesh colour.
HEN: Lighter colouring; throat bright buff. Black markings less well defined.

Distribution and Habitat

United States and Mexico, Central America and the West Indies. Inhabits scrub, grassland, cultivated areas and woodland edges. Introductions have taken place in many areas, some of which have been successful.

**Subfamily Phasianinae**

In this subfamily are the 'typical' Old World quails of the genus *Coturnix*; some authors also include *Excalfactoria* and less frequently *Synoicus*. Collectively these quails have a distribution from Europe through the Ethiopian region and Asia, to Australasia. They are small, rather rounded birds with weak bills and legs. With the exception of the Common or Migratory Quail (*C. coturnix coturnix*) they are sedentary, although some Ethiopian and Asian forms travel considerable distances when moving into areas to breed after rainfall. The bush quails (*Perdicula*) of the Indian subcontinent have larger stronger bills and legs and are really small partridges.

## Genus *Coturnix*

This is a genus of five species, four of which are currently available to aviculturists. These include the Eurasian subspecies *C.c. coturnix* which is a summer visitor to the UK and as a 'British' species, is not included here. *Coturnix* species are completely terrestrial and therefore cause no disruption in a mixed collection. Two cocks should never be kept in the same enclosure and conflict may arise if they are housed with other terrestrial species. The incubation and rearing of the chicks is carried out by the hen.

### HARLEQUIN QUAIL *Coturnix delegorguei* **Plate 43**

Three subspecies are recognised.

This quail has never been a frequent import, although occasionally small shipments have arrived from Africa — I obtained some in 1965. They are free breeding given the right conditions and my small group bred for ten years. Eventually they failed because fresh blood was unobtainable and the cocks in *C. delegorguei* broods outnumber hens by six or seven to one. This imbalance of the sex ratios is also found in some other *Coturnix* species and in *Excalfactoria*. Small numbers of captive-bred stock, either imported or UK bred, are occasionally available. They should be wintered with enough heat to keep their accommodation at 7°C (40°F).

#### Description

150 mm (6 in), sexually dimorphic.
COCK: Bill brown; irides light brown; top of head brownish black with a yellowish brown stripe in the centre; black stripe runs above the eye to the nape; white eyebrow stripe down to neck; cheeks white; throat white edged in black; a black stripe running from bill across cheeks; in centre of throat a black triangular spot; centre of breast black; neck and sides of body reddish brown; upper part of body dark brown with yellow-brown transverse stripes; buff stripes on shoulders and back; wings dark brown; legs and feet yellowish brown.
HEN: Light brown eyebrow stripe and cheeks; abdomen rust with pale feather edging; throat white, edged black, sometimes there is an ill-defined 'necklace' of dark spots.

## Distribution and Habitat

Southern Arabia, Senegal to Ethiopia, South Africa, São Tomé island. Inhabits open plains and grass country.

## Breeding

PERIOD: Wild birds make irregular migrations dependent on rainfall within their vast area of distribution; they appear in areas to breed then move on. Roberts records a breeding period of August to October. In outside aviaries in the UK nesting commences in April/May and continues until October, with two or three broods being reared.
NEST: A scrape lined with grasses and located under a tuft of grass or other herbage; aviary nests are made in similar sites. Harlequin quails will also nest in open-fronted boxes or under a raised board. The hen makes a scrape and will usually add material; the cock sometimes sits in the scrape but I have not seen the male birds take any material to the site.
EGGS: Ground colour varies from light buff to olive brown, usually heavily spotted and blotched with darker brown or reddish brown. Lightly marked and immaculate eggs are sometimes laid. Clutch size 6–9, occasionally up to 12.
INCUBATION: Carried out by the hen. Period 17–18 days.
CHICKS: The precocial, downy chicks are brooded by the hen in the scrape for a few days; those hatched in the early morning are following the hen by about midday. Any chick leaving the scrape is 'called back' by the hen and tucked under her plumage. When they leave the scrape, the hen will usually brood them in the site that night, then cover them in any sheltered area thereafter. On hatching, the chicks' down is yellow-buff, with darker brown stripes on the upperparts. The chicks' development is rapid — they can fly quite well at 10–11 days and can be sexed at 5–6 weeks. The young cocks give adult vocalisations and will try to copulate with the hens, so if the adult cock is still present, the chicks should be removed at this stage.

## Behaviour

The cock Harlequin plays no part in rearing the chicks and

when the chicks are hatched will often harass the hen in attempts to copulate. It is generally accepted that the *Coturnix* quails are polygamous and they have been successfuly bred as trios of two hens to one cock. If kept as monogamous pairs for 'natural' breeding, the cock should be removed just before the chicks hatch, although on rare occasions I have left the cock with the hen without disruption. If fertile eggs are removed for artificial incubation, the cock housed with two or three hens will give the best results.

Harlequin quails are ideal birds to house with passerines and doves, providing species with terrestrial behaviour are avoided. They adjust well to aviary life and will often become tame enough to take mealworms from your hand.

RAIN QUAIL *Coturnix coromandelica*
OTHER NAMES: Black-breasted Quail. There are no subspecies.

The Rain Quail is in many ways the Asiatic counterpart of the Harlequin Quail; in some areas of its distribution it suddenly appears to breed during the rainy season, a characteristic which gives the bird one of its common names. The breeding biology and behaviour of the two quails is also similar if not identical. In captivity the Rain Quail cock plays no part in the incubation or rearing of the chicks, and if monogamous pairs are kept, he is best removed when the chicks hatch. This species was once imported in large numbers from the Indian subcontinent, but now, like the Harlequin, only captive-bred imports or birds that have been captive bred in the UK are occasionally available. They are attractive birds which will breed freely in aviaries once established. Like the Harlequin, I have found that in the majority of broods the cocks outnumber the hens — sometimes a hatch of seven chicks have all proved to be cocks.

Description

150 mm (6 in), sexually dimorphic.
COCK: Bill greyish horn; irides brown; centre of head chestnut, with two black stripes from base of bill to nape; white eyebrow marks and a dark line through the eyes; cheeks and throat white, edged with black; black moustachial lines with a triangular black marking on the chin; upperparts buff and

dark brown; underparts pale yellowish-buff striated with black and a large black mark in the centre of the breast; legs and feet flesh colour.
HEN: Bill brownish-horn. The hen lacks the black marking on head, chin and breast; also the buff striations on the upperparts.

## Distribution and Habitat

India, Sri Lanka, Burma. Frequents open country, grass and cultivated areas, often close to villages.

## JAPANESE QUAIL *Coturnix japonica* **Plate 44**

OTHER NAMES: 'Coturnix' Quail. There are no subspecies.

The Japanese Quail was formerly considered to be a subspecies of the Common or Migratory Quail (*C. c. coturnix*). A domesticated strain has been reared in Japan for several centuries and these birds have also been bred in Europe, the USA and elsewhere for meat and eggs, and since the 1950s in laboratories. In aviculture several colour variations have been bred including a white morph. The cock's call is different to the clear ringing notes of other *Coturnix* species and can be described as a croak or crow. They have been hatched by bantams and in incubators for so many generations that hens in aviaries will seldom incubate naturally. The rapid maturation and reproductive rates of the Japanese Quail have been improved upon in the domestic strains and sexual maturation can be at six weeks.

## Description

N.B. As this species is noted for its variable plumage, the following can only be considered as commonly encountered examples.
150–180 mm (6–7 in)
COCK: Bill brownish or brownish horn; irides brown; upperparts brown, striated and barred with buff and rufous brown; underparts and throat whitish, becoming darker with age; breast uniform brown, abdomen paler; legs and feet flesh colour.
HEN: Similar to the cock, but the breast is paler and speckled with grey and black.

Distribution and Habitat

Sakhalin, Japan to Indochina. Inhabits grasslands and cultivated areas.

**Genus** ***Excalfactoria***

This is a genus of two species, the well-known Asiatic Chinese Painted Quail (E. chinensis) and the Ethiopian-region Blue Quail (*E. adansonii*). This latter species is little known and a very rare import; I can find no published record of a captive breeding. The Chinese Painted Quail is well established in captivity and various colour morphs are bred. This genus has been placed in *Coturnix* but currently most works retain its generic status. *Excalfactoria* species differ from the *Coturnix* in two obvious ways; they have shorter and more curved bills and a larger number of tail feathers. There are also ethological differences: the Chinese Painted Quails are contact birds and unlike the *Coturnix* will frequently 'clump' together to roost, and mutual preening is also frequently observed. *E. chinensis* cocks will also tend the chicks by finding food and brooding them after they leave the scrape. Occasionally Chinese Painted cocks have covered the eggs for brief periods in my aviaries but I have never known *Coturnix* species do this. Their vocalisations are a series of mainly crowing notes, nothing like *Coturnix* calls.

CHINESE PAINTED QUAIL *Excalfactoria chinensis* **Plate 45**
OTHER NAMES: Blue-breasted Quail, Indian Blue Quail, and erroneously 'Button Quail' (see Turnicidae). There are nine subspecies.

Captive-bred stock is always available and importations from the countries of origin no longer occur in the UK (at least on a commercial scale). The smallest species in the Phasianidae, the Chinese Painted Quail is an attractive bird, free breeding and reasonably hardy, although it should not be wintered in outside aviaries without adequate protection and heat at about 8°C (45°F). Like the *Coturnix* quails, some breeders winter them without heat if it is a mild one, and provided there is adequate shelter no harm will result. However, being terrestrial birds they can easily suffer from frost-bite on the toes, and in my opinion they winter more successfully in moderately heated accommodation. Like *Coturnix* they are completely terrestrial and can share accommodation with small passerines and doves.

Description

130 mm (5 in), sexually dimorphic.
COCK: Bill black or greyish black; irides reddish brown; throat black surrounded by a broad white band edged with black; forehead, face, side of neck, breast and flank bluish grey; abdomen russet brown in centre; tail dark brown; legs and feet yellow.
HEN: Upperparts mottled black and rufous brown; underparts pale buff, heavily barred with black on the breast and flanks; lower abdomen rusty brown.

Distribution and Habitat

South and east Asia through Indonesia to Australia. Inhabits grasslands, marshy areas and swamps. In Burma they have bred on polo grounds and race courses (Smythies 1960).

# 10
# Turnicidae — Hemipodes (Button Quail)

These quail-like birds are represented by 15 species, including the somewhat aberrant Quail Plover (*Ortyxelos*) of Africa. This Old World group, although they are members of the Gruiformes, are often confused with the true quails (*Coturnix* spp). This confusion is largely due to the use of the name 'button quail' for the group, as many importers, aviculturists and sometimes ornithologists refer to the true quails as 'button quail'. The use of the alternative name hemipodes would largely obviate this undesirable confusion, for although they resemble quails in appearance, there are anatomical, reproductive and behavioural differences.

The family differs from the true quails and the Phasianidae in general by the lack of a hind toe and a crop. Females are more brightly coloured than males and larger. Hemipodes are polyandrous, the females competing against rivals for males, and giving booming or drumming advertising calls to attract the male partners. Limited evidence from field observations and captive breedings indicates that the female courts a number of males, lays a clutch of eggs, then leaves each male to incubate and rear the chicks, although in studies of captive Barred Hemipodes (*Turnix suscitator*) females paired with one male have retained a pair bond and helped to rear the chicks (Trollope). Unlike the large clutches of eggs laid by quail, the clutch size of hemipodes is three or four (two in *Ortyxelos*). Development of the chicks and reproductive maturity is rapid, adult size, weight and plumage being attained at five to six weeks. Flieg compared the growth and maturation rates of the African subspecies of *Turnix sylvatica* with that of the Chinese Painted Quail (*Excalfactoria chinensis*) and his data indicated that the *Turnix* species had a much faster growth and maturation rate.

Hemipodes have never been popular with aviculturists, for although attractive and interesting birds, the females lack the brighter colours of the male Chinese Painted Quail and the free-breeding *Coturnix* species. This is a pity because there is much to learn about the behaviour of the Turnicidae and this is a classic case of where observations of the aviculturist can supplement and even replace field studies in some areas. The observations of the naturalist and aviculturist David Seth-Smith early in this century provided much valuable information on the reproduction and reproductive behaviour of the Turnicidae.

## Care and Breeding

In this section information is given on the care and breeding of the two species which are most often seen in captivity in this country. Other species have occasionally been kept in the larger and well established zoological gardens, for example the Painted Hemipode (*Turnix varia*). Commercial importations have always been erratic and small in number but they have been available in 1989–90.

Hemipodes are certainly not hardy in the literal sense of the word and although my birds have been kept in an outside planted aviary between April and November, after that time, or before, if severe weather occurs, they are removed to a bird room heated to approximately 10°C (50°F). They are kept in box cages during the winter, the cages measuring a minimum 120 × 45 × 45 cm high (4 × 1½ × 1½ ft). Ideally the birds should be kept in outside aviaries with a heated shelter attached, inside which they can be shut during periods of very wet weather, frost and fog. Newly imported birds should be isolated in quarters maintained at 15–20°C (60–65°F) until they become adjusted to their environment. The cages can be fitted with hessian tops or padded roofs, to prevent injury if the birds should fly up in panic. The aviaries should be well drained and although protected from heavy rain and suchlike, access to direct sunlight should be available in some areas, as these birds are avid sunbathers. They also enjoy dust-bathing, which is a social affair and most amusing to watch, especially when both parents and well-grown chicks indulge in hurried scufflings and pivot-turns such that they resemble phrenetic and uncontrolled clockwork toys. I can always stimulate the birds to dust-bathe by tipping fine sand or dry soil on the aviary floor. In my experience, best results are obtained in a fairly large aviary measuring approximately 2.4 × 1.8 × 1.8 m high (8 × 6 × 6 ft). The height is important, for like quail newly imported birds can be nervous, and may fly directly upwards if frightened, which can result in damage to their heads. However, they soon settle down and panic flights are not as great a problem as with imported *Coturnix* species. Any very nervous birds can be protected by cutting a few primary feathers short on one wing to prevent such flights.

The newly hatched chicks of species such as the Barred Hemipode (*Turnix suscitator*) and the Little Button Quail (*Turnix sylvatica*) are as small or perhaps slightly smaller than those of the Chinese Painted Quail. So if the mesh size of the aviary wire is 12 mm (½ in) or greater, the aviary sides must be boarded up to approximately 30 cm (12 in) high to prevent their escape.

Hemipodes like *Coturnix* quail can be kept in the same aviary with finches, waxbills and doves — in fact any birds which are not terrestrial, aggressive or predatory. However, adult females will fight and should not be kept together, especially female Barred Hemipodes, which are particularly aggressive. Hemipodes do not perch, so therefore frights to small passerines such as waxbills and finches are not a problem. Flieg kept three pairs of the South African Hemipode *Turnix sylvatica lepurana* in a cage measuring 3.1 × 1.1 m (10 × 3 ft) along with lovebirds, sand-grouse, sand plovers and sparrow larks, and found the group compatible.

## Food and Feeding

I have always fed adult birds on mixed millets, maw, commercial chick crumbs and canary mixture; live food is provided in the form of mealworms and white worms with the addition of collected insects during the spring and summer. I also put a heap of dead grasses and weeds in the aviary and regularly fork this over. Small insects, spiders and other invertebrates are essential for the young chicks during the first few days after hatching and green food should always be provided in the form of seeding grasses, chickweed and sprouted and growing seeds. My stock of Ocellated Hemipodes (*Turnix ocellata*) have taken commercial softbill mixture, but not the Barred Hemipode (*T. suscitator*) or the Little Button Quail (*T. sylvatica*). Flieg fed his *T. sylvatica* on Purina game bird chow mixed with Purina trout chow and small seeds; small mealworms were given when breeding. Seed should be provided in shallow glazed earthenware dishes, mealworms in deeper dishes, the rim having a slight overhang on the inside to prevent their escape.

### Water

Hemipodes like pigeons and sand-grouse drink by sucking; the bill is gently dipped just below the water surface, and the water taken with a 'bibbling' action of the mandibles, the head is then raised to the 'normal' position. In captivity water should be provided in flat earthenware dishes which are shallow enough to prevent young chicks drowning. Pieces of flat tile or flat stone can be placed in dishes as a further precaution against accidents. I have never observed captive hemipodes water bathing or rain bathing.

**Genus** *Turnix*

BARRED HEMIPODE *Turnix suscitator*

OTHER NAMES: Barred Button Quail, Bustard Quail, Common Button Quail, Blue-legged Bustard Quail.

### Description

115–140 mm (4½–5½ in), sexually dimorphic in size and plumage, the hen being larger and more brightly coloured.

COCK: Bill grey; irides yellow; upperparts rufous brown, above marked with light buff and dark brown; cream-coloured throat and breast barred with black; abdomen buff; legs and feet bluish grey.

HEN: Bill grey, thicker and less attenuated than the cock's; forehead, crown and cheeks spotted with light grey; throat and middle of the breast black, the barring heavier and more widely spaced than with the cock; legs and feet as for the cock.

Although in bird literature the black throat and breast markings of the hen are referred to as nuptial plumage, all the female chicks I have bred have moulted into this plumage pattern, without further change during the following adult seasonal moults.

## Distribution and Habitat

Wide distribution, including the Indian subcontinent, northern Sri Lanka, Malaysia, Thailand, China and Taiwan. Ali (1955) records the habitat for the Indian subcontinent as every type of country excepting dense forest and desert, with a partiality for scrub-jungle, light deciduous forest and the neighbourhood of cultivation.

## Breeding

PERIOD: From June until September for successful breeding, although eggs have been laid in May.

NEST: The nests built by my birds have varied from a cave-like construction at the base of a thick pile of dried grasses and weeds to a scrape in the soil lined with stems. These rudimentary nests are probably the results of keeping a hen with a single cock, thus preventing the complete polyandrous reproductive cycle. All the nests, irrespective of the amount of material used, were well concealed, e.g. at the base of weeds, in an earth clod or bush. The well constructed nests often had stems sticking out from the top of the dome like a canopy — during incubation this was often pulled down to obscure the sitting cock. The materials used were dried grasses and weeds, and dead convolvulus stems.

Both sexes take part in the nest building which is rapidly completed; stems were held in the bill tip and pulled to the site with sharp jerks, sometimes the stem would be across the bird's back. One partner, usually the cock, would sit in the nest and take the material from the gatherer, pulling the stems into place with the same sharp jerks.

EGGS: Light stone or greyish-white ground colour, blotched and spotted with dark brown and a few purplish red spots. Clutch size 3 or 4.

INCUBATION: Carried out entirely by the cock. Period 12–13 days. With the monogamous pairs the hen will lay further clutches, but these are wasted as the cock is already incubating the first clutch.

CHICKS: Newly hatched chicks are brown with darker streaks above and light brown underparts. They are very light, almost cream coloured in the facial area, with a single dark stripe from crown to bill. The chicks remain in the nest for approximately six to ten hours and are brooded by the cock. On leaving the nest they are very active, the cock and the hen offering them small insects etc. on the tip of the bill. They can take commercial chick starter crumbs and seed about five or six days after hatching. Both parents brood the chicks up to approximately 14 days after hatching and from this age a lateral clumping position is adopted with the chicks between the parents. It is usual for each parent to take charge of the feeding of one or two of the chicks. Those that are cared for by the hen will follow her and run to her when she gives a food call. The same behaviour applies to the chicks looked after by the cock who, by this stage, are almost as large as their male parent.

## Behaviour

I was unable to create a successful polyandrous group with this species. In an aviary 2.4 × 1.8 × 1.8 m high (8 × 6 × 6 ft) any combination of pair introductions or the placing of two cocks and a hen together always resulted in the cocks fighting, or the hen chasing one cock to near exhaustion. However, I was successful with *T. sylvatica*, indicating that *T. suscitator* is a much more aggressive species.

Courtship feeding by the hen occurs frequently and often precedes copulation, the hen offering the tit-bit to the cock on the bill tip in the same manner as the parents feed the chicks. The hen strides rapidly around the aviary then stops suddenly and rocks her body forwards and backwards. If the cock approaches, courtship feeding takes place, then the hen crouches and the cock mounts and copulates. On one occasion reversed copulation was observed, the hen mounting the cock.

Egg-rolling behaviour has often been observed in this species; it is always performed by the hen walking backwards and pushing the egg in the desired direction with the underside of her bill. This differs from the egg-rolling behaviour of the Chinese Painted Quail (*Excalfactoria chinensis*) where the egg, although pushed along with the bill, is guided by the legs.

## ANDALUSIAN HEMIPODE *Turnix sylvatica*

OTHER NAMES: Little Button Quail, Striped Button Quail.

### Description

115–130 mm (4½–5 in), sexually dimorphic in size, the female being larger. There is also some indication that cocks are more heavily spotted than hens with the buff on the breast paler. With this species having such a wide geographical distribution there is variation in the markings and size of subspecies.

Bill light horn to brownish; irides pale yellow; crown brown with darker streaks, back of head rufous; upperparts chestnut brown, barred with black and yellowish. Underparts whitish, the breast buff, browner in the centre. Sides spotted with black and chestnut; tail rather pointed. Legs and feet flesh coloured.

### Distribution and Habitat

From the Iberian Peninsula through Africa and Asia. Habitats can vary from sandy plains with palmetto scrub, thickets, planted fields and stubble to grassy plains, marshy country and open scrub-jungle.

### Breeding

PERIOD: Successful breeding has occured from May to August, with eggs laid in September.
NEST: Most nests were a scrape lined with grass stems, although on one occasion a crude dome of stems was made which was sited at the base of a pile of dead grasses and weeds.
EGGS: Ground colour greyish white, creamy white or yellowish, speckled and spotted with greyish brown, with a few purple spots or blotches. Clutch size 3 or 4.
INCUBATION: Carried out by the cock. Period 12–13 days. The hen lays further clutches while the cock is incubating the first.
CHICKS: Newly hatched chicks are similar to those of *T. suscitator* but darker on the ventral surface; they also appear to be slightly smaller. The rearing patterns are the same as for *T.*

*suscitator*, the cock brooding the chicks in the nest for some hours after hatching, and both cock and hens calling them to feed from the parent's bill tip. The hen's feeding of the chicks was infrequent for the first three or four days after hatching and she rarely brooded the chicks.

Behaviour

A polyandrous group of two cocks and a hen was established with this species, both cocks successfully hatching and rearing broods. The hen also fed the chicks but her attention was spasmodic. In Flieg's larger group of three pairs, a male hatched young successfully on only one occasion, the other clutches laid were removed and artificially incubated. The lack of success of the incubating cocks was attributed to the constant harassment by the hens until the sitting cocks deserted the eggs. As with *T. suscitator* courtship feeding and body-rocking display by the hen precedes copulation.

Egg-rolling behaviour has been frequently observed; it would appear that in this species the egg is tucked between the legs, otherwise the method of rolling is the same as for *T. suscitator*.

# 11
# Columbidae — Pigeons and Doves

There are no ornithological differences between pigeons and doves. In the UK and some other parts of the world the larger members of the family are called pigeons and the smaller, doves. The species covered in this book are the smaller seed-eating species which are generally referred to as doves. These and many other members of the family are similar in their breeding biology and behaviour. The majority build flimsy nests, lay two or sometimes one egg and both parents share the duties of incubation and care of the young. Diurnal incubation is divided between the sexes, the cock sitting from about mid-morning until late afternoon, the hen then taking over and sitting through the night. In captivity either sex may cover the eggs for brief periods if their partner leaves the nest to feed.

The Columbidae are a successful family, in spite of their weak bills and the rather delicate appearance of many forms, helpless young and flimsy nests. Reproductively they are very successful with a pattern of 'small profits but rapid returns'. Most species have a short incubation and fledgling period so if the nest is found by a predator, they have lost a flimsy nest and two eggs or young, quickly replaced. The rapid growth rate of the young is due to the parent's production of crop milk which is considered to be a major factor for their reproductive success. Crop milk means that, unlike other breeding seed-eating species, doves do not have to provide vast quantities of live food for their young. However, as pointed out by Goodwin (1970), crop milk is only one of the several ways in which seed-eating birds have solved the problem of feeding their young. He considers that other factors — rapid reproductive rate, effective escape behaviour, hardiness and longevity — contribute more to their success than crop milk. In my experience, many species of doves in captivity will take live food whether breeding or not. Wild doves, especially the more terrestrial forms, also eat invertebrates. Apart from some rock-dwelling and terrestrial species doves are arboreal, nesting, roosting and seeking shelter in trees.

## Accommodation and Breeding

The majority of dove species can be kept successfully with seed-eating passerines and breeding will take place without conflict. As a general rule only one species should be housed in each aviary. If more than one pair is kept in the same enclosure, they should be unrelated and the aviary as large as possible, with plenty of potential nesting sites. I have had good results in aviaries 3.1 × 1.1 × 2.4 m high (10 × 3½ × 8 ft) housing one pair of doves, two pairs of small passerines and one pair of small terrestrial quail such as the Chinese Painted Quail (*Excalfactoria chinensis*). One third of the aviary was covered with translucent plastic sheeting, and the birds were protected from predators and the attentions of mice by the methods described in Chapter One. A sheet of heavy-duty clear plastic sheeting fixed approximately 50 mm (2 in) beneath the true roof will prevent the doves injuring their heads on the wire, if frightened.

The nesting sites favoured in my aviaries are clumps of cut gorse branches hung up under cover. Wire baskets and flat boxes with a rim of about 25 mm (1 in) are also used. Although the majority of species in the wild build a nest largely of twigs and occasionally, plant stems and other material, I have found my birds will seldom use twigs, even though a wide variety of every size has been provided. They use instead dried grasses, plant stems and artificial material such as wood-wool.

Most of the free-breeding dove species will rear at least three or four broods in a season. As each brood leaves the nest the cock will take over most of their feeding and I separate the young when the following brood is hatched, as by this time,the first brood can feed themselves, and the cock will in most cases harass them. The chicks are fed on crop milk for the first few days, then small seed and soft foods are given in addition to the crop milk. The parent takes the chick's bill into its own and the crop milk is regurgitated with a gentle pumping motion. Sometimes both chicks are fed 'in tandem', their bills in the parent's at the same time.

## Food and Care

Doves swallow seeds whole, so it is no good providing large seeds such as maple peas for the small species. The smaller doves such as the Diamond (*Geopelia cuneata*) and the Masked Dove (*Oena capensis*) are fed on millets, small canary seed, maw, niger and seeds of similar size. In a separate dish I provide a dove 'tonic' mixture consisting of Dari, 'finch' seeds and very small cut maize. The larger species will take milo in addition to the other seeds, and in all cases green food and seeding grasses when in season should be provided. Diced cheese is recommended by several authors and doubtless would provide an excellent protein source for breeding pairs, if they will take it, but my doves will not. Chick crumbs are taken by some pairs when they get used to them and provide an excellent nutritional base for the chicks. Small mealworms should also be provided for breeding pairs — all my doves take live food, with some species taking large quantities when breeding. The main advantage in 'mixed' aviaries is that passerines and doves will often take the other's 'diet' and benefit from the variety.

Mineralised grit and Kilpatrick's pigeon minerals should always be available, also fine grit, oystershell and crushed cuttle fish bone. Water for drinking and bathing should be given in heavy shallow dishes, a few pieces of flat stone or tiles will ensure that newly fledged chicks will not drown.

Although some aviculturists winter foreign doves without heat, from November until April in my shelters heat at 8°C (45°F) is provided. Doves are not delicate when established, but I have found that they are fitter the following season if moderate heat is provided.

When catching doves great care must be exercised; they are nervous, soft-feathered birds and clumsy handling will result in them losing a good deal of their plumage, besides suffering unnecessary stress.

### Genus *Streptopelia* (Turtle Doves)

This genus contains several species well known in aviculture including the domesticated variey of *S. roseogrisea*, the Barbary Dove. It has been said that this dove has been domesticated longer than any other avian 'species'. They are widely kept and bred and have been used (with varying degrees of success) as foster parents for the more difficult species of foreign seed-eating doves. The generic name of *Turtur* was formerly used for these doves, but is now used for the African wood doves.

Although turtle doves nest, roost and shelter in trees, they are primarily ground feeders. Like most species in the family they are sunbathers and often lie along the dusty verges of roads and open spaces — behaviour which (as remarked by Goodwin) has led to incorrect records for dust-bathing in this genus.

Several Asiatic and African species of *Streptopelia* used to be frequently imported, now perhaps two are regularly available and one other occasionally.

RED COLLARED DOVE *Streptopelia tranquebarica*
OTHER NAMES: Red Ring Dove, Red Turtle Dove, Dwarf Turtle Dove. There are three subspecies.

This species shows a more marked sexual dimorphism than other *Streptopelia* and is probably the smallest member of the genus. They are attractive little doves and are imported fairly frequently but not regularly. Like many other members of the genus, they are free breeding in captivity, usually building a typical dove nest of twigs in an open site, occasionally using a nest box. I have not bred them myself, but Kendall (1973) has been very successful with these doves, finding them hardy once established as well as free breeding. Two pairs bred successfully in an area of ten square metres, both pairs establishing territories without serious conflict occurring.

Description

200 mm (8 in), sexually dimorphic.
COCK: Bill black; irides dark brown; entire plumage mauvish pink, paler below except for the head and back which are grey and the tail which is grey and white; broad, black half-collar on hind neck; legs and feet red brown.
HEN: Entire plumage greyish brown with half collar, as cock.

Distribution and Habitat

Tibet, India to Indochina and the northern Philippines.

Inhabits open country with trees, scrub-jungle, dry woodland and areas of cultivation.

LAUGHING DOVE *Streptopelia senegalensis*
OTHER NAMES: Palm Dove, Senegal Dove, Little Brown Dove. There are eight subspecies.

This once frequently imported dove has a wide African and Asiatic distribution; they adjust well to captivity and are free breeding. The Laughing Dove would make an excellent subject for establishment in captivity, they are attractive, can be sexed visually and will rear four broods or more between April and November in outside aviaries.

### Description

250 mm (10 in), sexually dimorphic.
COCK: Bill blackish or greyish black; irides brown; orbital ring whitish; plumage mainly dark mauve-pink, lower abdomen white; lower back, rump and wings grey; front and sides of neck has a black-and-white checked collar; central tail feathers greyish brown, the outer are white and grey; legs and feet purplish red.
HEN: Slightly smaller than cock, plumage generally duller.

### Distribution and Habitat

Africa, Arabia and Asia Minor to India. Inhabits arid scrub and thornbush country in the vicinity of water. In many areas of its range found in cultivated oases, gardens, villages and towns.

### Breeding

PERIOD: Irregular and extended in the wild, Whistler records from January to October for the Indian subcontinent. In captivity they will breed literally every month of the year. In outside aviaries in areas such as northern Europe breeding attempts usually fail after late October and November. The birds should be removed to winter quarters at this time and the sexes housed separately.
NEST: Thin twigs, grass stems and roots form a fragile

platform built in a variety of sites, including trees, bushes and the window sills and beams of houses, very occasionally on the ground. Aviary nests are built mainly of grass and plant stems — my birds seldom use the twigs provided. They will nest in wire baskets and shallow wooden trays, but the favoured site is in thick clumps of gorse fixed under cover. Nests have varied from shallow depressions in gorse, with the addition of a few stems, to quite substantial structures of grass and plant stems. The hen sits in the site apparently selected by the cock and arranges the material he brings.

EGGS: White and glossy. Clutch size 2; on the rare occasions my birds have laid 3 eggs, only 2 have hatched.

INCUBATION: The usual dove pattern of shared incubation, the cock sitting from about 09.00 hours until 15.00–16.00 hours, the hen then taking over and sitting throughout the night. If one partner comes off the nest to feed during the day, the other will cover the eggs, especially during periods of colder weather. Incubation period 13–14 days.

CHICKS: Fed and brooded by both parents. They are seldom left uncovered for the first few days of life, even in warm weather. The chicks often leave the nest as early as 11 or 12 days, before they can fly. The cock feeds them and the hen often commences a second clutch the day after the chicks leave the nest, usually in the same site. The chicks commence feeding themselves at about 12 days out of the nest although the cock will continue to feed them. The chicks should be removed from the aviary when the next brood hatches.

### Behaviour

Laughing Doves become quite steady in an aviary and will only panic if startled by 'unusual' movements made without warning or at the sight of a cat suddenly appearing. Although not aggressive to small passerines, they should not be housed with other doves, unless the aviary is very large. I have tried housing them with unrelated dove species and for a time there is no conflict, but sooner or later the cock Laughing Doves will become aggressive. The cock has a bowing display, and copulation is usually preceded by billing — that is, the hen's bill enters the cock's and he makes a pumping motion, as if he is feeding a chick.

**Genus *Turtur* (Wood Doves)**

The genus *Turtur* is composed of five species of African doves, which together with the closely related Masked Dove (*Oena capensis*) form a group known as African Spot-Wing Doves (Goodwin).

Four species of these medium-sized doves are available, the most frequently imported being *Turtur chalcospilos*, *T. afer* and *T. abyssinicus*. This trio adjust well to aviary life and can be free breeding. Their main avicultural disadvantage is that the sexes are alike and they are apparently impossible to sex visually. The morphological similarity of this homogenous trio often leads to confusion and the newcomer to aviculture must be wary of being offered a 'pair' consisting of two species. The Tambourine Dove (*T. tympanistria*) is imported in small numbers every year and is the only member of the genus which is sexually dimorphic. *T. brehmeri*, the Blue-headed Wood Dove, is the least known member of the genus and rarely imported.

BLACK-BILLED WOOD DOVE *Turtur abyssinicus*
OTHER NAMES: Black-billed Blue-spotted Wood Dove, Abyssinian Wood Dove.There are no subspecies.

This dove along with the very closely related *T. chalcospilos* and *T. afer* (which differs from them mainly in bill colour) has been considered a superspecies. Certainly the trio are alike in appearance and voice. Their breeding biology and behaviour would also appear to be the same from the information available, and therefore the details given for this species also apply to the other two species. *T. abyssinicus* will take seeds up to the size of wheat and cut maize; live food is also taken.

Description

200–215 mm (8–8½ in), sexes alike.
Bill black, with a narrow dark line extending from gape to eye; irides brown or dark brown; forehead, cheeks, ear-coverts and orbital skin light grey; crown and nape bluish grey; upperparts light brown, shading to light grey below with a mauve tinge, more pronounced on the breast; closed wing shows five

iridescent spade-shaped spots, a group of three on the greater coverts, and two on the secondaries (these spots are joined at the larger end of the 'spade', giving an appearance at any distance of two small blotches); tips of primaries blackish; underside of wing chestnut, sometimes showing a chestnut edge when wing is closed; two greyish-black bars across base of tail; tail feathers grey with black tips; legs and feet dark red or dark purplish-black.

## Distribution and Habitat

The drier parts of tropical Africa, from Senegal to Eritrea and northern Ethiopia. Frequents dry scrub and woodland.

## Breeding

PERIOD: Nesting in January is recorded for East Africa; probably extensive breeding at any time of the year, as reported for *T. afer*. In aviaries Black-billed Wood Doves will nest from April until November or later if the weather is mild, but late nesting is seldom successful and they should be housed in winter quarters at that time. Two or three broods are reared.
NEST: A typical dove nest in a tree or shrub; aviary nests are usually made of grasses and plant stems, and sometimes a few twigs are used. The favoured sites are in clumps of gorse hung up at a height of about 1.2–2 m (4–7 ft); wire baskets and shallow wooden boxes are sometimes used. The site is selected by the cock, who then brings nest material to the hen for her to arrange while sitting in the chosen spot.
EGGS: Colour varies from cream to light buff. Clutch size 2, rarely 3.
INCUBATION: The usual pattern of shared incubation between the sexes. Period 12–13 days, although 14 has been recorded.
CHICKS: Fed and brooded by both parents. The chicks leave the nest at 12 to 17 days, the time in the nest appearing to be dependent on the weather in captivity. Broods hatching after August/September in the UK spend a longer period in the nest. The young commence feeding themselves at 20 to 22 days after hatching.

### Behaviour

When the cock has selected a nest site, he will sit in the site and flick (or twitch) both wings, with head lowered and tail raised. The iridescent wing markings are conspicuous as the wings are moved. When the hen is approached on a perch or the ground the wing nearest to her is flicked and she will sometimes flick her wing. Copulation is usually preceded by billing — often the bills merely touch without the hen's bill entering the cock's. These doves are excellent subjects for housing with passerines, and could possibly be housed with other unrelated dove species in a large aviary.

## GREEN-SPOTTED WOOD DOVE *Turtur chalcospilos* **Plate 46**

OTHER NAMES: Emerald-spotted Wood Dove. There are two subspecies.

This dove is the most frequently imported species of the genus and if a true pair can be selected are free breeding in captivity.

### Description

200 mm (8 in), sexes alike.
Very similar to *T. abyssinicus*, the iridescent wing marking in this species consisting of two large patches on the closed wing. The patches are usually shining emerald green or golden green, rarely bluish green. These birds are also slightly darker on the underparts than *T. abyssinicus*.

### Distribution and Habitat

From Ethiopia and northern Somaliland in the east, Katanga and Angola in the west, south to the Cape. Inhabits dry veld, thornscrub and dry woodland.

## BLUE-SPOTTED WOOD DOVE *Turtur afer*

OTHER NAMES: Red-billed Wood Dove, Red-billed Blue-spotted Wood Dove, Sapphire-spotted Dove. There are no subspecies.

Not as frequently imported as the two preceding species, this dove has also proved to be free-breeding and an excellent subject for aviaries.

Description

200 mm (8 in), sexes alike.
This species differs from *T. chalcospilos* and *T. abyssinicus* by its bill colour which is red, paler and yellowish at the tip, purplish at the base. When observed in the same enclosure as the preceding species their appearance is generally browner and less greyish. Those I have seen also appear to be slightly smaller.

Distribution and Habitat

Africa south of the Sahara, east to Ethiopia and south to Angola, Zimbabwe and the Transvaal. Lives in wooded country, especially wood and scrub near streams and rivers. Replaced by *T. chalcospilos* and *T. abyssinicus* in drier areas and by the Tambourine Dove (*T. tympanistria*) in denser forest.

TAMBOURINE DOVE *Turtur tympanistria* **Plate 47**
OTHER NAMES: White-breasted Wood Dove, Forest Dove, White-breasted Pigeon. There are two subspecies.

The Tambourine Dove is an attractive species which becomes very steady when established. They are occasionally imported and have the great advantage of being visually sexable. Breeding records, however, are few and I kept this species for six years before they reared young. It would appear they take a long time to settle down and unlike some other dove species, will not breed the first season in captivity. Malcolm Ellis told me of an aviculturist in East Africa who has been very successful with these doves. He bred them in a heavily planted aviary which was rather dark, probably resembling the birds' natural forest habitat. My birds take a lot of live food and it is possible their dietary needs are different from those of the other members of the genus.

The first pair I obtained, although they appeared fit and healthy, did not call or make any attempt to nest for six years. When a second pair was obtained, both the cocks began to give advertising calls. The new pair (obtained from another aviculturist who had had them for three years without any reproductive activity) bred that season, so it is possible the stimulus of auditory and visual contact with conspecifics is a vital factor. Their advertising and nest-calls are similar to those of the other wood doves, but deeper in tone. The wing-flicking display and billing action are also similar but the head is not lowered when the cock is sitting in the nest site.

Description

190–200 mm (7½–8 in), sexually dimorphic.
COCK: Bill reddish-purple with blackish tip; irides dark brown; a black line from the gape to the eye; upperparts dark brown with blue-black spots on the wings; white forehead, eyestripe and underparts; short tail; legs and feet dark purplish-red.
HEN: White parts washed with grey; wing spots lack metallic gloss.

Distribution and Habitat

Africa from Sierra Leone and southern Ethiopia southwards, and the Comoro Islands. Inhabits forest, riparian woods and dense scrub.

**Genus *Oena***

MASKED DOVE *Oena capensis* **Plate 48**
OTHER NAMES: Cape Dove, Namaqua Dove, Long-tailed Dove. There are two subspecies.

This elegant little dove is the single species of this monotypic genus; they are more frequently imported than any other African dove. Although sexually dimorphic, like the Tambourine Dove they are not often bred and take a long time to become established. I have not had a pair breed until the second or third season in captivity, then some pairs will rear two or three broods, sometimes breeding successfully as late as November (in an average UK season). My birds are moved into heated accommodation with a temperature of 8–10°C (45–50°F) in November, or earlier if the weather is severe. They should not be subjected to the long nights and low temperatures of mid-winter. There is no doubt the climate of northern Europe is not the best for these sun-loving doves and the better breeding results have been achieved in California. Probably the most favourable housing in northern Europe would be inside accommodation, dry and warm with plenty of light.

Masked Dove behaviour is similar to that of the *Turtur* species; the wing-flicking display is accompanied by the long tail being moved rapidly up and down in unison with the wing movements. They are excellent companions for the smaller passerine species and even imported birds are very steady. When I feed my birds they often perch on my hand, arm or head and have to be gently lifted off, perched on a finger, and put back on the feeding platform.

### Description

200 mm (8 in) including tail of approximately 100 mm (4 in), sexually dimorphic.

COCK: Bill purple, sometimes orange-red at the base with yellow-orange tip; irides brown; orbital skin grey; forehead, throat, chest and tail black; tail long and graduated; shoulders grey; wing coverts grey with violet-blue spots; mantle brown; rump crossed with dark bands; underparts white or whitish; legs and feet purple.

HEN: The same as the cock but lacks the black forehead, throat and chest.

N.B. In shape and size these doves resemble the Australian Diamond Dove (*Geopelia cuneata*) which is a domesticated species.

### Distribution and Habitat

Africa, from Senegal to Arabia and Cape Province; also Madagascar. Frequents dry, open scrub country, open wood areas, cultivated areas, gardens, villages and towns.

## Genus *Chalcophaps* (Emerald Doves)

This genus consists of two species of plump, rather long-legged doves. They are largely terrestrial and feed on the ground although they roost and usually nest in trees. Some of the various subspecies of the Emerald Dove (*C. indica*) are imported in small numbers, but the little known Brown-backed Emerald Dove (*C. stephani*) has probably never been commercially imported.

## EMERALD DOVE *Chalcophaps indica* **Plate 49**

OTHER NAMES: Green-winged Dove, Little Green Pigeon, Green-backed Dove. Thirteen subspecies of this widely distributed species are recognised.

The Emerald Dove has been bred fairly frequently. They are active, fast flying birds, best housed in large aviaries with ample cover. Because of their terrestrial habits they should not be kept with quail and although not aggressive birds, they are fairly large and will disturb passerine species when they fly up to roost. In my aviaries I had a pair that built a nest consisting of a few stems and twigs on the ground, and inside two light buffish eggs were laid. After five days of incubation I found the hen dead — she had been frightened and had flown into the wire. The cock made spasmodic attempts at covering the eggs for another two days, then took no further interest in the nest. The usual nest sites in captivity are in bushes, although wire baskets and flat boxes with low sides have been used. The nests have often been substantial and new material has been added when a second or third clutch has been laid. The incubation period for the two eggs is 14 days (16 days has also been recorded); the young are fledged at 12–13 days, becoming independent some 18 days after leaving the nest.

The advertising call of the cock is a deep, distinctive 'hoon, tuk-hoon' — 'hoon'. When approached by the hen he will move his head up and down in a bobbing motion and often bill-click, which can be heard at some distance. In display the head is lowered below the perch, the wings and tail raised. Sometimes the tail is raised and the wings slightly opened displaying the grey bands across the lower back.

### Description

255–280 mm (10–11 in), sexually dimorphic.

COCK: Bill orange-red or red; irides dark brown; orbital skin flesh-coloured. Forehead and eyebrows white, crown and nape grey; back of neck, throat and breast deep maroon; wings and upper back green with white patch on shoulder; lower back blackish with two grey bands; tail grey with broad black band; legs and feet red.

HEN: Neck, throat and breast chestnut brown; no white eyebrows. The white wing patch of the cock indicated by a faint grey mark or absent.

### Distribution and Habitat

India through South-east Asia to northern and eastern Australia. Inhabits wooded country in both flat and hilly areas.

## Genus *Geopelia*

There are three species in this genus: the domesticated Diamond Dove (*G. cuneata*) which has not been imported into the UK from its native Australia for many years; the Zebra Dove (*G. striata*) which has a wide Asiatic and Australasian distribution and is still imported fairly frequently; and the Bar-shouldered Dove (*G. humeralis*) which has not been commercially imported to my knowledge.

## DIAMOND DOVE *Geopelia cuneata* **Plate 50**

OTHER NAMES: Little Dove. There are no subspecies.

The Diamond Dove is widely kept and bred in aviaries in many parts of the world. They are prolific and will breed in large cages, and have been used as foster parents for other small dove species. They will nest in practically any type of basket or box with a low rim, fixed under shelter. The usual materials used are small, slender twigs and grass stems but they will use anything from paper to coconut fibres.

### Description

180 mm (7 in), including tail of approximately 90 mm (3½ in), sexually dimorphic.

COCK: Bill horn grey; irides red or orange-red; orbital skin orange-red; head, neck and breast mainly pearly grey fading to white on the underparts; nape, back and scapulars dull brown; wing coverts spotted white; tail dark-grey, outer feathers white-tipped; legs and feet reddish.

HEN: Slightly smaller than cock. Plumage browner; wing spots larger; orbital skin of the eye paler than the cock's.

### Distribution and Habitat

Northern and inland Australia. Inhabits open woodland, mulga scrub, gum creeks and open country with some scrub and bushes within reach of water.

ZEBRA DOVE *Geopelia striata*
OTHER NAMES: Barred Ground Dove, Barred Dove. Is known as the Peaceful Dove in Australia. There are seven widely distributed subspecies.

The Zebra Dove has proved to be as prolific as the Diamond Dove in captivity, but they are not so popular and are difficult to sex. They should be kept one pair to an aviary and cannot be kept with other doves unless the aviary is large.

Description

180–200 mm (7–8 in), which includes tail of approximately 100 mm (4 in). Difficult to sex visually.
COCK: Bill horn-coloured; irides whitish; orbital ring bluish grey; upperparts pale brown with black-barred mantle, wings and back; forehead, cheeks and throat ash grey; back of head and nape dull reddish-brown; sides of neck, breast and flanks with dark brown and buff white bars; breast pink, shading to white below tail; tail brownish grey with black outer tail feathers, white-tipped; legs and feet flesh-coloured.
HEN: Slightly smaller than cock; underparts paler.

Distribution and Habitat

Malaya through Indonesia to Australia and introduced in other areas. Inhabits open country with trees and bushes, gardens and agricultural land.

**Genus *Columbina***

There are seven species in this genus of small New World doves, and together with three other genera they are collectively called the American ground doves. They are not too happily named, for although ground feeders, they are not as terrestrial as the quail doves and other forms. Three species of the genus are the most frequently imported of the New World doves. They are plump, rather short-tailed, and have iridescent wing-spots, and like *Turtur* and *Oena* species they flick (or twitch) their wings in display. *Columbina* species have proved to be free breeding in captivity and are not delicate when established.

GOLD-BILLED GROUND DOVE *Columbina cruziana*
OTHER NAMES: As usual with imported doves, this species is known by many common names; these include Peruvian Ground Dove, Gold-ringed Ground Dove and Croaking Ground Dove. In dealers' lists they are often called Yellow-billed Ground Dove, Yellow-billed Pigmy Dove and Peruvian Pigmy Dove.

These species are among the best breeding of any imported seed-eating doves and they will rear as many as six broods in a season. They are lively and attractive, and once established can be wintered outside between April and November in the UK. Their only avicultural disadvantage is that they can be aggressive and disruptive towards unrelated species as well as other doves.

Description

165–190 mm (6½–7½ in), sexually dimorphic.

N.B. Sexual dimorphism occurs in plumage as well as size, but because only a small number of the birds have been measured and examined, no mention of sexual dimorphism in size has been found in bird literature.

COCK: Bill about two-thirds from the base orange-yellow or bright yellow, the remainder black. There is some indication that the yellow-orange area intensifies in colour when the males are in breeding condition, the bill appearing to be thicker in this coloured area in the male. Outer zone of irides red, then concentric zones of green, yellowish-brown and brown; orbital skin pale yellow; head bluish grey (white on the chin), shading to brownish grey or paler bluish grey; closed wings show a reddish-purple bar and a variable number of blue-black spots and blotches; outer secondaries and primaries tipped with black; breast and underparts pink; outer tail feathers tipped with black; legs and feet pink.

HEN: Bill pale yellow; outer zone of irides greyish white, then concentric zones of orange-red and pale yellow; orbital skin pale yellow; upperparts light brown, shading into light grey or whitish grey below. A variable number of feathers have light buff-brown edging, mainly on the abdomen and undertail coverts. Compared with cock, the closed wings show a similar but shorter reddish-purple bar, with a narrow, buff-brown upper margin. Spots and blotches not so well defined and lighter in colour than in the males.

## Distribution and Habitat

From coastal Ecuador to northern Chile, extending east in Peru to the valley of Maranon. Found in arid scrub, oases and gardens.

## Breeding

PERIOD: Extensive in the wild; in Ecuador nests are started in every month except August to October. The period is not so prolonged in other areas and starts after the first good rainfall. Aviary birds will breed or attempt to breed throughout the year; I bring them in in November (unless they have chicks) and keep them indoors till April, with sexes separated.
NEST: Feral nests are built in bushes, trees, also on the ledges of buildings, low cliffs, banks, half-open nest boxes and sometimes on the ground. Aviary nests are also built in a wide variety of situations including nest boxes and baskets. My birds favour gorse clumps and occasionally build very substantial nests of grasses and stems.
EGGS: Glossy white. Clutch size 2, sometimes 3.
INCUBATION: Typical dove pattern of sharing between the sexes during the day. Period 14 days.
CHICKS: Fed and brooded by both parents, they grow rapidly and leave the nest at 12 days, sometimes earlier. They begin to feed themselves at 18–20 days after hatching and are usually independent at 25–26 days. Usually the hen has another clutch either hatched or near hatching at this time, so the young should be removed to prevent the cock harassing them.

## Behaviour

The wing-flick display is given when the cock is nest-calling at a potential site and often when approaching the hen. Both sexes wing-flick and the cock also gives a bowing display. Billing and mutual preening usually precede copulation and there is some indication that the cock actually feeds the hen when billing. These birds are often aggressive to the larger passerines such as cardinals and will buffet them with their wings if they approach their nest.

RUDDY GROUND DOVE *Columbina talpacoti*

OTHER NAMES: Blue-headed Ground Dove, Cinnamon Dove, Stone Dove. Often called Pigmy Dove by dealers in common with congenerics such as *C. minuta*. Four subspecies are recognised.

Importations are now rare, but the Ruddy Ground Dove is not such a popular aviary bird as, for example, the Diamond Dove and certain *Streptopelia* species.

Breeding in captivity has occurred quite often, but published records are very few; probably the first in this country was in 1903–4.

### Description

180 mm (7 in), sexually dimorphic.

COCK: Bill horn coloured; irides dark brown with outer ring of red; orbital skin grey; top and sides of head and nape bluish grey; throat greyish white; rest of plumage pinkish chestnut, looking very red in sunlight; black spots of variable size and shape on wings; primaries blackish with narrow brown tips on the outer feathers; tail feathers black, tipped with light brown; legs and feet a light flesh colour.

HEN: Irides dark brown with outer ring of yellowish- or buffish-brown. The pinkish-chestnut plumage of the male is replaced by brown on the upper surface and lighter brown below. Wing and tail markings, leg and foot colour as for cock.

### Distribution and Habitat

The drier parts of the Guianas, Venezuela and Colombia, south to northern Argentina, accidentally as far south as Tucuman and Buenos Aires, also Margarita Island, Trinidad and Tobago. Habitat is recorded as shrubby savanna, pastures, gardens and towns.

PLAIN-BREASTED GROUND DOVE *Columbina minuta*

OTHER NAMES: Pygmy Dove, Grey Ground Dove, Little Ground Dove. Three subspecies are recognised.

This little New World dove is still occasionally imported and is often confused with its sibling species, the Scaly-breasted or Passerine Ground Dove (*C. passerina*). Both species are called pygmy doves by dealers. *C. minuta* can be distinguished from *C. passerina* as it lacks the spotty or scaly appearance of the feathers on the head and neck of *C. passerina*, which is not so often imported. Both species are excellent aviary birds and I have found *C. minuta* to be free breeding, building a tiny nest which is often little more than a few stems of grass. Unlike *C. cruziana* they are not aggressive towards unrelated species, and can be kept with passerines.

Description

150 mm (6 in), sexually dimorphic.
COCK: Bill grey or greyish brown; irides yellowish or yellow-brown; plumage mainly brownish grey; forehead, crown and nape bluish grey; wings chestnut, coverts tinged wine-red and metallic with blue-black spots; short rounded tail; outer feathers dark grey, white tipped; sides of head, neck and underparts wine-red; legs and feet red.
HEN: Browner than the cock; throat and underparts whitish.

Distribution and Habitat

Wide geographical range, but local and patchily distributed, from Mexico to northern Colombia, Venezuela, Guyana, Brazil, Paraguay and the Pacific coastal region. Inhabits savanna, open wastelands, second growth woodland and cultivated areas.

# Appendix — Imported Birds and the law in the UK

**The Convention on International Trade in Endangered Species of Wild Fauna and Flora (CITES)**

The United Kingdom signed CITES, in Washington in 1973, the convention came into force in July 1975 and was ratified by the UK on 2 August 1976. The species covered by the convention are grouped into three appendices.

CITES Appendices

| | |
|---|---|
| Appendix 1 | Species threatened with extinction which are, or may be, affected by trade. There is presumption against all trade in species on this Appendix (trade means all international movements of species whether commercial or not). Only in certain extenuating circumstances is trade permitted. |
| Appendix 2 | Contains species which although not necessarily now threatened with extinction may become so unless trade in them is strictly regulated (by licensing) to prevent over-exploitation and to facilitate monitoring. Also contained in this category are species which may be confused with those listed on Appendix 1 by virtue of their visual similarity. |
| Appendix 3 | This Appendix contains species listed at the request of particular countries in order to secure international assistance in enforcing their domestic legislation. |

It is prohibited to sell or offer for sale endangered species unless an exemption has been granted by the Department of the Environment (International Trade in Endangered Species Branch). The DoE will provide a list of endangered species on request. Enquiries should be directed to the DoE, Tollgate House, Houlton Street, Bristol BS2 9DJ.

**Wildlife and Countryside Act 1981**

Under the above act it is illegal to release or allow to escape into the wild any animal which is not ordinarily resident in Great Britain in a wild state. Aviculturists who wish to release birds from an aviary, knowing they will return (e.g. parent birds released from a controlled batch in an aviary to seek live food for their young) are advised to obtain a licence from the Department of the Environment, Tollgate House, Houlton Street, Bristol BS2 9DJ.

**Species on the British List**

The following species listed in this book at the time of writing, are on the British list as accidentals.

EMBERIZIDAE — BUNTINGS

Red-headed Bunting (*Emberiza bruniceps*)
Black-headed Bunting (*Emberiza melanocephala*)
Blue Grosbeak (*Guiraca caerulea*)
Painted Bunting (*Passerina ciris*)

The Bobwhite Quail (*Colinus virginianus*) is on the British list as a feral breeding species. The population has developed from either accidental or deliberate release. Aviculturists wishing to show these species may do so provided that the bird's breeding parents were lawfully held in captivity, when the egg, from which it was hatched, was laid.

**The Importation of Birds, Poultry and Hatching Eggs Order 1979. (As amended)**

Under UK law, all birds entering the UK must be licensed before landing and they must be quarantined. Applications for licences and details of quarantine requirements should be directed to the Ministry of Agriculture, Fisheries and Food, Government Buildings (Toby Jug Site), Hook Rise South, Tolworth, Surbiton, Surrey KT6 7NF.

# Bibliography

ALBRECHT-MOLLER, J. L. (1977) 'Sporophila' In *Encyclopaedia of Aviculture* (Vol. 3) Blandford Press, Poole

ALI, S. (1955) *The Book of Indian Birds* Bombay Natural History Society (Bombay)

ALI, S. & DILLON RIPLEY, S. (1968–74) *Handbook of the Birds of India and Pakistan* (Vols 1–10) Oxford University Press

BECKETT, C. D. (1964) 'Chinese Hawfinches' *Foreign Birds* 30 (2): 76

BECKETT, C. D. (1980) 'Breeding the Himalayan Greenfinch' *Foreign Birds* 46 (4): 108–10

BICE, C. W. (1955) 'Millets for Cage Birds' *All-Pets Magazine* 26 (3): 72–84; 26 (4): 109–26

BICE, C. W. (1956) 'Observations on Budgie Feeding' *Budgerigar Bulletin* 113: 19–27

BLEWETT, E. (1980) *Care & Breeding of Australian Finches* Rigby Publishers Limited, Melbourne

BOND, J. (1960) *Birds of the West Indies* Collins, London

BOOSEY, E. J. (1962) *Foreign Bird Keeping* (2nd Edition) Iliffe, London

BRICKNELL, N. (1986) *Introduction to Southern African Cage and Aviary Birds* (Vol. 1) Nadine Publishers, South Hills

BRUGGERS, R. L. & ELLIOTT, C. G. H. (Eds) (1989) 'Quelea Quelea *Africa's Bird Pest*' Oxford University Press

CAMPBELL, B. & LACK, E. (Eds) (1985) *A Dictionary of Birds* Calton (Poyser) and Vermillion (Buteo)

CARMICHAEL LOW, G. (1929) *The Vertebrated Animals Exhibited in the Gardens, 1828–1927* (Vol. 2 *Birds*) Zoological Society of London

COOPER, D. M. (1976) 'The Japanese Quail' In *The Care and Management of Laboratory Animals* (UFAW Handbook, 5th Edition) Livingston, Edinburgh and London

COUPE, M. F. (1964) 'Breeding the Red-billed Weaver (*Quelea quelea*)' *Avicultural Magazine* 70 (6): 229

CUMMINGS, W. D. (1964) 'Breeding Results at Keston Foreign Bird Farm' *Avicultural Magazine* 70 (2): 56–8

CURZON, M. (1982) 'Breeding the Golden-Breasted Bunting' *Foreign Birds* 8 (3): 72–3

DECOUX, A. (1927) 'Breeding the Red-Crested Finch in France' *Avicultural Magazine* 4th series, (5): 107–8

DECOUX, A. (1931) 'The Breeding of the Blue-headed Waxbill' *Avicultural Magazine* 4th series, 9: 37–9

DELACOUR, J. (1943) 'A Revision of the Subfamily Estrildinae of the Family Ploceidae' *Zoological Magazine* 28: 69–86 (New York)

DE PASS, G. (1956) 'Breeding of the Rose-breasted Finch (*Carpodacus erythrinus*)' *Avicultural Magazine* 62 (3): 118

DE SCHAUENSEE, R. M. (1970) *A Guide to the Birds of South America* Oliver & Boyd, London

EVANS, S. & FIDLER, M. (1990) *Parrot Finches. The Aviculturist's Guide* Blandford Press, London

FLIEG, M. C. (1973) 'Breeding Biology and Behaviour of the South African Hemipode in Captivity' *Avicultural Magazine* 79 (2): 55–9

GIBSON, L. (1980) 'Some Sources of Live Food' *Avicultural Magazine* 86 (1): 33–9

GLEGHORN, C. (1969) 'Breeding Orange Weavers' *Foreign Birds* 35 (4): 135–6

GOODWIN, D. (1970) *Pigeons and Doves of the World* British Museum (Nat. Hist.), London

GOODWIN, D. (1982) *Estrildid Finches of the World* British Museum (Nat. Hist.), Oxford University Press

GREEN, R. (1986) 'Breeding the Five-colored Mannikin *Lonchura quinticolor*' *Avicultural Magazine* 92 (4): 181–3

GRUSON, E. S. (1976) *Checklist of the Birds of the World* Collins, London

HALL, B. P. & MOREAU, R. E. (1970) *An Atlas of Speciation in African Passerine Birds* British Museum (Nat. Hist.), London

HARRAP, K. S. (1970) 'Breeding of the Lark-Like Bunting' *Avicultural Magazine* 76 (1): 4–5

HARRISON, C. J. O. (1967) 'Apparent zoographical dispersal patterns in two avian families' *Bulletin of the British Ornithologists Club* 87: 63–72

HARRISON, C. J. O. (1973) 'Observation on the Behaviour and Breeding of the Saffron Finch (*Sicalis luteola*)' *Avicultural Magazine* 79 (6): 201–13

HARRISON, C. J. O. (1975) *A Field Guide to the Nests, Eggs and Nestlings of British and European Birds* Collins, London

HARRISON, C. J. O. (1978) *A Field Guide to the Nests, Eggs and Nestlings of North American Birds* Collins, London

HARRISON, C. J. O. & DORMER, B. P. (1962) 'Notes on the Display and Behaviour of Peters' Twin-spot and the Brown Twin-spot' *Avicultural Magazine* 68 (4): 139–43

HARRISON, C. J. O., RESTALL, R. & TROLLOPE, J. (1965) 'The Egg-rolling Behaviour of the Painted Quail' *Avicultural Magazine* 71 (4): 127–30

HERKLOTS, G. A. C. (1961) *The Birds of Trinidad and Tobago* Collins, London

HODGES, M. (1979) 'Breeding Results for 1979' *Foreign Birds* 45 (4): 6–7

HOWARD, R. & MOORE, A. (1980) *A Complete Checklist of the Birds of the World* Oxford University Press

IMMELMANN, K. (1977) *Australian Finches* Angus and Robertson, London

IVEY, W. D. & HOWES, J. R. (1967) 'The Coturnix Quail (*Coturnix coturnix*)' In *The Care and Management of Laboratory Animals* (UFAW Handbook, 3rd Edition) Livingston, Edinburgh and London

KEAST, A. (1958) 'Intraspecific Variation in the Australian Finches' *Emu* 58: 219–46

KENDALL, S. B. (1973) 'The Dwarf (Red) Turtle Dove (*Streptopelia tranquebarica*)' *Avicultural Magazine* 79 (6): 197–9

KING, B., WOODCOCK, M. & DICKINSON, E. C. (1975) *A Field Guide to the Birds of South-East Asia* Collins, London

LEE, A. J. (1987) 'Breeding the Fischer's Whydah' *Foreign Birds* 53 (2): 33–5

LEITCH, L. (1970) 'Breeding Black-crested Finches or Pigmy Cardinals (*Lophospingus pusillus*)' *Avicultural Magazine* 76 (4): 137–8

LONG, J. L. (1981) *Introduced Birds of the World* David & Charles, Newton Abbot & London

LOW, R. (1987) *Hand-rearing Parrots and Other Birds* Blandford Press, Poole

LOWE, J. R. (1959) 'Half-masked Weaver (*Ploceus vitellinus*)' *Avicultural Magazine* 65: 27

LYNCH, G. C. (1956) 'House Finch (*Carpodacus mexicanus*)' *Foreign Birds* 22: 240–1

LYNCH, G. C. (1958) 'Purple Finch (*Carpodacus purpureus*)' *Avicultural Magazine* 64: 137–9

MACKWORTH-PRAED, C. C. & GRANT, C. H. B. (1960) *African Handbook of Birds* (Vol. 2, *Birds of Eastern and North-Eastern Africa*) Longman, London

MARSHALL, A. J. (1959) 'Internal and Environmental Control of Breeding' *Ibis* 101 (3–4): 456–78

MARTIN, A. (1961) 'Breeding the Brown Mannikin' *Avicultural Magazine* 67 (3): 89–90

MARCHANT, S. (1960) 'The Breeding of Some South-Western Equadorian Birds' *Ibis* 102 (4): 584–99

MEADEN, F. (1979) *A Manual of European Bird Keeping* Blandford Press, Poole

MOBBS, A. J. (1985) *Gouldian Finches* Fanciers Supplies Ltd., Liss

MULLER, K. (1967) 'The South American Crimson Finch (*Rhodospingus cruentus*)' *Avicultural Magazine* 73 (1): 1, 2

MUNDY, P. J. (1987) 'What is the World's Most Abundant Bird Species?' *Avicultural Magazine* 93 (4): 240–41

MURRAY, H. (1966) 'Breeding the Pileated Song Sparrow (*Zonotrichia capensis*)' *Avicultural Magazine* 72 (5): 131–2

NEWTON, I. (1975) *Finches* Collins, London

NICOLAI, J. (1977) 'Der Rotmaskenastrild (*Pytilia hypogrammica*) als Wirt der Togo-Paradieswitwee (*Steganura togoensis*)' *Journal fuer Ornithologie* 18: 175–88

PALMER, D. J. (1990) 'Breeding the Crested Bunting' *Foreign Birds* 52 (2): 56–7

PARIS, P. (1970) 'Notes on Parakeets and Seedeaters' *Avicultural Magazine* 76 (4): 168

PARTRIDGE, W. R. (1964) 'Breeding the Cayenne Seed-Eater (*S. frontalis*)' *Avicultural Magazine* 70 (3): 111–13

PETERSON, R. T. (1941) *A Field Guide to Western Birds* Riverside Press, Cambridge, Massachusetts

RESTALL, R. (1987) 'Neo-Tropical Finches' *Avicultural Magazine* 93 (4): 207–22

RIDGLEY, R. S. & TUDOR, G. (1989) *The Birds of South America* (Vol. 1) Oxford University Press

ROBBINS, C. E. S. (1989) *Quail, Their Breeding and Management* World Pheasant Association

ROBILLER, L. (1974) *Cage and Aviary Birds* Almark Publishing Co., London

ROOTS, C. (1968) 'Maggots and Mealworms' *Avicultural Magazine* 74 (1): 186–9

RUTGERS, A. (1977) *The Handbook of Foreign Birds* (Vol. 1, 4th Edition) Blandford Press, Poole

RUTGERS, A. & NORRIS, K. A. (Eds) (1977) *Encyclopaedia of Aviculture* (Vols 1–3) Blandford Press, Poole

SERLE, W., MOREL, G. J. & HARTWIG, W. (1977) *A Field Guide to the Birds of West Africa* Collins, London

SETH-SMITH, D. (1903) 'On the Breeding in Captivity of *Turnix tanki* with some notes on the Habits of the Species' *Avicultural Magazine* 2 (3): 317–24

SETH-SMITH, D. (1905) 'On the Breeding of *Turnix varia*' *Avicultural Magazine* 2 (3): 295–301

SHORE-BAILEY, W. (1926) 'The Breeding of the St Helena Seed-eater (*Serinus flaviventris*)' *Avicultural Magazine* (4) (4): 328–9

SKEAD, C. J. (1960) *The Canaries, Seed-eaters and Buntings of Southern Africa* The Trustees of the South African Bird Book Fund, Cape Town

SMYTHIES, B. E. (1953) *Birds of Burma* Oliver & Boyd, London

SMYTHIES, B. E. (1960) *Birds of Borneo* Oliver & Boyd, London

SUMMERS-SMITH, J. D. (1963) *The House Sparrow* Collins, London

TELL, M. (1983) 'Breeding the Crested Black Bunting (*Melophus lathami*)' *Avicultural Magazine* 89 (3): 133–5

THOMASSET, B. C. (1931) 'Breeding the Pileated Finch (*Coryphospingus pileatus*)' *Avicultural Magazine* 4 (9): 303–4

TIMMIS, W. H. (1973) 'Breeding the Red-headed Bunting (*Emberiza bruniceps*) at Chester Zoo' *Avicultural Magazine* 79: 3–7

TIMMIS, W. H. (1973) 'Breeding the Crimson-rumped or Sundervall's Waxbill (*Estrilda rhodopyga*) at Chester Zoo' *Avicultural Magazine* 79 (1): 25–7

TOLLEFSON, C. I. (1969) *Nutrition in Diseases of Cage and Aviary Birds*, Ed. Petrak, Margaret L., Lea and Febiger (Philadelphia)

TROLLOPE, J. (1963) 'Bird Escapes from London Airport' *Avicultural Magazine* 69 (3): 134

TROLLOPE, J. (1966) 'Some Observations on the Harlequin Quail (*Coturnix delegorguei*)' *Avicultural Magazine* 72 (1): 5–6

TROLLOPE, J. (1966) 'Breeding the Red-crested Finch (*Coryphospingus cristatus*)' *Avicultural Magazine* 72 (6): 149–53

TROLLOPE, J. (1967) 'Breeding a Hemipode (*Turnix suscitator*)' *Avicultural Magazine* 73 (6): 184–8

TROLLOPE, J. (1974) 'The Breeding and Behaviour of the Talpacoti Dove (*Columbina talpacoti*)' *Avicultural Magazine* 80 (3): 86–92

TROLLOPE, J. (1974) 'The Breeding and Behaviour of the Gold-billed Dove (*Columbina cruziana*)' *Avicultural Magazine* 80 (5): 181–8

TROLLOPE, J. (1978) 'The Breeding and Behaviour of the Black-billed Wood Dove (*Turtur abyssinia*)' *Avicultural Magazine* 84 (2): 64–8

TROLLOPE, J. (1979) 'Breeding Results and Photoperiod' *Avicultural Magazine* 85 (2): 89–92

TROLLOPE, J. (1979) 'Breeding the Yellow-throated Sparrow' *Avicultural Magazine* 85 (3): 135–8

TROLLOPE, J. (1983) *The Care and Breeding of Seedeating Birds* Blandford Press, Poole

TROLLOPE, J. (1984) 'Breeding the Collared Warbling Finch (*Poospiza hispaniolensis*)' *Avicultural Magazine* 90 (1): 27–32

TROLLOPE, J. (1987) 'The Wood Doves of Africa' *Foreign Birds* 53 (4): 97–8

TROLLOPE, J. (1990) 'Some Birds of Tanzania' *Foreign Birds* 56 (3): 77–9

WALTERS, M. (1980) *The Complete Birds of the World* David & Charles, Newton Abbot

WEEKS & WEEKS, J. G. (1968) 'Breeding the Paradise Whydah (*Steganura paradisaea*)' *Avicultural Magazine* 74 (1): 5

WEEKS & WEEKS, J. G. (1968) 'Breeding of the Shaft-tailed Whydah (*Tetrenura regia*)' *Avicultural Magazine* 74 (1): 6

WHISTLER, H. (1963) *Popular Handbook of Indian Birds* Oliver & Boyd, London

WHITE, C. M. N. (1963) 'The Indigo Birds' *Bulletin of the British Ornithologists Club* 83: 83–8

WHITTAKER CARR, V. (1964) 'Chinese (or Asian) Hawfinches' *Foreign Birds* 30 (1): 37

WOOLHAM, F. (1987) *The Handbook of Aviculture* Blandford Press, Poole

WÖSTENDIEN, U. (1965) 'Crimson Winged Finches' *Foreign Birds* 31 (4): 131, 132, 136

ZACKRISSON, R. (1972) 'Breeding *Poospiza ornata* in Sweden' *Avicultural Magazine* 78 (4): 113–17

# Index of Scientific Names

Figures in **bold** refer to colour plates

# Index of Common Names

Figures in **bold** refer to colour plates

## INDEX OF COMMON NAMES